everyday
REIKI

About the Author

Dawn McLaughlin graduated from Minot State University with a degree in mathematics, but along the way, she fell in love with yoga, meditation, and energy healing. For more than a decade, she has developed her Reiki skills and has taught countless others this powerful healing modality. Dawn lives in Rhode Island with her husband, Kevin, and their lively Italian Greyhound, Dharma. Visit her website at Intuitive-Hearts.com to explore her offerings.

everyday
REIKI

a self-healing routine for mastering the
teachings and practice of reiki

Dawn McLaughlin

Llewellyn Publications · Woodbury, Minnesota

FIRST EDITION
First Printing, 2023

Book design by Donna Burch-Brown
Cover design by Kevin R. Brown
Interior figure illustrations by Mary Ann Zapalac
Interior Chakra and Reiki symbols by the Llewellyn Art Department

Llewellyn Publications is a registered trademark of Llewellyn Worldwide Ltd.

Library of Congress Cataloging-in-Publication Data (Pending)
ISBN: 978-0-7387-7544-9

Llewellyn Worldwide Ltd. does not participate in, endorse, or have any authority or responsibility concerning private business transactions between our authors and the public.

All mail addressed to the author is forwarded, but the publisher cannot, unless specifically instructed by the author, give out an address or phone number.

Any internet references contained in this work are current at publication time, but the publisher cannot guarantee that a specific location will continue to be maintained. Please refer to the publisher's website for links to authors' websites and other sources.

Llewellyn Publications
A Division of Llewellyn Worldwide Ltd.
2143 Wooddale Drive
Woodbury, MN 55125-2989
www.llewellyn.com

Printed in the United States of America

Forthcoming Books by Dawn McLaughlin

Spirit Allies and Healing Guides:
Create Your Divine Support System (Llewellyn, 2024)

A special thanks to my Reiki teachers:
Helen Chin Lui, Angela Cote, and Trish Matthies.

This book is dedicated to my husband, Kevin McLaughlin.

Contents

Part 6: Reiki Forty-Day Immersion Experience: Reiki Mastery

Disclaimer

Please note that the information in this book is not intended as a substitute for professional medical advice from licensed healthcare professionals. The practices outlined in this book are not intended to prevent, diagnose, or treat any illness. Both the author and the publisher recommend consulting a licensed medical practitioner before attempting the techniques outlined in this book.

Introduction

As students of Reiki, we are exposed to complex concepts about energetic healing over a compact period of time in our initial Reiki training, often just a day or two at most. The quality of Reiki training varies from teacher to teacher. Sometimes there is little consideration for the ability of the student to internalize these powerful lessons. Frequently, the only suggestion made to students after the initial Reiki Level One training is to practice self-healing for twenty-one days. That's it! Although a daily self-healing routine is a necessary cornerstone for embracing Reiki as a part of life, there are many intrinsic benefits to taking a deeper dive into all facets of the jewel that is Reiki energy.

Rooted in my personal practices, I developed this comprehensive guide based on the core concepts of Reiki with the intention of providing an opportunity not only to understand but also to integrate these topics into your life. By giving ample time to explore each key component individually with an opportunity to have a personal experience related to each topic, you develop more insights into effectively using this healing power and cultivate a personal relationship with the healing energy itself. The outcome of this process will be a solid connection to Reiki energy and more powerful healing sessions.

This book is suitable for beginners as well as seasoned Reiki healers who want an opportunity to renew and revitalize their relationship with Reiki energy. The focus of this book is to hone and develop your Reiki skills.

Anatomy of This Book

Everyday Reiki is designed for anyone interested in deepening their connection to Reiki energy and focusing on their personal healing journey. Whether you are brand new to Reiki or a seasoned healing professional, this book has something to offer you.

Exploring the Format

This book is not another Reiki training manual. For each level of Reiki, this book has two sections, totaling six parts. Parts one, three, and five focus on the theory of Reiki healing, covering key topics you may have been exposed to during your Reiki training. Parts two, four, and six are forty-day immersion experiences designed to foster an intimate awareness of the transformative power of Reiki, allowing for the integrating of these key concepts. For forty days, you will be presented with a prompt to connect with your personal Reiki intention, a unique five to ten–minute meditation, and a guided journaling exercise. I recommend completing your daily practices with a full Reiki self-healing session.

Why Forty Days?

The forty-day time period is significant. In the Vedic and Buddhist traditions of the East, forty days is the length of time dedicated to certain spiritual disciplines, such as Sanskrit mantra practices, to receive maximum benefits. In the West, the forty-day period also plays an important role, such as the Christian religious observance of Lent. In "The Ballad of Thomas Rhymer," forty days is the amount of time that the central figure spends in the underworld with the fairies. Forty days is also the amount of time associated with quarantine, a topic we have all become intimately familiar with during the recent COVID-19 pandemic.

Integrating new habits into daily life takes time. Be patient with yourself during this period. Consider the time spent during the forty-day immersion experiences as an investment in your future, resulting in a healthier you and a more powerful connection to Reiki energy.

Setting Intentions

Backed by consistent action, intention setting is a powerful way to co-create with the universe. Setting an intention to form a personal connection to Reiki energy and reinforcing that commitment with both meditation and journaling provides a structure for successfully integrating this healing modality into daily life.

Reiki Theme of the Day

The Reiki Theme of the Day will be explored by taking a deep dive into a critical concept of Reiki. This topic will be further examined during the daily meditation and journaling exercise.

Meditations

As a meditation teacher, I have firsthand experienced the innumerable benefits of meditation. Even for brief periods of five to ten minutes a day, meditation can have significant physical, mental, emotional, energetic, and spiritual benefits.

Journaling

Journaling is an excellent way to invite more creativity into daily life. By recording your insights, you'll be able to reflect on and document your unique journey through the Reiki landscape. Your journal provides a forum for personal growth, insights, and the internalization of Reiki's healing powers. Before starting, be sure you have a dedicated Reiki journal, notebook, or three-ring binder to record insights received during your immersion experiences.

Exploring the Benefits

By the end of your forty-day period, you will have established a firm foundation for future Reiki adventures. Benefits to following this forty-day Reiki immersion experience include the following:

- Strengthening your connection to Reiki energy
- Healing on all levels: physical, emotional, mental, energetic, and spiritual
- Increasing mindfulness and focus
- Internalizing the Reiki principles: also known as the Reiki prayer
- Exceeding the suggested self-healing protocol of twenty-one days for Reiki 1 practitioners
- Establishing a daily meditation practice
- Developing a daily journaling practice
- Promoting relaxation
- Developing greater self-awareness
- Reducing stress and anxiety
- Creating a deeper connection with the Reiki hand positions for self-healing
- Cultivating intuition
- Promoting spiritual growth and development
- Providing a greater sense of inner balance and harmony

Where to Begin

This book is divided into a text section associated with a specific level of Reiki and a corresponding forty-day immersion experience to deepen your understanding of that level of Reiki through your own personal experience.

If you are newer to Reiki, you may find it helpful to read through part one in its entirety before embarking on the daily practices in the immersion experience. However, if you feel called to jump into the forty-day guided practices before completing part one, it's recommended that you start with the last chapter in part one, "The Power of Intention." Beginning with a focused, personal intention will ensure that your practices will be meaningful for your personal healing journey.

I'm so excited that you are embarking on this amazing journey with me. Let's begin!

Part 1
Reiki Foundations: Reiki Level One

Chapter 1

What Is Reiki?

Reiki is a term that describes both the healing energy and the healing modality that promotes physical, emotional, mental, energetic, and spiritual healing through the connection to the universal healing energy. A general translation of the Japanese word *reiki* is "universal life force energy." Although laying of hands for healing purposes has an ancient history, Reiki is a relatively recent technique.

In the 1890s, a Japanese Buddhist monk, Dr. Mikao Usui, discovered Reiki on a religious pilgrimage to Mount Kurama outside Kyoto. The legend describes the story of how Dr. Usui received the transmission of the Reiki symbols and the knowledge of the symbols' potential for healing during a period of fasting and meditation. Dr. Usui traveled throughout Japan, sharing his healing gifts with others and teaching his healing technique to eighteen students, the first Reiki Masters. Since its inception, Reiki has grown in popularity and spread throughout the world.

The Levels of Reiki

Based on the Usui Ryoho Reiki system, there are three levels of Reiki. Reiki Level One teaches the foundations of Reiki. During Reiki Level One, the student will learn about the history of Reiki and the anatomy of the energy body. Through the first attunement process, the Reiki Master-Teacher will facilitate the transmission of universal healing energy to the student. Additionally, the self-healing hand positions and the hand positions for healing others are explained during Reiki Level One training.

Reiki Level Two strengthens the connection to Reiki energy and assists with the Reiki practitioner's spiritual growth and personal development. Reiki students will learn about the three sacred Reiki symbols: the Power symbol, the Mental/Emotional symbol, and the

Distance symbol, which are used to transmit Reiki energy. The Reiki student will also be taught how to send remote healing to others across distance, time, and space. A second attunement is passed to the student for the expansion of Reiki energy.

Reiki Level Three may be subdivided into two classes: Master-Practitioner, in which the students learn the third-degree symbols, the five elements, and the circuit of ki energy; and the second, Master-Teacher, for those who feel called to teach the gift of Reiki.

There are over fifty nontraditional schools of Reiki. Although these healing modalities fall outside the scope of this book, it's worth noting that these systems are valid and access the same universal healing energy. However, they may employ different symbols and use other processes. If you are curious, feel free to experiment with various types of Reiki and practice the one that resonates with you.

Attunement Process

To become a channel for Reiki energy, you must receive an attunement from a Reiki Master-Teacher. Once you receive an attunement, it is with you forever. There is no need to repeat an attunement unless you feel called to do so.

During the attunement process, the Reiki Master-Teacher, with the use of the Reiki symbols and your personal intention to receive the attunement, synchronizes your personal vibrational frequency to that of the level of Reiki for which you are being attuned. By adjusting your personal energetic signature, you can act as a channel for the high vibrational Reiki energy. The attunement process can be done in person or remotely.

During your Reiki attunement, you will experience significant shifts in energy that may express themselves in various ways. Since no two people are identical, your individual experience will be personal to you. You may not notice these energetic changes, or you may have a physical response. The ways in which your new energetic frequency may express itself include the following:

- Pulsating energy in your physical body
- Seeing colors of swirling energy behind your closed eyes
- Warmth and/or tingling in your hands and/or feet
- Feelings of tranquility, inner peace, and/or joy
- Shifting emotions

- A sense of lightness or floating
- Hearing a slight hum or ringing in the ears

After your Reiki attunement, you will be asked to practice Reiki self-healing sessions for twenty-one days. This period of time is referenced in Dr. Mikao Usui's personal history as the length of time of his meditation practice on Mount Kurama.

For weeks after your attunement, you may undergo a personal transformation as you adapt to Reiki energy and the self-healing practices. You may develop a healthier lifestyle as negative patterns of behavior begin to change into more positive ones. You may find that you are out-growing old friendships that are not aligned with your current path. Your dreams may become more vivid and meaningful. You may need more alone time to process all these shifts in energy. Be patient with yourself during this period of adjustment and allow the process to unfold for you. Practice self-care and drink plenty of water to help support yourself during this time.

Reiki Principles

The core teachings of Reiki are the Reiki Principles, which Dr. Usui presented to his students. These Reiki Principles are also known as the Reiki Prayer or the Reiki Precepts. Although Reiki is not a religion, it does provide ethical guidance on how to live. The Reiki Principles are not commandments but invitations to be mindful of our daily actions and make sage decisions.

There are several variations of the Reiki Principles. The closest to the original version might be the one provided in Diane Stein's *Essential Reiki*. In it, she provides in Hawayo Takata's own words, as described in *The History of Reiki As Told to Me by Mrs. Takata* (Vision Publications, transcript page 11):

Just for today, do not anger.
Just for today, do not worry.
We shall count our blessings and honor our fathers and mothers,
our teachers and neighbors and honor our food.
Make an honest living.
Be kind to everything that has life.[1]

---

1. Diane Stein, *Essential Reiki: A Complete Guide to an Ancient Healing Art* (New York: Crossing Press, 1995), 26.

The version I use in my daily practice is below:

> *Just for today, I will be grateful.*
> *Just for today, I will not worry.*
> *Just for today, I will not anger.*
> *Just for today, I do my work honestly.*
> *Just for today, I will be kind to all living things.*

The wisdom of these principles is the focus on today, approaching each day with renewed focus and determination to make ethical decisions. Interestingly, these principles are not focused directly on healing but on living a noble life. By living a life in alignment with our values, we can be in a position to give of ourselves more openly in service to others. We can be powerful facilitators of healing energy from a place of service.

My suggestion would be to begin and end each day reciting the Reiki Principles.

Chapter 2

Energy Anatomy Basics

As we begin our exploration of Reiki and how it works, we should first consider our energy body, also known as the subtle body. It is through our energetic body that Reiki healing energy flows. When we have blockages or congestion in our energetic body, the symptoms of these blockages may express themselves in the form of mental or emotional issues and even physical illness. By knowing how the energy body works, we, as healers, can better understand where the potential blockages are located and understand Reiki healing in a more in-depth manner.

Our aura is the energy field surrounding us at all times. It extends beyond our physical body in all directions. Our auric field isn't stagnant. It morphs and changes based on our physical, emotional, mental, and spiritual health. When an aura is healthy, it radiates strong, vibrant energy. When there is illness or disease, the auric field shrinks and becomes smaller. There might even be holes or tears in our auric field due to unhealed trauma or severe illness. Reiki, meditation, and practices such as yoga can significantly strengthen the auric field and greatly increase our energetic health.

Consider the many different types of maps that exist: a topography map will not help you drive to New York, but a surveyor designing a new road would find the information invaluable. The map of the energy body we will be exploring is the chakra system map. This map won't tell you where your spleen is located, but it will provide you with knowledge about your energy anatomy, essential for all Reiki healers.

The subtle energy that flows throughout the body is called various names in different cultures: you may know it as prana, chi, ki, or life force energy. This subtle energy travels over energetic pathways called *nadis*, a Sanskrit word meaning "channel," "stream," or "flow." It is estimated that there are more than 72,000 nadis in the body through which subtle energy flows.

Our exploration of the energy body begins with the central channel that runs from the tailbone to the crown of the head. This energetic pathway is called the sushumna nadi. It is our energetic connection to the earth and the heavens. Some traditions call this central channel the Hara line. The seven main chakras we will explore in the section lie on the sushumna nadi.

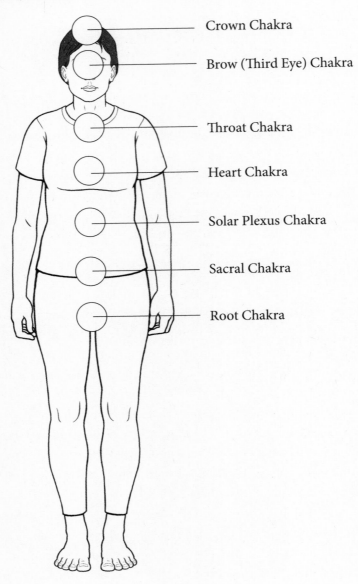

Crown Chakra

Brow (Third Eye) Chakra

Throat Chakra

Heart Chakra

Solar Plexus Chakra

Sacral Chakra

Root Chakra

The word *chakra* is a Sanskrit term that translates to "wheel." Chakras are vortices of energy in constant motion. These energy centers assist us with processing our own internal energies and energies from our outer environment. We can connect to these energy centers using the techniques of meditation, visualization, chanting, and mindfulness practices such as yoga.

Root Chakra
Sanskrit name: Muladhara
Meaning: Root Support
Location: Sacrum/tailbone
Energy state: Solid
Psychological function: Survival
Color: Red
Element: Earth
Planets: Earth and Saturn

The root chakra is your foundation chakra. It's the lowest chakra located at the base of your spine, your tailbone. It has the densest vibration of all the energy centers, but being the densest doesn't make it any less important than the other chakras. It is the most closely aligned with the energies of our physical world, the earth.

This chakra is associated with survival, the sense of security and stability, the physical body, and financial health. When this chakra is balanced and operating effectively, we know we have the right to exist and thrive on this planet. We feel grounded and secure in our physical bodies. Our home life is stable, and we feel financially secure. Additionally, we can easily manifest our goals and desires by bringing our inner vision into reality in the physical world.

When the root chakra is under-active or blocked, we may live in an ungrounded state. Emotions such as fear, anxiety, and insecurity may interfere with daily activities. There may be a financial lack or the inability to manifest or attract our wishes and desires. This imbalance may even have us question our very existence or our right to achieve success during this lifetime.

In contrast, when this chakra is overactive, it may manifest as extremes in behaviors or be expressed in several ways. There can be a tendency to engage in hoarding behavior to overcome the fear of not having enough. Aggression may replace fear as the overactive root chakra forcefully asserts the right to be here on the planet.

Balancing this chakra may benefit the following conditions:

- Adrenal gland issues
- Eating disorders
- Fatigue
- Spinal issues/back pain
- Leg issues
- Foot problems
- Fear
- Insecurity
- Financial hardships
- Inability to manifest your inner vision into the material world

Balancing this chakra may strengthen the following:

- Sense of grounding
- Connection with the earth
- Connection to your physical body
- Inner security
- Satisfying home life
- Financial security
- Ability to manifest an inner vision into the material world

Sacral Chakra

Sanskrit name: Svadhisthana

Meaning: Sweetest

Location: Two inches below the navel

Energy state: Liquid

Psychological function: Desire

Color: Orange

Element: Water

Planet: Moon

The sacral chakra is the energy center focused on creativity, emotions, and pleasure. It's the second chakra located approximately two inches below your belly button in your lower abdominal region.

The element associated with this energy center is water. Our ability to thrive is greatly enhanced if we are adaptable to the ever-changing nature of this world. Consider how you flow through life. Do you readily embrace change? Can you surrender yourself by releasing the reins of your control and allowing situations to unfold organically? By embracing the concepts of adaptability, change, fluidity, and surrender, we can draw on the essence of the sacral chakra and invite more creativity, intimacy, and connection into our lives.

When the sacral chakra functions in a balanced and healthy way, we can express our authentic, creative selves. We are connected to our emotions and our sexuality. Additionally, we can routinely experience genuine joy, pleasure, and emotionally satisfying relationships. We can move with the flow of life, adapting to the changing environment around us.

When this chakra is not aligned properly, we are not functioning from a place of emotional balance. If blocked or underperforming, there may be a disconnect from our feeling state, resulting in sexual repression, lack of passion, and addiction issues. We might not be able to express ourselves creatively. General apathy and boredom may affect the quality of daily life.

In contrast, over-performance of this energy center manifests in many different ways, including an excess of sexual energy resulting in hypersexual behavior devoid of emotional intimacy present in healthy relationships, or intense mood swings and erratic behavior connected with extreme highs and lows in emotional states that may adversely affect day-to-day living.

Balancing this chakra may benefit the following conditions:

- Sexual dysfunctions
- Reproduction issues
- Addiction problems
- Blocked creativity
- Control issues
- Repressed or blocked emotions
- Resistance to change

- Feelings of guilt and/or shame
- Apathy

Balancing this chakra may strengthen the following attributes:

- Adaptability
- Enhanced creativity
- Ability to nurture
- Fertility
- Sexual health
- Greater intimacy
- Ability to feel joy and pleasure
- Clairsentience

Solar Plexus Chakra

Sanskrit name: Manipura
Meaning: Lustrous Gem
Location: Solar Plexus
Energy state: Plasma
Psychological function: Will
Color: Yellow
Element: Fire
Planets: Mars and the Sun

The solar plexus chakra is the vortex of energy centered around your personal power. It is associated with determination and drive, which manifest as the ability to take action in the physical world. It's the third chakra located in your core, in the body's solar plexus region.

The element associated with this energy center is fire. How active is your own internal fire? Does it flicker like a candle in a dark room? Does it resemble a hearth fire, providing warmth and support? Does it burn like a wildfire destroying everything in its path?

We act purposefully and confidently when the solar plexus chakra is optimally functioning. Our vitality and strength radiate throughout our being. We operate from a place of personal power, and through our own inner fire, we can transform ourselves.

Alternatively, when this chakra is out of balance or blocked, we are not correctly utilizing our personal power. If blocked or underperforming, we may experience a lack of willpower or an inability to assert ourselves. Excessive shyness, excessive fatigue, and overall lack of self-confidence may affect the quality of life.

In contrast, an over-active solar plexus chakra may be experienced as an authoritarian point of view in which control needs to be exerted over others. Excessive ego development is another hallmark of an over-performing solar plexus chakra.

Balancing this chakra may benefit the following conditions:

- Stomach issues
- Ulcers
- Acid reflux disease
- Diabetes
- Heartburn
- Pancreas issues
- Liver issues
- Hypoglycemia
- Gallstones
- Control issues
- Fatigue/lack of energy
- Shyness

Balancing this chakra may strengthen the following attributes:

- Self-confidence
- Energy levels
- Metabolism
- Willpower
- Vitality
- Personal power

Heart Chakra
Sanskrit name: Anahata
Meaning: Unstuck
Location: Heart center
Energy state: Gas
Psychological function: Love
Color: Green
Element: Air
Planet: Venus

The fourth energy center is the heart chakra, focusing on love and compassion. Located at the center of your chest, this energy vortex is also the energetic balancing point of the chakra system, with three lower chakras below it and three higher chakras above it.

The element associated with this energy center is air. Consider the vital role air plays in our lives. Without air, we can't breathe, and our lives would end. Air also represents movement, openness, and freedom.

When the heart chakra is functioning in a state of equilibrium, we are open to love and compassion not only for others but also for ourselves. We have a sense of freedom, openness, and willingness to be tolerant of others who may have different views or beliefs. Overall, we operate from a place of emotional balance.

However, when this chakra is not appropriately aligned, the energies of the heart do not express themselves in a balanced, harmonious way. If blocked or underperforming, there may be a disconnect from feelings of love and compassion, resulting in the inability to engage in loving, supportive relationships. This imbalance may manifest as feeling profound loneliness or being overly critical toward oneself or others. A lack of self-care or the ability to nurture oneself may also be present.

In contrast, the over-performance of this energy center may be experienced in many ways. For example, there may be issues with jealousy, possessiveness, or narcissistic tendencies. Typically, unstable or one-sided relationships are a hallmark of a heart chakra imbalance.

Balancing this chakra may benefit the following conditions:

- Cardiac issues
- High blood pressure
- Coronary artery disease

- Arrhythmia
- Angina
- Lung issues
- Asthma
- COPD
- Bronchitis
- Jealousy
- Possessiveness
- A judgmental/critical perspective

Balancing the chakra may strengthen the following attributes:

- Love
- Compassion
- Ability to nurture
- Tolerance
- Emotional balance
- Openness

Throat Chakra

Sanskrit name: Vishuddha
Meaning: Purification
Location: Throat
Energy state: Vibration
Psychological function: Communication
Color: Blue
Element: Ether
Planet: Mercury

The fifth energy center is the throat chakra, focusing on communication, self-expression, and the ability to speak our truth. The throat chakra is the first of the three higher chakras (throat, brow, and crown) and is the gateway to the higher realms of consciousness and spirituality.

The element associated with this energy center is ether, the vast void of space itself. Through the ether, we are connected to the higher planes of spirit. Of all the elements, ether is the most subtle.

When the throat chakra is functioning in an optimal state, we can express ourselves clearly and confidently. We are also able to listen to others effectively. Since the ears are also related to the throat chakra, we can hear and access our inner wisdom and intuition through this energy center. There is a balance between your ability to speak and your ability to listen.

Imbalances in this energy center can lead to a host of issues. If blocked or stagnant, there may be communication issues expressed as a weak speaking voice, stuttering, fear of speaking in public, not trusting intuition, and not listening to inner wisdom. As a result, your ability to express yourself creatively and authentically is compromised.

In contrast, an excess of throat chakra energy may manifest as an overly aggressive communication style and lack of listening skills. There may be an inability or unwillingness to express one's truth through lying, deceit, or exaggeration. These poor skills of communication and self-expression can lead to issues with relationships, both personal and professional.

Balancing this chakra may benefit the following conditions:

- Mouth issues
- Throat issues
- Tonsillitis
- Laryngitis
- Thyroid and parathyroid issues
- Jaw problems
- Teeth grinding
- Speech problems
- Fear of public speaking
- Neck issues
- Hearing problems
- Stuttering
- Allergies

Balancing this chakra may strengthen the following attributes:

- Speaking clearly and effectively
- Self-expression
- Effective listening
- Inner hearing
- Intuition
- Truthfulness
- Authenticity

Brow (Third Eye) Chakra

Sanskrit name: Ajna
Meaning: Command center
Location: Center of forehead
Energy state: Luminescence
Psychological function: Intuition
Color: Indigo
Element: Light
Planets: Jupiter and Neptune

The sixth energy center is the brow chakra, also called the third eye chakra. This energy vortex is in the middle of your forehead, slightly above your eyebrows. Its focus is on inner vision, imagination, intuition, and psychic abilities. It also connects to our thinking abilities and the delicate balance between the brain's left hemisphere (rational thought) and the right hemisphere (creative thought).

When the brow chakra operates in a balanced way, we have access to our inner wisdom and trust our intuition. We can visualize what we wish to manifest and actively use our imagination in creative ways. Our thoughts are clear and focused.

Imbalances in this energy center can lead to both physical and mental challenges. If blocked or underperforming, there may be issues with sight: both literally in the form of eye problems and metaphorically in the form of the inability to visualize solutions to problems. There might be an inability to see the big picture or a general lack of clarity. Additionally, without access to your intuition and inner wisdom, you can easily be deceived, possibly leading to unhealthy relationships and other challenging situations.

In contrast, an excess of brow chakra energy may appear as excessive daydreams or living in a constant state of illusion disconnected from the material world. In addition, there may be anxiety or the tendency to over-think or over-analyze problems. These issues can affect our mental state, relationships, and professional life.

Balancing this chakra may benefit the following conditions:

- Blurred vision
- Glaucoma
- Eye strain
- Eye issues
- Migraines
- Headaches
- Nightmares
- Disconnection from intuition
- Illusions
- Inability to see the big picture
- Lack of clarity
- Anxiety
- Over-thinking

Balancing this chakra may strengthen the following attributes:

- Inner vision
- Intuition
- Insight
- Psychic abilities
- Clarity
- Greater access to dreams

Crown Chakra
Sanskrit name: Sahasrara
Meaning: Thousand-fold
Location: Top of the head
Energy state: Consciousness
Psychological function: Understanding
Color: Violet and white
Element: Thought
Planet: Uranus

The seventh energy center is the crown chakra located at the top of your head. This energy center governs our connection to the Divine, our ability to understand, our thoughts, and our higher consciousness.

When the crown chakra operates in a balanced way, we feel a solid connection to the Divine and our relationship to all things. We operate from a place of inner peace and tranquility rooted in the knowledge that we are in a state of unity with the Divine.

Imbalances in this energy center can lead to spiritual crises and feelings of isolation. If blocked or underperforming, there may be issues with apathy, mental disorders, and learning difficulties. Moreover, without access to the Divine, there may be a deep fear of the unknown and an inability to see that you are a part of a large whole: a community. Excessive materialism may also be a result of a crown chakra imbalance since the physical world may become our sole focus.

In contrast, an excess of crown chakra energy may appear as a compulsion toward spirituality at the expense of living a full life in this world. This imbalance may manifest as obsessively looking for signs or synchronicities to justify a spiritual path. Alternatively, it may be spending too much time in meditation or ritual practices while neglecting earthly responsibilities.

Balancing this chakra may benefit the following conditions:

- Mental disorders
- Issues with the central nervous system
- Fear of the unknown

- Materialism
- Memory issues
- Learning disabilities
- Apathy
- Exhaustion
- Spiritual crisis of any sort
- Disconnection from humanity

Balancing this chakra may strengthen the following attributes:

- Inner peace
- Understanding
- Unity
- Spiritual connection
- Wisdom
- Open-mindedness

Reiki healing can assist with the removal of energy blockages in the nadis and chakras, restoring balance and optimal health. Additional ways of connecting with and healing the chakras are provided in detail in the Forty Day Immersion Experience: Reiki Foundation located in part two.

Chapter 3

How Reiki Energy Works

Entrainment is the process by which Reiki works on the subtle body. It's possible to observe entrainment in the motion of clock pendulums: several clocks placed together with pendulums that are swinging out of sync with each other will eventually synchronize.

Since Reiki energy vibrates powerfully at the high frequency of unconditional love, the energy of the object or person receiving the Reiki energy will adjust to this higher level of vibration. This vibrational current can remove stagnant or blocked energy and assist with healing on an energetic level. As the energetic body is restored to health, healing may also occur in the physical, emotional, mental, and spiritual bodies.

Turning Reiki On and Off

Reiki energy flows from the divine source, into the Reiki practitioner, and out through the healer's hands. To begin the flow of this healing energy, the Reiki practitioner should set an intention for the healing session and start channeling Reiki using their own method to "turn on" the flow of Reiki. Different visualizations can assist with this process, so experiment to see which variation works best for you or develop your own visualization tool. You might try the following:

- Visualize an on/off light switch. Flip the switch on to start the flow of Reiki energy and flip the switch off to stop the energy channeling.
- Visualize a radio button and turn the dial to start or stop the flow of Reiki.

- Imagine a portal of light opening up in the universe and streaming Reiki energy emerging from it. At the end of the session, imagine the portal closing and the energy flow ceasing.

The Current of Reiki

Reiki flows from the divine source through the crown chakra of the Reiki practitioner, into the heart center, and then down through their hands into the person or object receiving the healing energy. Reiki permeates the body of the individual receiving the Reiki energy and travels through their energetic pathways (nadis) and into their chakras. Reiki energy flows where it is needed, and since its high vibrational frequency corresponds with divine love, it cannot be misused.

Reiki energy exists all around us and has an innate intelligence. You may find instances where Reiki energy may start flowing without you consciously turning it "on." For example, you may be sitting with your pet on the couch and place your hand on your pet's back when you notice your hand heats up or becomes tingly—a sign that Reiki energy is flowing through your hands. This phenomenon may signify that your pet is in need of healing energy, and you can simply allow the Reiki energy to flow through you into your pet.

Grounding Energy

The current of Reiki energy is gentle yet powerful. Grounding yourself before, during, and after a Reiki healing session is essential. Grounding allows the Reiki practitioner to stay connected to the earth and be in the present moment while channeling high vibrational Reiki energy. It also assists with maintaining energetic balance for the Reiki practitioner, who may experience periods of high energy intake as the healing session progresses. Grounding should also be done at the end of a healing session to ground and seal the Reiki energy.

Gassho meditation is a simple yet effective technique Dr. Mikao Usui taught to assist with grounding and centering. Gassho meditation may be used daily as a standalone meditation practice and before every healing session. The following steps guide you through the Gassho meditation process:

- Sit or stand with a straight spine and your head in a neutral position.
- Allow your eyes to close or have a soft gaze in front of you.

- Bring the palms of your hands together in prayer position with your thumbs touching your heart center.
- Notice the natural flow of your breath without altering it in any way.
- Bring your awareness to the place where the middle fingers touch.
- If your mind wanders or drifts, return your focus to the place of connection of your middle fingers.
- End the meditation when you experience a sense of balance and focus.

Clearing Energy

As energy Reiki flows from the hand of the Reiki practitioner into the healing partici-pant, stagnant energy will begin to flow, and energetic blockages will start to dissolve. As these processes take place, lower vibrational energy may be released. The Reiki prac-titioner may experience this lower vibrational energy as a heaviness or thickness in the air or, for those visually inclined, as gray mist or smoke. If this occurs, energy clearing practices may be used to help disperse the energy. The following techniques are helpful when clearing energy:

- Sweeping the area with your outstretched arm or a smudge fan.
- Visualizing Reiki-infused rain lightly showering your healing space, washing away the negative energy.
- Using a Tibetan singing bowl to clear the room's energy.

After a Reiki session, the person receiving Reiki should have their auric field swept by your outstretched arm or smudge fan at least three times to clear away stagnant or negative energy that has been released. Additionally, you may want to consider clearing the energy of your healing space using the above techniques.

Benefits of Reiki Energy

There are innumerable benefits to receiving Reiki energy. Since Reiki energy heals on an energetic basis, there are opportunities for healing on all levels of being: physical, emo-tional, mental, and spiritual. However, since healing will occur according to the highest good of the healing participant, it is impossible to know the precise nature of the healing benefits an individual will receive.

Benefits that a healing participant may experience include the following:

- Stress reduction
- Pain relief
- Improved quality of sleep
- Balancing of the mind, body, and spirit
- Assistance with preventative care
- Relaxation
- Improvement in overall well-being

For the Reiki practitioner, there are also benefits to performing Reiki. In addition to being of service to others, performing Reiki healing strengthens your own connection to the universal healing energy. This connection supports your energetic field and raises your personal vibration. As your own energetic frequency rises, you may experience spiritual gifts of all kinds.

Chapter 4

Spiritual Gifts, Sacred Imagination, and Sacred Intuition

As your energetic body becomes accustomed to the high vibrational energy of Reiki, you may notice an enhancement or access to various "spiritual gifts." I use the term differently than religious organizations, but some overlap exists. When I speak of spiritual gifts, I'm referring to the personal qualities, talents, and abilities that become more accessible to us as our vibrational frequency naturally increases when engaging in our healing process and regular meditation.

Before diving deeper into the spiritual gifts relevant to Reiki healing, consider what you believe your spiritual gifts are and how they express themselves in your life. You might want to pause here and take a moment to write down your spiritual gifts in your Reiki journal to track their development as you progress along your life path and record new gifts as they appear. Do not limit yourselves to only the blessings described in this section.

Knowledge is the expertise gained through instruction or life experiences. The gift of spiritual knowledge is divinely inspired knowledge that assists you with your personal evolution, as well as an awareness of how to heal yourself and others. This knowledge may come in the form of channeling or "downloading" information directly to your mind. Alternatively, you can obtain this knowledge by finding the right teachers, books, or courses to assist with your personal growth and help you along your unique path. Regarding Reiki, spiritual knowledge can be obtained by finding teachers, books, and classes about Reiki that resonate with you.

Understanding describes our ability to grasp the meaning of something. The gift of spiritual understanding is comprehending the meaning behind the facts, information, and skills leading to personal growth and transformation. Understanding is a uniquely personal experience. Teachers and other guides can assist with the understanding process, but it's up to the individual to actively pursue the deeper meaning behind the knowledge. For those learning about Reiki, spiritual understanding may happen when the techniques and mechanics are mastered and the deeper level of why we perform them are grasped. This process can be envisioned as moving the information from the mind's intellect to the heart center, where a profound understanding takes place.

Wisdom occurs when an individual has both knowledge and understanding. Spiritual wisdom leads to actions aligned with our highest potential. Once the knowledge of Reiki is both known and understood, material changes may occur in your daily life. More informed decisions may be made regarding relationships, habits, attitudes, modes of thinking, and behaviors that align with our ultimate goals and promote a healthier lifestyle.

Sacred Imagination

We are all born with imagination: some individuals have very active imaginations, while others are less engaged with this part of themselves. You may think of time spent daydreaming is a mere waste of time and discount the vital role imagination can play in your personal evolutionary process as well as your development as a Reiki healer. Your imagination may also be considered a spiritual gift. With sacred imagination, you use your imagination to assist with your personal development, including your ability to perform Reiki.

There are several ways in which imagination can be useful in Reiki healing, including the following:

- Imagine the chakra energy centers within yourself or your healing participant.
- Imagine the colors of the chakras behind your closed eyes to connect deeper with their energetic frequency.
- Imagine the Reiki energy descending from Source and flowing through you.
- Imagine creating your own inner healing temple where you can perform distance healing sessions.

- Imagine being surrounded by angels and spirit guides as you perform Reiki.
- Imagine yourself or your healing participant in perfect health.

A component of your imagination is your ability to visualize and create images in your mind's eye. Visualization is a skill you can develop. If visualization doesn't come naturally to you, don't worry or stress about creating the mental images. Instead, imagine what the experience would be like if you could call up the desired image. Be patient with yourself as your mind's eye becomes more focused; the skill will develop in time.

The uses of sacred imagination to help create the future you desire and to obtain a healthier version of yourself is unlimited. So engage your imagination and experience the results for yourself.

Sacred Intuition

The last of the spiritual gifts we will be exploring is the concept of sacred intuition. Intuition is our capacity to comprehend something spontaneously without the involvement of our rational mind. Simply put, intuition is your gut response. We are all born with an intuitive nature but unfortunately, society has placed a greater value on the rational mind and logic. Once we begin to ignore our intuitive hits, we become disconnected from our intuitive abilities. Fortunately, when we begin to actively listen to these subtle signals, we can restore our connection to our intuitive guidance.

Reiki healers who are connected to their intuition may receive guidance on alternative hand placements, guidance on whether to use crystals or aromatherapy in conjunction with Reiki healing sessions, and additional insights regarding the healing journey of others as well as their own healing paths. Be open to how you can develop and act on your own intuitive guidance: both for your own development and for assisting others.

As you consciously work on your own healing and the health of your energetic body, your connection to your sacred imagination and sacred intuition will develop. You may experience additional spiritual gifts in the form of psychic senses. Psychic senses mirror the physical senses, but the source of the psychic information is unknown or inexplicable by conventional standards. A more detailed explanation of the psychic senses appears in part three, but a summary of the psychic skills that may begin to develop may be found here:

- Clairvoyance (clear seeing) is the ability to see using a second sight that may be perceived through the mind's eye in the form of inner visions or external through your physical eyes.
- Clairaudience (clear hearing) is the ability to hear with either your physical ears as sounds from outside yourself or as inner hearing.
- Claircognizance (clear knowing) is the ability to know by receiving a download of information directly into your brain without any external means of obtaining the information.
- Clairempathy (clear feeling) is the ability to share in the feelings of another as if those feelings are your own.
- Clairsentience (clear sensing) is the ability to sense the energetic signature or vibes of another person, object, or place.
- Clairalience (clear smelling) is the ability to smell something not present in your physical environment.
- Clairgustance (clear tasting) is the ability to taste something that is not in your mouth.
- Clairtangency (clear touching) is the ability to receive information previously unknown by touching a person or object.

Chapter 5
The Art of Reiki Self-Healing

One of the most essential practices of Reiki is self-healing. When you perform Reiki on yourself, you are not only participating in your own healing process but also sending a signal to the universe that you are prioritizing your own self-care.

The hand positions for self-healing vary among traditions and from Reiki book to Reiki book. However, these are the self-healing hand placements that you may consider using for optimal healing benefits.

Self-Healing Hand Position 1

In the first hand placement when doing a Reiki self-treatment healing session, place the palms of your hands gently over your eyes with the fingers positioned on your forehead.

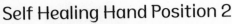

Self Healing Hand Position 2

The second hand placement typically performed when doing a Reiki self-treatment healing session is placing the palms of your hands gently on each side of your jaw line with your fingers positioned over a portion of your ears.

Self-Healing Hand Position 3

The third hand placement typically performed when doing a Reiki self-treatment healing session is gently placing the palms of your hands over your throat center. One version of this hand placement places one hand on your neck and the other covering the first hand. Alternatively, you can place your inside wrists together, letting the heels of your hands rest on the center of your neck, allowing your fingers to wrap along either side of it.

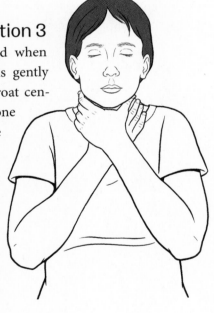

Self-Healing Hand Position 4

The fourth suggested hand position in a Reiki self-treatment practice focuses on the area around the back of the head. Your hands form a triangle shape by placing your thumbs touching your skull's base and your index finger resting on the middle skull region. An alternative hand position is to cradle the back of your head with one hand and place the other hand right above it.

Self-Healing Hand Position 5

The heart center of the body is the focus of the fifth suggested hand position in a Reiki self-treatment practice. Lay one hand on the center of your chest with the other slightly above it. Alternatively, you may place one hand over your heart and cover it with your second hand.

Self-Healing Hand Position 6

The ribs and upper abdomen are the focus of the sixth hand position in a Reiki self-treatment practice. Gently rest your hands below your breasts on your lower ribs.

Self-Healing Hand Position 7

The abdomen is the focus of the seventh hand position. Place your hands on the center of your core for this hand placement. Your fingers should be facing toward your belly button.

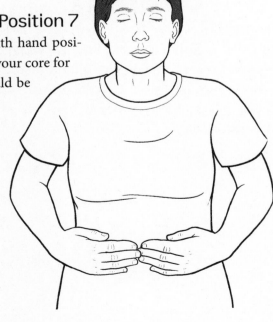

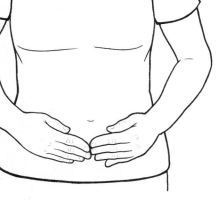

Self-Healing Hand Position 8

The eighth hand position focuses on the lower abdomen. Place your hands on your lower belly region slightly below your navel.

Self-Healing Hand Position 9

The ninth hand position in a Reiki self-treatment practice focuses on the upper back. Place your hands on your upper back region with your fingertips on your shoulder blades.

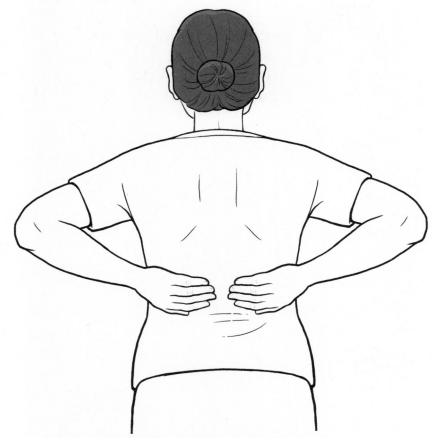

Self-Healing Hand Position 10

The tenth hand position focuses on the middle back. For this hand placement, place your hands on your middle back region. It may not be possible for both hands to reach your middle back. If that's the case, try using just one hand at a time or hover your hands slightly away from the area.

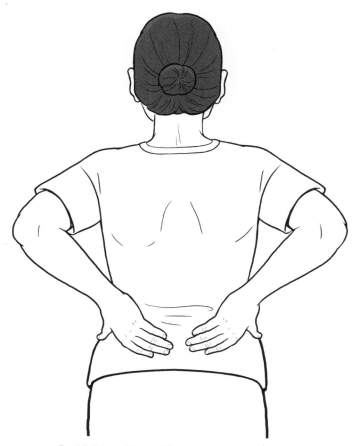

Self-Healing Hand Position 11

The eleventh hand position focuses on the lower back. Place your hands on your lower back region for this hand placement with your fingers pointing in a downward direction.

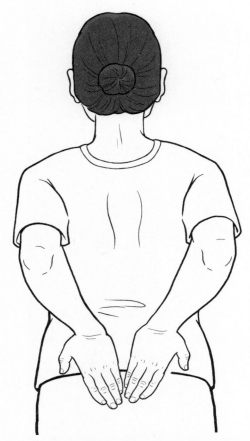

Self-Healing Hand Position 12

The twelfth suggested hand position in a Reiki self-treatment practice focuses on the sacrum (tailbone). For this position, place your hands on your sacrum almost as if you were sitting on your hands.

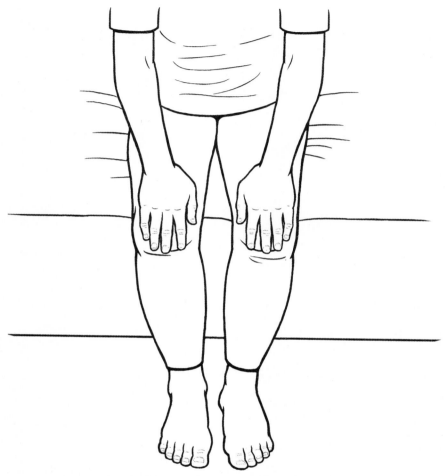

Self-Healing Hand Position 13

The thirteenth suggested hand position in a Reiki self-treatment is focused on the knees. For this hand position, place your hands on each kneecap.

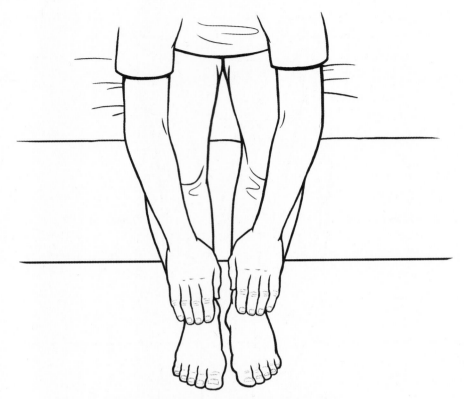

Self-Healing Hand Position 14

The fourteenth and final hand position in a Reiki self-treatment practice focuses on the feet. For this one, place your hands over your ankles and feet.

Performing a Reiki Self-Healing Session

The process of performing a self-healing session should be approached in the same manner as you would if you were healing another person: with an open heart and focused attention. Some guidelines to assist you with performing a meaningful and successful Reiki self-healing session are outlined below.

Step 1: Create your sacred healing space

Creating a sacred healing place to perform your Reiki self-healing treatments doesn't require complex rituals. When we create a sacred healing space, we designate an area as a safe, calming environment to explore our inner worlds, participate in our own healing, and connect with Reiki's divine energy. Ideally, the area should be clean and free from clutter. Outside distractions should be minimized, and cell phones should always be silenced. You will need a chair or meditation cushion to sit on while performing the self-healing Reiki session. Additional components to add to the ambiance of this healing space are candles, incense, or essential oils. The most critical element of your sacred healing space is you.

Step 2: Set your intention

Your intention has innate power within it. Our intention directs our will and our energy. Setting an intention before your self-healing Reiki healing session is an essential step in the process. Consider what you hope to accomplish during your Reiki healing session: perhaps you have a physical ailment or illness, experiencing a high degree of stress, or having trouble sleeping. Each day is different, so check for what parts of yourself need your attention today.

Based on your analysis, you can craft your daily healing intention. A sample may be found below.

"My personal intention for my self-healing Reiki session today is for full-body healing and for deep relaxation to assist with releasing the anxiety I have been experiencing. May this healing session be aligned with my best and highest good."

Step 3: Ground yourself

Connecting to the earth and centering yourself is a crucial step in all Reiki healing sessions. It assists with maintaining focus and energetic stability. Grounding doesn't have to be a time-consuming process. Anywhere from a minute to a few minutes will suffice.

Gassho meditation with your hands in prayer positive and your thumbs resting on your heart center is the traditional way to ground before a Reiki session. Still, you can experiment to see if other techniques resonate with you.

Step 4: Start the flow of Reiki energy

After you feel grounded and centered, you can start the flow of Reiki energy by setting your intention to "turn on" Reiki. Visualization techniques such as imagining a light switch turning on or a dial rotating from "off" to "on" might be helpful. After you start the flow of Reiki, rub the palms of your hands together a few times as you visualize the flow of Reiki energy entering the crown of your head, flowing down your spine into your heart center, through your arms, and into your hands. You may experience tingling or warmth in your hands at this time. If you don't feel physical sensations, don't worry: the Reiki energy is still flowing through you.

Step 5: Perform your self-healing session

Now you are ready to begin your self-healing Reiki session. You can refer to the self-healing hand positions for a traditional Reiki treatment session. You can let your hands rest in a particular position for as long as you feel that the Reiki energy is needed in that area. There is no need to rush or move too quickly. Listen to your inner guidance and pay attention to any shifts in energy that may occur during your session.

Instead of using the traditional self-healing hand placements, you can let your intuition be your guide and place your hand where you instinctively feel they should be. You have the freedom to customize the hand positions, the order of the hand positions, and the duration of time spent in each hand position. Experiment to see what works best for you. Consider keeping a journal of your self-healing sessions to track your use of hand placements and any insights you receive during your treatments.

Step 6: Stop the flow of Reiki energy

When you feel your Reiki session is complete, set the intention to turn off the flow of Reiki energy. If you used visualization to assist with turning Reiki "on," consider using the same visualization to turn the flow of Reiki energy "off."

Step 7: Clear stagnant or negative energies

During your Reiki self-healing treatment, you may be releasing energy that has a heavy quality and/or may feel negative or oppressive. Sweep your auric field at least three times with your hand or an herb bundle to assist with moving any released energy away from you.

You may decide to energetically cleanse the room after your Reiki self-healing treatment. There are several ways to approach this practice, including using a Tibetan singing bowl or misting sprays of rose water or Florida water.

Step 8: Ending your Reiki self-healing session

After you clear the room's energy, give thanks for the healing gift of Reiki energy. Also, express gratitude toward yourself for taking an active role in your healing process.

I highly recommend journaling your direct experience of your Reiki healing sessions: describe any shifts in energy that may have occurred physically, emotionally, mentally, and energetically. You may also wish to record any insights you receive during your session. These notes are invaluable for tracking your personal transformation and providing documentation of your unique hand placements as well as your energetic response to those hand placements.

If you're in a time crunch, it's better to do an abbreviated self-healing Reiki session than to eliminate the practice altogether. For example, you might want to use a timer and do a Reiki session based on an allotted time or do random Reiki spot-treatments throughout the day.

Benefits of Using Reiki for Self-Healing

There are innumerable benefits to performing Reiki every day. In addition to the typical benefits outlined in chapter three, the Reiki practitioner develops a deeper understanding of Reiki: both as a Reiki practitioner and Reiki recipient. The following list shows some ways these insights may be invaluable to you as you progress along this path of healing:

- First-hand experience of the benefits of Reiki healing
- A deeper understanding of the energy body
- A deeper connection to Reiki energy and how it flows
- Experience using your intuition as a guide in the Reiki healing process
- Strengthening and balancing the chakras
- Greater alignment with your higher self and sense of purpose

As you gain first-hand experience of using Reiki for self-healing, you will find a more profound understanding of how this energy healing modality works. Your understanding may lead to a great source of wisdom regarding Reiki healing, the energy body, and your personal connection to the Divine.

Chapter 6

The Art of Healing Others with Reiki

Offering Reiki healing to others is a beautiful gift. However, there are certain matters that must be considered before beginning a Reiki healing session.

Do you have permission to perform Reiki healing? You should not perform Reiki healing unless you have the explicit consent of the receiver of Reiki energy. The person to whom the Reiki healing energy is being sent must actively participate in the healing process and want to receive the healing energy. For this reason, I refer to the recipient of Reiki healing as a healing participant instead of a client. Know that if you choose not to obtain permission, you are essentially imposing your will on others and, as a result, affecting your own karma. If there is a reason why the person can't provide consent (e.g., the person is in a coma), consider using your imagination: in your mind's eye, picture yourself asking for their permission. In this instance, allow your intuition to guide you on whether the person is consenting to receive Reiki healing.

Do you need a waiver? You might not need a release if you are performing Reiki on friends and family members. That said, it's always best practice to require a waiver before the beginning of a Reiki treatment session, since it provides a level of protection against lawsuits. A sample waiver is provided in the appendix (page 337), or you can find additional samples online.

Hand Positions for Healing Others

The hand positions below are a guide. Before placing your hands on your healing participant, ask them if they would prefer a hands-on healing session or for you to hover your hands instead. If they choose for you to hover your hands, you may use the same hand placements but place your hands a few inches above the body part receiving the

Reiki energy. If they elect to have a hands-on treatment, follow up by asking if there are any parts of the body that they would prefer you do not touch. Please keep in mind that you should *never* touch the private areas of your healing participant's body.

The following hand positions can be used if your healing participant is lying down or modified if they are sitting in a chair.

Front Body

Hand Position 1: Eyes
Both palms rest gently over the healing participant's eyes, with your fingers lying over the cheekbones.

Hand Position 2: Temples
Both palms cradle the sides of the head with the fingers resting on the temples.

Hand Position 3: Ears
Both palms gently cup the participant's ears or are hovered near the ears. Direct contact covering the ears may be triggering to some individuals.

Hand Position 4: Throat
The throat is a very sensitive area for most individuals. Therefore, the suggested hand placement is with the fingertips on either side of the collarbone (clavicle bones) without directly touching the throat. Alternatively, you can hover your hands over the throat chakra.

Hand Position 5: Heart
Place your hands on top of each other on your healing participant's heart center. Please be sensitive to a female client's chest area; if there is a chance of touching her breasts, hover your hands instead.

Hand Position 6: Ribs
Place your hands on one side of your healing participant's ribs. Treat only one side of the ribs at a time unless you have the arm length to reach both sides simultaneously.

Hand Position 7: Core
Place your hands next to each other at your client's core, solar plexus area.

Hand Position 8: Lower Abdominal Region

Place your hands at your healing participant's navel.

Hand Position 9: Hips

Place your hands at your healing participant's hip points.

Hand Position 10: Thighs

Place your hands at your healing participant's thigh above the knees, and then move your hands down to the knees.

Hand Position 11: Feet and Ankles

Cup one foot and ankle of your healing participant before moving on to the second foot and ankle.

Back of the Body

The following hand positions can be used to treat the back of the body. If you choose not to have your healing participant turn over, that is fine since Reiki energy will flow through the energy channels wherever it's needed.

Hand Position 12: Upper Back

Place both hands on the upper back above the shoulder blades.

Hand Position 13: Shoulders

Place both hands on the shoulder blades.

Hand Position 14: Middle Back and Lower Back

Move your hands to the middle of the back and then continue down to the lower back.

Hand Position 15: Tailbone

Rest your hands at your healing participant's base of the spine, which is known as the tailbone or sacrum. Be mindful not to touch the buttocks of your healing participant.

Hand Position 16: Knees

Gently rest your hands on your healing participant's back of the knees.

Hand Position 17: Ankles
Place your hands on the back of the ankles and cradle the ankles lightly.

Hand Position 18: Soles of the Feet
Place your hands over the soles of the feet.

Evaluating Your Healing Participant's Energy

Two methods are commonly used for evaluating subtle energy for a Reiki session: the first uses your hands, and the second uses a pendulum.

If using your hands to scan energy, allow them to hover about six to eight inches from the body of your healing participant. Start with the crown of the head, and slowly let your hand move downward toward the feet. You may experience hot or cold spots. You may also feel a heaviness or denseness of energy in certain areas. These are places where energy blockages or unbalanced energy is pooled. These are areas that should receive extra Reiki energy during your healing session.

Alternatively, a pendulum can help assess the energetic health of the healing participant, especially the chakra centers. Hold the pendulum over each chakra center and observe the movement. A balanced energy center will have the pendulum move in a clockwise direction. Imbalanced or blocked energy centers will cause the pendulum to move in another manner, such as in a line, counter-clockwise, or remain still.

Performing a Reiki Healing Session

General guidelines for creating a healing space for your Reiki sessions include ensuring the surface your healing participant will be lying on or sitting in is clean and disinfected. The room should be inviting and free of clutter. You may want to consider using a white noise machine or meditation music during your healing session. Ask your healing participant before using any essential oils since there are allergies and sensitivities to certain aromas. All cell phones should be silenced before beginning.

Intake Form/Waiver
If it is your first time seeing a healing participant, consider spending a few moments talking about the purpose for the healing session. You can have a participant complete an intake form and a waiver if that is your preference. If you do decide to use intake

forms, respect your healing participants' privacy and file these forms away in a safe place. Do not discuss an individual's health concerns with others.

The Reiki Session: Step by Step

What follows is a suggested step-by-step outline of a Reiki session. Feel free to experiment and develop your unique style.

Invite your healing participant to sit or lie down. Reiki healing participants should remain fully clothed; shoes can be removed.

Confirm whether your healing participant would like hands-on or hands-off treatment and if there are any areas they would prefer you not to touch.

Ask if your healing participant would like a blanket for warmth or a bolster under the knees to relieve pressure on the lower back.

Once your healing participant is comfortable, recite aloud your intention for this Reiki session. Allow your intuition to guide how you phrase your healing intention. For example: "It is my heartfelt intention that this Reiki healing session is for the best and highest good for [participant's name] and provides healing for the body, mind, and soul."

Ask your healing participant if there is anything they would like to add to that intention and if they are willing to receive the gift of Reiki healing.

Ground yourself using the Gassho meditation technique and start the flow of Reiki using your intention and visualization.

Scan your healing participant's energy field with your hands or with a pendulum.

Place your hands on your healing participant's shoulders as a way of connecting to their energy and allowing your healing participant to adjust to the pressure of your hands.

When you feel ready, you can use the suggested hand placements or place your hands where your intuition guides you. Remember not to touch any sensitive areas of your healing participant, including any specific body parts or areas you were asked to avoid.

Using your hands or a pendulum, scan your healing participant's auric field and chakras to evaluate the energetic response to your healing session.

Turn off Reiki at the session's close using your intention and visualization. Proceed to sweep your healing participant's aura (about 6 inches to a foot over the physical body) three times using your hand or an herb bundle.

Inform your healing participant that the session has ended. You may want to consider placing your hand on your healing participant's shoulders as you did when you started the Reiki session. Consider saying a phrase or two acknowledging the end of the treatment, such as: "At the close of this healing session, we want to express gratitude for the gift of Reiki healing. Thank you. Thank you. Thank you."

Ask that your healing participant get up slowly at their own pace.

You may want to spend a few moments after the healing session to discuss your healing participant's experience and share your insights regarding the healing session.

Aftercare for Your Healing Participant

You may want to make some suggestions to your healing participant to help them assimilate to the Reiki energy they received, including the following: drinking plenty of water, eating nourishing foods, avoiding alcohol and non-prescription drugs, resting as needed, and taking a bath with sea salts or essential oils.

Aftercare for the Reiki Practitioner

After you perform a Reiki healing session, it's essential to restore your own energetic balance. After your healing participant has left, consider doing the following: washing your hands to remove unwanted energy (and for basic hygiene), performing a short grounding meditation, taking a walk or performing some basic stretches to bring your awareness back to your physical body, and resting as needed.

Chapter 7

The Power of Intention

I invite you to go deeper in self-exploration. Let's begin with developing your intention for the next forty-day immersion experience designed to deepen your understanding of Reiki by providing you with a personal experience of key foundational concepts. Dr. Wayne Dyer describes intention as "a strong purpose or aim, accompanied by a determination to produce a desired result."[2] Your intention is a force lit by your inner fire and fueled by your personal will.

Intention setting is a powerful practice that focuses energy on the desired outcome. When your intention is connected to your heart (emotional body), mind (mental body), and spirit (higher self), the results can be astonishing. To ensure that our intentions are aligned in this manner, we should perform a personal inquiry, without judgment, to assess our true motivations and desired outcomes.

Setting Your Intention: A Promise of Growth and Healing Made to Yourself

As a prelude to undertaking your forty-day journey into the foundational elements of Reiki, contemplate what you are hoping to gain from this process. Make a listing of goals, hopes, and wishes for your personal healing and, potentially, for healing others.

Craft a personal intention for the next forty days based on your unique aims. Intention setting assists with providing clarity and vision, aligning our daily actions with longer-term goals. We will connect with your intention daily to remind you of your commitment to yourself and your healing journey.

---

2. Wayne Dyer, *The Power of Intention: Learning to Co-Create Your World Your Way* (Carlsbad, CA: Hay House, 2004), 1.

Sample Heartfelt Intention

I, [your name], agree to follow the daily practices in these pages, including meditation, journaling, and self-healing for a minimum of forty days. I will say *yes* to activities, choices, and thoughts that align with my goals of learning the tools and techniques to heal myself and others on physical, emotional, mental, energetic, and spiritual levels.

Today, with a grateful heart for my unique journey, I am ready to commit myself to the study of Reiki healing and integrate Reiki energy into my daily life.

Signed: _____

Date: _____

Part 2

Forty-Day Immersion Experience: Reiki Foundations

Reiki Exploration Day 1

Daily Intention Review

Take a moment and connect with the ground beneath you. From a place of stability and inner stillness, recite aloud your heartfelt intention.

Grounding

Grounding is an essential practice for Reiki practitioners of all levels. Grounding refers to the ability to align your body, mind, and spirit with the energetic frequency of the earth. The act of grounding enhances your focus and your ability to stay present in the moment. Grounding also assists with maintaining energetic boundaries and letting go of blocked energy trapped in your subtle (energetic) body. If an excess of energy exists, grounding is a way of releasing extra energy back into the earth and cultivating energetic balance. When you are aligned with the earth element and firmly grounded, you can more easily manifest your inner vision and develop a solid foundation to channel Reiki energy.

There are many benefits to developing a consistent grounding practice, including the following outcomes: reduction of stress and anxiety, greater awareness of surroundings, living in the present moment, development of inner strength, and deepening the mind-body-spirit connection.

For Reiki practitioners, grounding also ensures that healing sessions occur from a solid foundation: a place of energetic balance and harmony.

Many signs and symptoms indicate that you may be in an un-grounded state. For example, feelings of being scattered or disorganized may be a sign that more grounding is needed. The inability to focus, ineffective communication skills, losing track of time, and feelings of exhaustion are all additional signals. Consuming food is a way to ground yourself, but it can have adverse health consequences when taken to an extreme; over-eating is an often overlooked symptom of a lack of grounding.

Your grounding practices may be as unique as you are, so experiment with what grounding practices are most effective for you. Develop your own grounding toolkit with your favorite and most effective techniques to connect with Mother Earth. For example, you may find that spending time in nature or gardening is the most effective way to ground yourself. Alternatively, perhaps you connect more closely with visualizations or meditations. Affirmations, repeated positive statements to elicit an effect, may be another approach that you'd like to explore. Suggestions you may wish to include in your personal grounding toolkit include the following:

✤ Activities

- Plant a garden.
- Spend time in nature walking or hiking.
- Walk barefoot on the grass, often called earthing.
- Lie in savasana (corpse pose) outside or inside, feeling a connection to the earth's grounded energy.
- Receive a massage.

✤ Meditations

- Visualize the colors associated with the earth element during meditation: green, brown, or red.
- Take your meditation practice outside and meditate while sitting on a rock or leaning against the trunk of a tree.
- Visualize roots growing from your tailbone and descending all the way down to the core of the earth, where the roots may draw up the grounding energy of Mother Earth.
- Meditate using Prithvi mudra by gently connecting your ring finger and thumb. (Mudras are hand gestures known to provide specific energetic results.) Your palms may be positioned upwards to receive energy or downwards for additional grounding.

✤ Affirmations

- "I am connected to the healing energies of Mother Earth."
- "I live in harmony and balance with the energies of the earth."

You can also purchase metaphysical tools to assist with achieving a more grounded state. What follows are some recommendations. Please keep in mind that flower essences are often made with brandy or vodka. If you have issues with alcohol, you may want to find a flower essence made with glycerin, use the flower essence as a room spray, or apply it topically instead of ingesting it.

✿ *Essential Oils*

- Cedarwood
- Rosewood
- Juniper
- Cypress
- Patchouli

✿ *Crystals*

- Petrified wood
- Smoky quartz
- Dalmatian jasper

✿ *Flower Essences*

- Pink Yarrow for establishing energetic boundaries
- Corn Flower for grounding

As a Reiki practitioner, you should implement a grounding practice before, during, and after a Reiki healing session. This practice can be as elaborate or as simple as you wish. You are only limited by your own imagination.

Grounding Practice Meditation

Find a comfortable seated position and settle in for a few moments. Then, take a complete inventory of yourself at this moment in time. Notice how you feel physically, emotionally, mentally, and energetically.

Set a timer for five to ten minutes, and silence your cell phone.

In your mind's eye, imagine roots growing from the soles of your feet (or your tailbone if you are seated in a cross-legged position). These roots travel through the layers of soil, air pockets, and underground streams all the way down to the center of the earth. Once at the earth's core, imagine your roots drawing up nurturing, grounded energy. This energy can be any color that resonates with you, but traditionally, earth energy is visualized as the color green. On each inhaling breath, picture the grounding energy of Mother Earth traveling up your roots into your body. And on each exhaling breath, visualize the healing energy of Mother Earth spreading throughout your body and auric field.

At the end of your meditation, thank Mother Earth for sharing her gifts with you and release the visualization. Sit for two to three minutes afterward in contemplation, observing your practice's ripple effects.

Journaling Practice

Reflect on your meditation practice. Describe your direct experience connecting to Mother Earth and infusing your auric field with her energy. How did this practice affect your physical, emotional, mental, energetic, and spiritual bodies? What are some opportunities for you to use a similar grounding practice in your daily life? How might you incorporate grounding as a part of your Reiki healing sessions?

Reiki Exploration Day 2

Daily Intention Review

Take a moment to reconnect with your heartfelt intention. Then, as you recite it aloud, picture it in your mind's eye as if it has already happened.

Self-Healing Hand Position 1: Eyes

Traditionally, the first hand placement when doing a Reiki self-treatment healing session is placing the palms of your hands gently over your eyes with your fingers positioned on your forehead. Because healing may occur across all dimensions of our being and not just our physical shell, it's worth exploring which areas are directly affected by this hand placement.

Consider what body parts physically receive Reiki energy during hand placement 1: the eyes, muscles surrounding the eyes, skeleton structure of the eyes, forehead, and cheeks. Additionally, consider the skull's interior, which contains the brain and three glands associated with the endocrine system: the pineal gland assists with the sleep cycle, the hypothalamus gland helps with regulating other glands, and the pituitary gland is responsible for the production of essential hormones. Finally, the nose and associated sinus cavities would benefit from this hand placement, improving the ability to breathe and assist with the process of respiration.

Energetically, this hand placement may stimulate the brow or third eye chakra. This energy center relates to our intuition and inner sight, which is commonly known as clairvoyance. In addition, our crown chakra located at the top of our head would also receive these healing energies resulting in a stronger connection to the Divine and enhancing our inner knowing abilities, often referred to as claircognizance.

This hand placement may benefit the following ailments:

- Eye injury or eye illness
- Cataracts
- Macular degeneration
- Tension headaches
- Hormone production
- Short-sightedness
- Not seeing the big picture
- Addictive behaviors
- Stress
- Anxiety
- Sleep disorders
- Allergies

This hand placement may strengthen or balance the following attributes:

- Intuition
- Clairvoyance
- Vision
- Intelligence
- Moral consciousness
- Focus
- Claircognizance
- Connection to the Divine

The above listing is not all-inclusive. Experiment with this hand position and track other potential applications.

Self-Healing Targeted Practice

Find a comfortable seated position and cultivate a moment or two of stillness. Silence your cell phone. Take a scan of yourself: notice how you are feeling physically and also observe your inner landscape.

Tune in to Reiki using your unique method of connection and feel the infusion of Reiki energy into your being. Using hand position 1 for self-healing, give yourself a five-minute targeted Reiki healing session. Hand position 1, for clarity, is with the palms of the hands lightly covering the eyes.

Sit for a few minutes afterward in contemplation, observing the after-effects of your self-healing treatment.

Journaling Practice

Reflect on hand position 1. How did this hand position land with you? Did it stir up any positive or negative sensations, feelings, or memories? How might your physical sight or your inner sight benefit from this hand placement? What did the targeted self-healing experience of hand position 1 inform you of how you may use this hand position for future Reiki healing sessions?

Reiki Exploration Day 3

Daily Intention Review

Cultivate feelings of gratitude for Reiki energy as you read aloud your heartfelt intention.

Reiki Principle Line 1: "Just for today, I will be grateful."

Recent scientific studies demonstrate that individuals who cultivate a thankful approach to life experience more significant physical and emotional health and greater overall happiness. For example, in their 2003 paper titled "Counting Blessing Versus Burdens: An Experimental Investigation of Gratitude and Subjective Well-Being in Daily Life," Robert Emmons and Michael McCullough document the benefits of performing a daily gratitude practice. During this experiment, the participating college students practicing daily gratitude experienced better physical and mental health than the control group.

Some benefits of a sincere, consistent gratitude practice include the following:

- Greater joy and happiness
- Increased levels of optimism and energy

- A greater sense of optimism about the future
- Improved sleep patterns and quality of sleep
- Healthier relationships
- Greater compassion for others
- Reduced stress levels and stress-related health issues
- Healthier lifestyle choices
- More confidence
- Greater self-esteem

Cultivating gratitude is a practice. You may consider this type of practice "endurance training for the heart." To assist you in developing your own attitude of gratitude, I've assembled a few of my favorite gratitude practices below.

Gratitude Journal: Every day, write down at least three things that give rise to feelings of gratitude within you. The challenge is never to repeat an item on your list. Use your imagination. Be creative. We are all blessed in so many ways.

Affirmations: Use an affirmation as part of your meditation practice or a simple reminder to be grateful throughout the day. Here are a few of my favorites.

- Thankfulness, appreciation, and heartfelt gratitude are significant parts of my identity.
- I am thankful for everything I have in my life today and for all the blessing I will receive in the future.
- I start my day with a grateful and open heart. (Try this affirmation at the beginning of the day.)
- I am grateful for all the experiences, opportunities, and interactions I had today. (Try this affirmation at the end of the day.)
- I am grateful for the challenges in my life, as they are opportunities for personal growth.

Thank-you Letter: Write a sincere letter of thanks to someone who has had a positive impact on your life. If this individual is alive, consider mailing them the letter. Often people have no idea of the beneficial influence they have had on the lives of others.

Gratitude Collage: Create a visual reminder of all your blessings. The collage (a collection of assorted pictures) can consist of words or images. Get creative! Look at the collage often to connect with the feelings of thankfulness and appreciation.

Meditation: Meditation is a powerful exercise on many levels. When combined with a gratitude practice, it has even more benefits. The following is a sample of a gratitude meditation taught in one of my classes:

> Take a comfortable seat. Relax and focus on the natural rhythm of your breath. When you are ready, begin to picture an object of your gratitude in your mind's eye. It can be a person, a situation, a pet, an element of nature—anything at all. Picture this object as clearly as you can. When you have a well-defined image, reach for this object and place it in your heart center. Pause for a moment in genuine appreciation before calling to mind another focus of your gratitude and repeat the process for five to ten minutes. After completing the meditation, you may want to write down your experience, thoughts, and feelings in a journal to reflect on later.

By taking gratitude beyond the superficial into a more heartfelt, conscientious approach to daily living, we can enhance all aspects of our being: physical, mental, emotional, energetic, and spiritual.

Reiki Principle Practice

Find a comfortable seated position and take a moment to settle in. Then, take a complete inventory of yourself at this moment in time. Notice how you feel physically, emotionally, mentally, and energetically.

Reflect on the first line of the Reiki Principle, which may be similar to the one below:

"Just for today, I will be grateful."

Set a timer for five minutes and use this line from the Reiki Principle as an affirmation, repeating it to yourself or out loud for the duration of that time. If your mind wanders during this practice, simply invite your mind to refocus on the affirmation.

Sit for a few moments afterward in contemplation, observing any shifts in energy that may have occurred.

Journaling Practice

Reflect on this line of the Reiki Principle. Does this line of the Reiki Principle resonate with you? Why or why not? How would you design a personal gratitude practice? How could you benefit from invoking more gratitude daily? How can gratitude play more of a role in your Reiki healing sessions?

Reiki Exploration Day 4

Daily Intention Review

Take a moment to reflect on your heartfelt intention. Then read it aloud and feel appreciation toward your dedication to your healing path.

The Root Chakra

The root chakra is your foundation chakra and is located at your tailbone. This chakra is associated with survival, our sense of security and stability, our physical body, and our financial health.

Let's explore your connection to your own root chakra. Consider these statements:

- "I am financially secure."
- "I easily manifest my heart's desires."
- "I am deeply connected to Mother Earth."
- "I feel safe and secure."
- "I have a right to exist."
- "I am at home in my physical body."
- "My home life is stable and peaceful."

If you noticed a statement does not feel true for you now, consider paying extra attention to your root chakra. Fortunately, there are many ways to balance and heal this energy center. For example, daily Reiki self-healing sessions or other energetic healing treatments would positively impact this energy vortex. Experiment with the suggestions below for additional ways to harmonize and strengthen your root chakra.

✿ Activities

- Spend time in nature walking or hiking.
- Practice grounding exercises and meditations.
- Recite the bija (seed) mantra associated with the root chakra: *Lam* (pronounced "lahm").
- Visualize a vibrant red color.

✿ Affirmations

- "I am supported."
- "I am safe and financially secure."
- "I have a right to exist and to thrive."

You can also purchase metaphysical tools to assist with energizing and healing your root chakra. What follows are some recommendations. Remember that flower essences are often made with brandy or vodka. If you have issues with alcohol, you may want to find a flower essence made with glycerin, use the flower essence as a room spray, or apply it topically instead of ingesting it.

✿ Essential Oils

- Sandalwood
- Juniper
- Frankincense
- Cypress
- Patchouli

✿ Crystals

- Red jasper
- Black tourmaline
- Smoky quartz

✿ *Flower Essences*

- Aspen for promoting feelings of security

Root Chakra Meditation Practice

Find a comfortable seated position and settle in for a few moments. Silence your cell phone and set a timer for five minutes.

In your mind's eye, imagine a rich, vibrant red mist surrounding you. This mist is attuned to the energetic frequency of your root chakra, the energetic center associated with safety, security, and stability. On each inhale, draw this healing mist inside you, and on each exhale, send this healing mist to your root chakra located at the base of your spine. As you continue to send this vibrant red mist to your root chakra, see a red sphere take shape there. Imagine this sphere growing brighter and bigger with each breath until you sit within a ruby-red sphere of healing light.

At the completion of your meditation, please end the visualization.

Sit for a minute or two afterward, observing any ripple effects of your meditation session.

Journaling Practice

Reflect on your meditation practice. Describe your direct experience of connecting to the energy of the root chakra. How did this practice affect your physical, emotional, mental, and energetic bodies? What is your relationship to the topics of stability, security, and structure? How might you incorporate your knowledge about the root chakra into your Reiki healing sessions?

Reiki Exploration Day 5

Daily Intention Review

You are five days into your healing immersion. Congratulations! Take a moment to connect with your heartfelt intention. Read it aloud. Does it still resonate with you? If it feels appropriate, feel free to modify or reword your intention. Intention setting is a dynamic practice. If your intention starts to feel stale, feel free to change it so your daily intention can adapt as you evolve as a healer and as a receiver of Reiki energy.

Self-Healing Hand Position 2: Jaw

The second hand placement typically performed when doing a Reiki self-treatment healing session is placing the palms of your hands gently on each side of your jawline with your finger positioned over your ears.

Consider how this hand placement would direct Reiki energy across all dimensions of your being. For example, as the hands cover the jaw and fingers rest on the ears, the ears, the structure and musculature of the jaw, skeleton structure of the cheeks, teeth, gums, and tongue would receive healing energy.

Energetically, this hand placement may stimulate minor energy centers found at the ears and may also balance the throat chakra.

This hand placement may benefit the following conditions:

- Vertigo
- Dizziness
- Ear infections
- Tinnitus
- Hearing loss
- Allergies
- Gum disease
- Tooth cavities
- Tonsillitis
- Lock jaw
- Tension
- Anxiety
- Inability to listen
- Low concentration
- Confusion

The hand placement may strengthen or balance the following characteristics:

- Clairaudience
- Ability to listen
- Memory

- Receptivity
- Curiosity
- Clairgustance
- Balance

Self-Healing Targeted Practice

Find a comfortable seated position and settle in for a few moments. Then, silence your cell phone and set a timer for five minutes, the duration of your targeted self-healing session today.

Take a complete inventory of yourself at this moment in time. Notice how you feel physically, emotionally, mentally, and energetically.

Turn on Reiki using your unique method of connection and feel the infusion of Reiki energy into your being. Using hand position 2 for self-healing, give yourself a five-minute targeted Reiki healing session. For hand position 2, place the palms of the hands lightly covering the sides of your jaw with fingers placed on the ears.

Sit afterward in reflection, observing your treatment's after-effects. Take a moment to scan your body and observe any subtle shifts of energy that may have occurred.

Journaling Practice

Contemplate hand position 2. What associations do you have—positive or negative—regarding this hand placement? What potential for self-healing or healing others do you think would benefit from this hand position? What characteristics would you like to strengthen or balance using this hand position? What did the targeted self-healing experience of hand position 2 reveal to you regarding how you could use this hand position in future Reiki healings?

Reiki Exploration Day 6

Daily Intention Review

Begin today by remembering why you embarked on this adventure of self-healing and discovery. Then, when you are ready, state your heartfelt healing intention aloud.

The Power of the Word *Reiki*

Words contain power. The ancients knew this fact. The biblical creation story reports that God created the world by his spoken word alone: "In the beginning was the Word, and the Word was with God, and the Word was God. He was in the beginning with God. All beings came into being through him, and without him not one thing came into being"(1 John 1–3).

The Bible isn't the only ancient record of the importance of the spoken word in the creation process. According to ancient Egyptian mythology, the god Thoth, is "the Source of the Word," and it was through the power of his spoken word that our reality was crafted.[3]

The inherent power of the spoken word is the key to the chanting practices of eastern religions, where Sanskrit words are repeated for a specific number of repetitions, typically 108, the number of beads on a mala. These chants are used to elicit specific outcomes.

We don't have to be a sage or mystic to tap into the power of the spoken word. When we speak a word slowly and with a deep voice, we can feel the word's syllables vibrate within us. This process can help us tap into the power of the word and forge a deeper understanding of the essence of the word itself.

Consider the word "Reiki" and its essence, which represents the universal healing energy. Close your eyes and take a deep inhale. As you exhale, begin intoning "Reiki" in a slow, powerful voice from the pit of your belly. This simple practice, when performed regularly, can help foster a deeper connection to Reiki energy and assist with raising your personal vibration to be more consistent with the essence of this dynamic word.

Reiki Chanting Practice

Find a comfortable seated position and take a few deep breaths. Silence your cell phone.

Take a complete inventory of yourself at this moment in time. Notice how you feel physically, emotionally, mentally, and energetically.

Connect with the power of the word "Reiki." Notice what thoughts and feelings come up for you as you state this word aloud. Set a timer for five minutes and slowly chant "Reiki" out loud for the duration. At the end of your practice, sit for a minute or two in silent contemplation, observing the after-effects of your chanting session.

---

3. Dennis William Hauck, *The Emerald Tablet: Alchemy of Personal Transformation* (New York: Penguin Books, 1999), 23.

Journaling Practice

Chanting is a powerful energetic practice that can affect the physical, emotional, mental, and energetic bodies. What was your direct experience of your chanting practice? Did you feel a more profound understanding or connection to the word "Reiki"? If so, describe these insights. Consider drawing a picture to illustrate your experience. How might you use this type of practice in the future?

Reiki Exploration Day 7

Daily Intention Review

To connect with your purpose in exploring Reiki energy, read your heartfelt intention aloud.

Self-Healing Hand Position 3

The third hand placement typically performed when doing a Reiki self-treatment healing session is placing the palms of your hands gently over your throat center. One version of this hand placement is placing one hand on your neck and the other covering the first hand. Alternatively, you can position your inside wrists together, letting the heels of your hands rest on the center of your neck, allowing your fingers to wrap along either side of your neck.

Now contemplate where this hand placement would direct the transmission of Reiki energy.

Since your hands cover the throat and neck region, the bones of the upper vertebrate, collar bones, neck muscles, windpipe, and larynx would all benefit from this hand placement. Additionally, two glands of the endocrine system, the thyroid gland that regulates metabolism and the parathyroid gland that regulates blood calcium levels, would also receive healing energy.

Energetically, this hand placement may balance the throat chakra.

Conditions that may benefit from this hand placement:

- Tonsillitis
- Issues with the esophagus and trachea
- Issues with the larynx
- Whiplash

- Neck mobility issues
- Collar bone injuries
- Thyroid problems
- Parathyroid problems
- Communication issues
- Stuttering

Characteristics that may be strengthened or balanced with this particular hand placement:

- Public speaking
- Enhanced communication skills
- Self-expression
- Speaking your truth

Self-Healing Targeted Practice

Find a comfortable seated position and settle in for a few moments. Silence your cell phone. Take a body scan beginning at the top of your head and concluding at the soles of your feet. Notice any areas that might require extra healing today.

When you are ready, start the flow of Reiki energy using your personal method of connection. Notice the strength of the Reiki energy. If you can't sense the energy flowing, don't worry—trust that it's there, and honor your experience without judgment.

Self-healing hand position 3 is focused on the throat and neck area. Using hand position 3 for self-healing, give yourself a five-minute targeted Reiki healing session. For example, for hand position 3, you may cover the throat region by placing one hand on top of the other on the center of the throat or placing hands on either side of the neck.

Sit for a few minutes afterward in reflection.

Journaling Practice

Reflect on hand position 3. This location is very sensitive for many people since our necks are a highly vulnerable part of our body. Did you find yourself more or less sensitive to the sensations and feelings when using this hand position? Did you notice any energetic shifts during your healing session? What insights did you gain that will be helpful in future Reiki sessions?

Reiki Exploration Day 8

Daily Intention Review

Take a moment to consider the rich history of Reiki healing. Then, from this place of connection to the Reiki lineage, read out loud your heartfelt intention as a reminder of your healing journey.

The Legend of Dr. Mikao Usui

When a person makes a contribution as significant as Dr. Usui, legends and myths often develop, emphasizing their contributions. For example, there is the legend of George Washington, the first president of the United States, telling his father that he was the one who cut down the family's cherry tree and Abraham Lincoln, the sixteenth president of the United States, often referred to as "Honest Abe," who could never tell a lie. These legends reflect the value society placed on the contributions of these remarkable individuals.

The legend of Dr. Usui is summarized below. It's the version one of my Reiki teachers used during her trainings. Although I could not independently verify the story is historically accurate, it emphasizes his special offering to the world.

A Japanese Buddhist monk, Dr. Usui went on a religious pilgrimage to Mount Kurama in the late 1800s. On this retreat, he went on a twenty-one-day fast. While in a period of deep contemplation, he was struck by a beam of light that entered his forehead. In this powerful encounter, he received visions of the Reiki symbols and how to activate this healing power.

As Dr. Usui left his mountain retreat, a miraculous event occurred. It happened as Dr. Usui was making his trek down the mountain. He stumbled and severely injured his knee. Enlightened by his vision of the Reiki symbols, he covered his injured body part with his hands, miraculously healing his knee. At the foot of the mountain, Dr. Usui decided to break his fast by eating at a restaurant, where his server had a painful toothache. Dr. Usui cupped his server's head in his hand, and the toothache was instantly healed.

Inspired by this experience, Dr. Usui began practicing and perfecting his healing technique on friends and family before expanding his healing services. He named this system of healing *Shin-Shin Kai-Zen Usui Reiki Ryo-Ho,* which translates to "the Usui

Reiki Treatment Method for Improvement of Body and Mind."[4] For the remainder of his days, Dr. Usui traveled throughout Japan healing those in need and sharing his healing techniques with others.

Dr. Mikao Usui Meditation Practice

For this meditation, you'll need an image of Dr. Usui (many are available online). When we meditate on a person's picture, we aren't worshipping them. Instead, we are honoring the individual and focusing our attention on the qualities in them we wish to emulate.

Before you begin, place a picture of Dr. Usui where you can view it without straining your neck. Set a timer for five minutes and sit in a comfortable position. With a soft gaze, look upon the image of Dr. Usui and allow yourself to connect with his healing energy. Actively cultivate a connection with the father of Reiki healing by meditating on his image. Sit for a few minutes afterward in contemplation and gratitude for the contributions of Dr. Usui.

Journaling Practice

Consider the contributions of Dr. Usui to the world of energy healing. What elements of Dr. Usui's life resonate with you? What attributes would you like to emulate? How does the story of Dr. Usui assist you in your healing journey? Finally, how might you use these insights in future Reiki healing sessions?

Reiki Exploration Day 9

Daily Intention Review

Take a few deep, clearing breaths anchoring yourself in this present moment. From this place of presence, read your heartfelt intention out loud as a reminder of your healing journey.

Self-Healing Hand Position 4: Back of Skull

The fourth hand position in a Reiki self-treatment practice focuses on the back of the head region. Your hands may form a triangle shape by placing your thumbs touching at the base of your skull and your index finger resting on the middle skull region. An alternative hand position is to cradle the back of your head with one hand and place

---

4. International Center for Reiki Training, "An Evidence Based History of Reiki," *Reiki News Magazine*, 24.

the other hand right above it. Consider how Reiki energy would flow using this hand placement.

Since your hands are covering the back of the head, the back of the skull, the brain, the muscles at the top of the neck, and the so-called nodding joint that connects your skull to your vertebrae are the primary areas to receive healing energy.

This hand placement may benefit the following conditions and areas:

- Brain injuries
- Neck issues, including "text neck"
- Alzheimer's disease
- Brain fog
- Neck mobility issues
- Migraines/headaches
- Cranial nerve issues
- Hippocampus: memory center
- Amygdala: the fear center
- Cerebellum: movement/muscle control/balance
- Brainstem: regulates automatic bodily functions

This hand placement may strengthen or balance the following characteristics:

- Neuroplasticity
- Mental clarity
- Focus
- Access to memories/past life regression

Self-Healing Targeted Practice

Find a comfortable seated position and take a few deep, cleansing breaths. Silence your cell phone.

Be curious as you take an inventory of yourself at this moment in time. Notice how you feel physically, emotionally, mentally, and energetically. Don't judge; just observe.

Turn on the flow of Reiki using your own method of connection and feel the infusion of healing energy into your being.

For five minutes, use hand position 4 on the back of your head as the focus of your self-healing Reiki session. As a reminder, hand position 4 can be performed by cradling the back of your head with one hand and place the other hand right above the first one.

Afterward, sit for a few moments in quiet reflection to completely absorb the benefits of this practice. Once you've completed your targeted self-healing session, scan yourself and record any shifts or changes you experienced: no matter how small or subtle.

Journaling Practice

Reflect on hand position 4. What is your direct experience with this hand placement? Did it stir up any sensations, feelings, or memories? What insights did you receive regarding the potential of healing using this hand placement? How might you use this information during future Reiki healing sessions?

Reiki Exploration Day 10

Daily Intention Review

Take a deep clearing breath, hold it for a moment, and then exhale completely. Now, with clarity of mind, state aloud your heartfelt intention.

Sacred Imagination and Healing

Children have extraordinary imaginative skills and access to unlimited creative energy. The entire world is a playground to be experienced and explored with curiosity and fascination. Yet as we move from childhood to adolescence, we are encouraged by society and perhaps some well-meaning family members to put aside childish things and "grow up." Often our imagination is sacrificed on the altar of responsibility and adulthood.

Imagination can be viewed as a spiritual gift. Reclaiming our imagination and creativity, we say *yes* to actively co-creating with the universe. Furthermore, we can make substantial changes that align with our aspirations by clearly envisioning what we desire and taking steps to bring this vision into reality.

I refer to the use of imagination to bring about positive, creative outcomes as "sacred imagination." Our sacred imagination is a compelling way to connect with Reiki energy and other healing energies. Envisioning what Reiki energy looks like and how it flows can influence our ability to connect with the energy itself and use Reiki more effectively. Moreover, we can more easily achieve our desired results by using our sacred imagination to envision our bodies absorbing the Reiki energy and picturing ourselves in radiant health. Our results are only limited by our imagination.

Reiki and Sacred Imagination Practice

Either in a comfortable seat or lying down, take a few deep, clearing breaths, and consider the concept of universal healing energy.

Silence your cell phone and set a timer for five minutes. Focus your attention on the source of Reiki. Relax and invite your mind to form a picture of the universal healing energy of Reiki. Based on your intuition, what color, texture, temperature, and scent would you attribute to Reiki energy? Remember, there are no right or wrong answers, only your sacred imagination guiding you into unseen realms. Create this mental picture in as much detail as possible and hold this visualization for five minutes. After completing this practice, sit for a minute or two in reflection.

Journaling Practice

Take a few moments to journal your direct experience of this sacred imagination experience. How did the image of the universal healing energy of Reiki appear to you? How did this picture make you feel? If you could see, hear, taste, or touch it, describe that experience.

Draw a quick sketch—in black and white or color—representing your experience.

How might the insights you have gained regarding your sacred imagination be useful in future Reiki healing sessions?

Reiki Exploration Day 11

Daily Intention Review

Your heart is your inner compass. So check in with your heart today as you recite your heartfelt intention.

Self-Healing Hand Position 5: The Heart

The heart center of the body is the focus of the fifth hand position in a Reiki self-treatment practice. You may lay one hand on the center of your chest with your second hand slightly above the other. Alternatively, you may place one hand over your heart and cover it with your second hand.

Image how the Reiki energy flows using this hand placement. When your hands cover the heart center, the heart, sternum, ribs, lungs, and breasts receive healing energy.

Energetically, this hand placement heals and balances the heart chakra increasing your capacity for love and compassion for yourself and others. It also assists with healing the energetic heart during the grieving process after a significant loss.

This hand placement may benefit the following conditions:

- Heart problems
- High/low blood pressure
- Circulation problems
- Arrhythmia
- Lung issues
- Asthma
- Breast issues
- Lactating issues for new moms
- Heartbreak/sadness
- Jealousy
- Co-dependence
- Lack of intimacy

This hand placement may strengthen or balance the following:

- Cardiovascular health
- Increased lung capacity
- Increased capacity for love and compassion
- Healthy relationships
- Self-worth
- Increased capacity for forgiveness

Self-Healing Targeted Practice

While seated comfortably, connect with the present moment and begin a body scan. Begin the flow of Reiki and invite the healing energy into your being.

Self-healing hand position 5 is for the area at your heart center. Using this hand position, give yourself a five-minute targeted Reiki healing session. Place one hand on the center of your chest with the other hand slightly above it. Another option is to lay one hand over your heart and cover it with your second hand. After completing your targeted self-healing session, pause for a few moments to observe your reaction to your targeted Reiki treatment, and observe your reaction to treatment.

Journaling Practice

Reflect on your experience with hand position 5. Does this hand placement stir up any positive or negative sensations, feelings, or memories? Did you notice any energy shifts during your self-healing session? How might this hand placement benefit you personally as you continue your healing journey? How might you incorporate these insights into future Reiki healing sessions?

Reiki Exploration Day 12

Daily Intention Review

Take a few deep breaths and reflect on your progress on your healing journey. Then, when you are ready, read your heartfelt intention out loud.

Reiki Principle Line 2: "Just for today, I will not worry."

Worrying is a state of mind where we are focusing on potential adverse or unpleasant future outcomes. When we direct our attention to what might happen, we can experience unnecessary anxiety and stress. There are health consequences to prolonged periods of consistent worrying, including the following:

- Fatigue
- Headaches
- Erratic mood swings
- Digestive issues
- Nausea
- Compromised immune system
- Heart ailments
- Depression

To assist with releasing your worries, I've assembled a few of my favorite anxiety-busting practices here.

Breathwork: The breath is always present, so it is a simple and practical method to stay connected in the present moment. By making the length of your inhale match the length of your exhale, you can cultivate a sense of calm and balance. Try experimenting with using a length of breath for a count of four, five, or six.

Affirmations: Use an affirmation as part of your meditation practice or as a touchstone that can be repeated throughout the day. You may want to consider using one of the affirmations below or develop your own based on your personal situation.

- "I effortlessly release my worries and concerns."
- "I am rooted in the present moment."
- "I am relaxed and peaceful."

Journal: We can often find some relief by writing down our worries and concerns. This practice provides a format to express our anxieties taking them out of the mental realm. Sometimes just this simple act of writing is enough to help us calm down.

Meditation: Meditation is a way of staying in the present moment and, when combined with visualization, can elicit a specific outcome. Below is a sample meditation that can be used to release worries and restore inner harmony. This visualization can be used outside of a formal meditation practice whenever you're worried about future events or potential outcomes.

Sit comfortably. Relax and focus on the natural rhythm of your breath. When you are ready, picture a box in front of you. It can be any shape, from a jewelry box to a treasure chest. Imagine your name written beautifully across the box. This is your worry box, and its purpose is to hold all your worries and troubles. You may find relief from your problems and concerns by placing your worries into this box. In your mind's eye, picture an object representing a worry that is causing you anxiety. See this mental image as clearly and in as much detail as possible. When you are ready to release it, say silently to yourself, "I intend to release myself of this worry and stay in the present moment. I trust that the future will unfold in alignment with my best and highest good." Imagine the image you created being placed in your worry box. Know that you can retrieve it from the box at a later date if it's ever needed. Repeat this visualization as often as needed for five to ten minutes. After completing the meditation, you may want to write down your experience, thoughts, and feelings in a journal to reflect on later.

Reiki Principle Practice

Silence your cell phone and find a comfortable seated position. Settle in for a few moments before setting your timer for five minutes.

Reflect on the second line of the Reiki Principle: "Just for today, I will not worry."

Use this Reiki Principle as an affirmation, either repeating it silently or out loud for the duration. If your mind wanders during this practice, simply invite it to refocus on the affirmation.

Reflect on your personal experience for a minute or two after completing your practice.

Journaling Practice

Contemplate the purpose of this Reiki Principle. Why is this line important? What role does worry play in your life? How could you benefit from worrying less and living more in the present moment? How might these insights assist you as a Reiki healer?

Reiki Exploration Day 13

Daily Intention Review

Take a moment to notice how you are feeling today. From this place of emotional connection, state aloud your heartfelt intention.

The Sacral Chakra

The sacral chakra is the energy center focused on creativity, emotions, and pleasure. It's the second chakra located approximately two inches below your belly button in your body's lower abdominal region.

Let's explore your connection to your own sacral chakra. Consider the following statements:

- "I am in touch with my feelings."
- "I easily express myself creatively."

- "I follow my passions."
- "I go with the flow."
- "I am open to pleasurable experiences."
- "I embrace my playful nature."
- "I am comfortable exploring my sensual side."

If one of these statements does not feel true for you at this time, consider spending extra attention to your own sacral chakra. In addition to Reiki self-healing sessions and other energetic healing treatments, there are many methods of balancing your sacral chakra. You can explore the following suggestions for ways to strengthen and connect with this energy center.

Activities

- Creative activities such as painting, drawing, creating collages, etc.
- Spending time near a body of water.
- Reciting the bija (seed) mantra associated with the sacral chakra: VAM (pronounced *vahm*).
- Visualizing the vibrant color orange.
- Listening to music that makes your heart sing.
- Dancing.

Affirmations

- "I embrace my sexuality."
- "I am deeply connected to my emotions."
- "My creativity is limitless."

There are metaphysical instruments available to assist you with balancing and strengthening your sacral chakra. Below are some recommendations. Please remember that flower essences are often made with brandy or vodka. If you have issues with alcohol, you may want to find a flower essence made with glycerin, use the flower essence as a room spray, or apply it topically instead of ingesting it.

Essential Oils

- Sweet orange
- Jasmine

- Tangerine
- Bergamot

❀ *Crystals*

- Carnelian
- Moonstone
- Amber

❀ *Flower Essences*

- Iris to enhance creativity
- Wisteria to assist with intimacy

Sacral Chakra Meditation Practice

Sit in a comfortable position. Take a few deep breaths and bring your awareness to the present moment. Set a timer for five minutes and silence your cell phone.

Using your imagination, picture a bright orange mist surrounding you. This mist is harmonized with the energetic frequency of the sacral chakra associated with creativity, sexuality, intimacy, and emotional connections. As you inhale, invite this healing mist into your being. As you exhale, send this healing mist to your sacral chakra approximately two inches below your belly button. As you continue to send this vibrant orange mist to your sacral chakra, see an orange sphere take shape below your belly button. Imagine this sphere growing brighter and bigger with each breath until you are sitting within an orange-colored sphere.

When you have finished your meditation, release the visualization.

Sit for a minute or two afterward in observation, noticing any shifts in energy that have occurred.

Journaling Practice

Reflect on your meditation practice. Describe your direct experience of connecting to the energy of the sacral chakra. Consider your relationship to your sacral chakra. What is your connection to pleasure? Do you find joy easily during your day? Are you able to express yourself creatively? How might healing and strengthening this energy center affect your physical, emotional, mental, and energetic bodies? How might you use your knowledge about the sacral chakra as part of Reiki healing sessions?

Reiki Exploration Day 14

Daily Intention Review

With a grateful heart for all the progress you've already made, recommit to your healing goals by stating out loud your heartfelt intention.

Self-Healing Hand Position 6: Ribs and Upper Abdominals

The ribs and upper abdomen of the body are the focus of the sixth hand position. To perform it, gently rest your hands below your breasts on your lower ribs.

Consider how the Reiki energy flows using this hand placement. Since your hands cover the ribs and upper abdomen, healing energy is directly sent to the rib cage and lower sternum, diaphragm, upper abdominal muscles, spleen, liver, stomach, and pancreas.

This hand placement may benefit the following conditions:

- Breathing issues: especially concerning issues with the diaphragm
- Infections
- Issues with the spleen
- Liver problems
- Stomach issues
- Acid-reflux disease
- Stress-related disorders
- Pancreas issues
- Diabetes
- Gallbladder stones
- GERD/stomach reflux
- Stomach ulcers
- Indigestion

This hand placement may strengthen or balance the following characteristics:

- Digestive health
- Increased lung capacity
- Healthy blood sugar levels

Self-Healing Targeted Practice

Find a comfortable position and take a few deep, cleansing breaths. Silence your cell phone.

Be curious as you take an inventory of yourself at this moment in time. Notice how you feel physically, emotionally, mentally, and energetically. Don't judge, just observe.

Turn on the flow of Reiki using your own method of connection and feel the infusion of healing energy into your being.

Self-healing hand position 6 is for the ribs and upper abdomen. Using the sixth hand position for self-healing, give yourself a targeted Reiki healing session for five minutes. For hand position 6, you may cover the lower rib cage with your hands with your pinky fingers resting on your bottom ribs and parallel to the floor.

After your self-treatment, pause for a minute or two to observe the after-effects of your healing session.

Journaling Practice

Reflect on the sixth hand position. What was your direct experience of your self-treatment session? Did it stir up any positive or negative sensations, feelings, and memories? What does this analysis and your direct experience of your self-healing session inform you of the potential for healing using the sixth hand placement?

Reiki Exploration Day 15

Daily Intention Review

Take a few deep breaths and connect to the present moment. When you are ready, state your heartfelt healing intention aloud.

We Are Energy!

You are a being of energy and energetic patterns. This concept isn't limited to New Age thinking or metaphysical practices. Within our cells is a universe of atoms, each with its own energetic experience as sub-atomic particles of electrons and protons dance in their energetic expressions. This energetic dance occurs in every object in our world: you, your car, coffee cup, the ocean, and the stars above.

From the perspective of energy healers and Reiki practitioners, energy is understood as the vital life force that flows throughout our being and is pervasive throughout the universe. Different cultures refer to this energy by various names; prana, chi, and ki. It is often called subtle energy. While it's currently impossible to measure via known scientific means, we can directly experience this subtle energy. It is the basis for energy healing modalities such as Reiki.

When these subtle energies are flowing freely in a balanced way, we are functioning optimally. On the other hand, if the flow of this energy becomes blocked or stagnant, imbalances in our lives and bodies occur that may lead to health problems and disease. Fortunately, many tools are available to restore balance and equilibrium to our life force energy. We can restore harmony to body, mind, and soul by consciously addressing these imbalances and blockages energetically.

Although specific blockages or imbalances may require more precise healing techniques, below are suggestions to restore overall energetic balance and revitalize your life force energy:

- Reiki and other energetic healing modalities
- Conscious body movement practices such as yoga, tai chi, or qigong
- Meditation
- Conscious breathwork

Subtle Body Exercise: Feel Your Energy!

Get in a comfortable seated position and take a few deep breaths to settle into your space. Silence your cell phone.

Take a complete inventory of yourself at this moment in time. Notice how you feel physically, emotionally, mentally, and energetically.

Your aura is the energy field surrounding your physical body. The exercise that follows will assist you in feeling your auric field with your hands.

Explore your auric field by placing your hands approximately three inches in front of your abdomen or rib cage, palms facing towards you. Take a big breath in, and on your exhale, imagine pushing your energy field into your hands. Repeat several times and notice if you can feel your aura growing. If your hands can sense the energy field, begin to move your hands away from your body a few inches at a time and repeat the exercise. Explore how far your energy field can expand.

Journaling Practice

Journal your direct experience of this practice.

How did you experience your energy field? Did you have physical sensations? Did you experience changes in your emotions? What thoughts ran through your mind? Did you see any colors in your mind's eye?

Next, take a few moments to sketch any impressions you had of your energy body. Consider using colored pencils if you'd like to select colors that intuitively reflect your experience of your aura.

How might the knowledge of subtle energy and our auric field assist you as a Reiki healer?

Reiki Exploration Day 16

Daily Intention Review

To help establish the mood for your day, take a moment to reconnect with your heartfelt intention and recommit to your healing path by reciting it aloud.

Reiki Principle Line 3: "Just for today, I will not anger."

I've had mixed emotions (pun intended) regarding this line of the Reiki prayer. In my experience, there is a place for anger: the righteous anger expressed for a worthy cause; the anger you may experience when your boundaries are not respected. When expressed in a healthy manner, this version of anger precipitates necessary change. However, most anger prevalent in society at large and perhaps within ourselves is not expressed constructively. It is either suppressed, internalized, or held onto like a badge of honor. In addition to relationship and employment problems, health issues can occur due to prolonged, unmanaged anger, including the following conditions:

- Coronary disease/heart ailments
- Weakened immune system
- Stroke risk
- Anxiety and stress
- Respiratory issues
- Compromised immune system
- Depression

To assist you with addressing your anger constructively, I've collected several practices which may provide calming relief during trying times.

Ho'oponopono Prayer: This short Hawaiian prayer is an easy, accessible way to release anger by cultivating forgiveness and love. Simply repeat the following sentences for three to five minutes: "I'm sorry. Please forgive me. Thank you. I love you."

Breathwork Practices: This breathwork practice invites a greater sense of relaxation by making your exhale a few moments longer than your inhale. Try experimenting by using a count of four for your inhale and a count of seven or eight for your exhale. This breathing pattern can be used anytime and anywhere you need instant relief, such as when you are stuck in traffic or dealing with a problem at your job.

Affirmations: This powerful technique can be used anytime throughout the day or as part of your meditation practice for a specific period of time. Sample affirmations for releasing anger appear here but feel free to experiment with crafting your own affirmation.

- "I easily release my anger and frustration."
- "I invite peace into my heart."
- "I am calm."

Exercise: Exercise can be an effective way of releasing anger with the added bonus of releasing your body's natural endorphins, the "feel good" hormones. In addition, mindfulness-based exercise options such as yoga, tai chi, and qigong may provide more calming benefits.

Reiki Principle Practice: Line 3

Sit comfortably and check in with yourself physically, mentally, emotionally, and energetically. Silence your cell phone.

Reflect on the third line of the Reiki Principle: "Just for today, I will not anger."

Set a timer for five minutes. Use this line from the Reiki Principle as an affirmation, slowly repeating it out loud for the duration.

Sit for a minute or two afterward in quiet reflection, noticing any subtle shifts in your energy that may have occurred during your practice.

Journaling Practice

Reflect on the third line of the Reiki Principles. What does this line mean to you? What role does anger play in your daily life or your past interactions? What would your life look like if you could more easily release angry feelings or channel your emotions more positively? How might you include these insights in your Reiki healing sessions?

Reiki Exploration Day 17

Daily Intention Review

Connect with your core, the very essence of your being. Then, from a place of personal power, state your heartfelt healing intention aloud.

Self-Healing Hand Position 7: Core

The body's abdomen is the focus of the seventh hand position in a Reiki self-treatment practice. Place your hands on the center of your core for this hand placement. Your finger should be pointing toward your belly button.

Let's contemplate how the Reiki energy moves using this hand placement. Since your hands cover the solar plexus, healing energy would be sent directly to the abdominal muscles, large intestine, small intestine, colon, kidneys, stomach, and adrenal glands. Energetically, this hand placement heals and balances the solar plexus chakra, the center of your personal vitality and power.

This hand placement may benefit the following conditions:

- Digestion issues
- Celiac disease
- Irritable bowel syndrome
- Constipation
- Stomach Issues
- Kidney stones/kidney issues
- Adrenal gland problems
- Stress related disorders
- Bowel disease
- Stomach ulcers

- Lack of willpower
- Lack of vitality
- Lack of self-esteem

This particular hand placement may strengthen or balance the following attributes or characteristics:

- Digestive health
- Better absorption of nutrients
- Immune health
- Increased determination and drive
- Strong willpower
- Healthy self-esteem

Self-Healing Targeted Practice

Settle into a comfortable seated position and take a few deep centering breaths. Silence your cell phone and set a timer for five minutes. Begin the flow of Reiki and appreciate its healing power as you are infused with its energy.

Self-healing hand position 7 is for the solar plexus, the center of your abdomen region. Using the seventh hand position for self-healing with your hands on either side of your belly button, give yourself a targeted Reiki healing session.

Sit for a few minutes afterward in reflection, observing the after-effects of your self-healing session.

Journaling Practice

Reflect on the seventh hand position. Describe your direct experience of your self-healing Reiki session. Did any memories, thoughts, or feelings rise to the surface? Did you experience any physical sensations? What does this analysis teach you about the potential for healing using this hand position? How might you utilize these insights during future Reiki healing sessions?

Reiki Exploration Day 18

Daily Intention Review

Pause to contemplate your own personal power, your will to act, your determination, and your drive. From this place of strength, recite your heartfelt intention out loud.

Solar Plexus Chakra

Located at your core, the solar plexus chakra is the vortex of energy centered around your personal power. It is associated with your determination and drive, manifesting as your ability to take action in the physical world.

Let's explore your connection to your own solar plexus chakra. Consider these statements:

- "I am worthy and confident."
- "I am connected to my personal power."
- "I am enough."
- "I am connected to my own inner fire."
- "My willpower is one of my strengths."
- "When I set a goal, I am confident that I will achieve it."
- "I am comfortable with who I am."

If one of these statements does not feel true for you now, consider paying extra attention to your own solar plexus chakra. There are many options to strengthen and balance this energy center. In addition to Reiki treatments, consider the following suggestions for connecting with and revitalizing this energy center:

✿ Activities

- Spending time in sunlight using the appropriate sunblock protection and a hat. Alternatively, consider using a light therapy lamp for seasonal affective disorders, which provides many of the sun's healing benefits without the exposure to the sun's harmful ultraviolet rays.
- Reciting the bija (seed) mantra associated with the solar plexus chakra: RAM (pronounced *rahm*).
- Visualizing a rich golden color or picturing your own inner fire.
- Engaging in physical activities that increase your energy.

✿ Affirmations

- "I stand in my own power."
- "I am connected to my inner fire."
- "I am worthy, confident, and powerful."

Additionally, here are some metaphysical tools that can assist you with connecting to your solar plexus chakra. Again, please remember that flower essences are often made with brandy or vodka. If you have issues with alcohol, you may want to find a flower essence made with glycerin, use the flower essences as a room spray, or apply it topically instead of ingesting it.

✿ Essential Oils

- Lemon
- Black pepper
- Cardamon
- Marjoram

✿ Crystals

- Citrine
- Sunstone
- Golden calcite

🪷 *Flower Essences*

- Sunflower to enhance confidence and success
- Paper Birch to aid in embracing individuality and healthy ego development

Solar Plexus Chakra Meditation Practice

Sit in a comfortable position. Take a few deep breaths and bring your awareness to the present moment. Silence your cell phone and set a timer for five minutes. Using your imagination, picture a vibrant golden mist surrounding you. This mist is harmonized with the energetic frequency of the solar plexus chakra associated with personal power, confidence, and self-worth. As you inhale, invite this healing mist into your being, and as you exhale, send this healing mist to your solar plexus chakra located at your core. As you continue to send this bright golden mist to your solar plexus area, visualize a glowing yellow sphere take shape at your core. Imagine this sphere growing more brilliant and larger with each breath until you sit within a golden-colored sphere.

When you have finished your meditation, release the visualization. Sit for a minute or two afterward in reflection, noticing any shifts in energy that have occurred.

Journaling Practice

Consider your meditation practice. Describe your direct experience of connecting to the energy of the solar plexus chakra. Consider your own inner fire. How brightly does it burn within you? How might balancing this energy center contribute to the health of your physical, emotional, mental, and energetic bodies? How might you incorporate your knowledge about the solar plexus chakra into your Reiki healing sessions?

Reiki Exploration Day 19

Daily Intention Review

Pause and honor the emotions you are feeling at this moment. Don't judge—just accept what is. From this place of honest introspection, recite your heartfelt intention out loud.

Self-Healing Hand Position 8: Lower Abdominals

The body's lower abdomen is the focus of the eighth hand position in a Reiki self-treatment practice. Place your hands on your lower belly region slightly below your navel for this hand placement.

Let's consider how the Reiki energy flows using this hand placement: Your hands are covering your lower belly, so the healing energy is channeled to the pelvis, lower abdominal muscles, hip joints, hip flexor muscles, the uterus and ovaries (females), testes (males), bladder, colon, and sexual organs. Energetically, this hand placement heals and balances the sacral chakra, the center of your creativity, passion, and joy.

Conditions that may benefit from this hand placement:

- Hip issues
- Sciatica
- Constipation
- Appendicitis
- Bowel disease
- Menstrual cramps
- Urinary tract infection
- Sexual issues
- Blocked creativity
- Loss of passion or desire

Characteristics that may be strengthened or balanced with this particular hand placement:

- Digestive health
- Sexual health
- Greater intimacy
- Passion
- Joy
- Creativity

Self-Healing Targeted Practice

Settle into a comfortable seated position and take a few deep centering breaths. Silence your cell phone and set a timer for five minutes. Begin the flow of Reiki and appreciate its healing power as you are infused with its energy.

Self-healing hand position 8 is for the lower abdomen and pelvic region. Using the eighth hand position for self-healing with your hands below your navel, give yourself a targeted Reiki healing session.

Sit for a few minutes afterward in reflection, observing the ripple effects of your self-healing session.

Journaling Practice

Reflect on the eighth hand position. What was your direct experience of your self-healing treatment? Do you feel a deeper connection to this region of your body? What effect did this self-healing treatment have on your energetic body: especially related to your sacral chakra? What does this analysis inform you of the potential for future Reiki healings using this hand position?

Reiki Exploration Day 20

Daily Intention Review

It's the twentieth day of your Reiki immersion experience! Congratulate yourself on the progress you are making on your Reiki journey. Take a moment to reflect on your heartfelt intention. Does it still resonate with you? Give yourself permission to modify the wording of your intention so that it reflects your current vision and then read it aloud to reaffirm your commitment to your Reiki path.

Energy Clearing

Energy clearing refers to the act of removing negative or stagnant energy. Energy clearing can be performed on you, your space, or both! This practice should be incorporated into your daily Reiki healing practices. By dispelling harmful energies, you are essentially cleansing yourself and your space. This practice sets the stage for more successful healing outcomes. Additional benefits of consistent energy clearing include removing toxic thought forms and negative emotions as well as raising your energy levels and vibration.

There are many ways to perform energy clearing. Below are some suggestions to get you started. Experiment with different versions to find one that resonates with you.

White Light Visualization: You don't need any extra tools or supplies for this one, just your imagination. Set your intention to clear yourself and your space of all negative and stale energies. In your mind's eye, imagine a bright light of the purest white descending from the heavens and completely filling up your room. Allow the light to saturate every element in the room, including yourself. Keep this visualization for a few minutes or until you feel the energy in the room shift. When you are finished, imagine the light ascending back up to the heavens, bringing lower vibrational energies with it.

Tibetan Singing Bowls: Tibetan or Himalayan singing bowls are sound healing tools that vibrate and produce unique tones when played. To start the cleansing process, set the intention to clear your space or yourself of any negative energies that may be present.

Simply place the singing bowl in the palm of your hand and gently strike the bowl's rim with a mallet. Wait a few moments for the vibrations to spread throughout your space, and repeat as often as needed until you feel the energy shift. Alternatively, you may take the mallet and circle the bowl's rim to produce a different, distinctive sound.

Shower of Reiki Energy: You don't need any paraphernalia for this practice, only your access to Reiki energy. Set your intention to turn on Reiki and use the healing power to clear your space and yourself of any negative energies. Visualize Reiki energy pouring down from the heavens as a cleansing rain of healing energy, purifying both you and your surroundings. Keep the visualization for a few minutes or until you sense that the lower vibration energies have been cleared. Afterward, with a grateful heart for the healing energy, turn off Reiki.

Selenite Crystals: Selenite is an excellent, high vibrational crystal. It facilitates the removal of lower and stagnant vibrational energies by raising the frequency of a room or individual. Selenite is a common form of the mineral gypsum and has a milky white appearance. It can be used to clear energy by "sweeping" yourself or a room by holding the selenite in your hand and slowly moving the crystal up and down.

Essential Oils: These are gifts from our plant allies, and many varieties can be used to remove harmful energies. Experiment with rosemary, lemon, cypress, neroli, jasmine, and cedar. Essential oils can be used in a diffuser or applied topically. If applying essential oils directly to your skin, use a carrier oil such as jojoba or almond oil to avoid irritating your skin. Never ingest essential oils.

Energy Clearing Practice

Clearing your energy and energetic space is essential for Reiki practitioners of all levels. It is part of your energetic hygiene and should be used as needed, especially before and after a Reiki healing session.

Find a comfortable seated position and settle in for a few moments. Silence your cell phone and set a timer for five minutes. Take a complete inventory of yourself at this moment in time: how do you feel physically, emotionally, mentally, and energetically?

In your mind's eye, imagine a shower of Reiki energy streaming into your room. This energy can be any color that calls to you, though many consider gold, violet, or the purest white light to be the most effective. See yourself sitting under this Reiki shower of healing light. As you are bathed in Reiki energy, imagine any negative energy attached to you or your auric field being washed away. At the end of the five minutes, thank the Reiki energy, request the negative energy be transmuted into positive energy, and release the visualization.

Sit for two to three minutes afterward in contemplation, observing the ripple effects of your practice.

Journaling Practice

Reflect on this energy clearing meditation. Did you have a physical, emotional, mental, or energetic response to your meditation? Did you notice any energy shifts in your physical surroundings? Describe these changes or consider drawing a quick sketch to illustrate your experience. What opportunities can you use similar clearing practices in your daily life? How might these insights assist you during future Reiki healing sessions?

Reiki Exploration Day 21

Daily Intention Review

Reconnect to your journey of healing and personal growth by reading out loud your heartfelt intention.

Dr. Chujiro Hayashi

Dr. Chujiro Hayashi was a retired naval officer and medical doctor who became a student of Dr. Usui, who was traveling throughout Japan and sharing his healing gifts with others. When Chujiro Hayashi was forty-seven years old, he received the highest level of Reiki training, the Master Level, Reiki Level Three, in 1925. The lineage of Reiki was passed on through Chujiro Hayashi after Dr. Usui passed away in 1930.

Dr. Hayashi expanded the accessibility to Reiki healing by opening a healing center in Tokyo and training others in the healing art of Reiki. In addition, Dr. Hayashi continued to refine how Reiki treatments were administered by having clients lie on tables rather than sit in chairs, the method employed by Dr. Usui. Moreover, Dr. Hayashi developed the Reiki attunement process for transmitting the accessibility of Reiki energy to others.

In his Tokyo clinic, Dr. Hayashi treated a client named Hawayo Takata, who was from Hawaii. Over time, Dr. Hayashi trained Hawayo Takata and allowed her to share her knowledge of Reiki healing with others in Hawaii.

In the tense climate before the outbreak of World War II, Dr. Hayashi visited Hawayo Takata in Hawaii. Upon his return to Japan, however, he took his own life on May 11, 1940 rather than provide the Japanese military information regarding his trip to the Hawaiian islands.

Chujiro Hayashi Meditation Practice

For this meditation, you'll need an image of Chujiro Hayashi (many are available online). Please remember that when we meditate on a person's picture, we aren't worshipping them. Instead, we are honoring the individual and focusing our attention on their unique qualities that we wish to emulate.

Before you begin, place a picture of Chujiro Hayashi where you can view it without straining your neck. Set a timer for five minutes, sit in a comfortable position, and silence your cell phone.

With a soft gaze, look upon the image of Chujiro Hayashi and allow yourself to connect with his healing energy. Actively cultivate a connection with this remarkable individual by meditating on his image.

Sit for two to three minutes afterward in contemplation and gratitude for his contributions to Reiki.

Journaling Practice

Consider Chujiro Hayashi's contribution to the world of energy healing. What elements of his healing path resonate with you? What qualities would you like to emulate? Finally, compose a thank you letter to Chujiro Hayashi for his many gifts to the world of healing and for the way his contributions have affected your personal healing journey. How might you incorporate knowledge about Chujiro Hayashi in your future Reiki healing sessions?

Reiki Exploration Day 22

Daily Intention Review

Take a few deep breaths and bring to mind why you embarked on this path of inner exploration and healing. From this place of connection to your goals, recite your heart-felt intention aloud.

Self-Healing Hand Position 9: Upper Back and Shoulders

The upper back region of the body is the focus of the ninth hand position in a Reiki self-treatment practice. For the ninth hand position, the hands are placed on your upper back area with your fingertips on your shoulder blades.

Now let's contemplate how the Reiki energy flows using this hand placement. As your hands rest on your shoulders, the healing energy is channeled into the lower neck, the shoulders, and the upper back. Consider the sentence, "the weight of the world rests on [someone's] shoulders." Energetically, this hand placement may help address issues with responsibilities and burdens too heavy to bear. Additionally, the upper back region is connected to emotional support and love.

Conditions that may benefit from this hand placement:

- Lower neck issues
- Whiplash
- Shoulder issues
- Upper back issues
- Kyphosis: rounding of the upper back
- Herniated disks
- Meningitis
- Issues with responsibility
- Issues with over-commitment
- Issues with the emotional connections
- Exhaustion

Characteristics that may be strengthened or balanced with this hand placement:

- Back health
- Neck health
- Work-life balance
- Emotional health
- Self-worth
- Inner peace

Self-Healing Targeted Practice

Sit in a comfortable, supported position and take a few deep, centering breaths. Silence your cell phone and set a timer for five minutes. Begin the flow of Reiki using your preferred method and feel the flow of healing energy stream into your being.

Self-healing hand position 9 is for the body's lower neck and upper back region. Using the ninth hand position for self-healing with your hands on your shoulders, give yourself a targeted Reiki healing session.

Sit for a few moments afterward in reflection, observing the after-effects of your self-healing session.

Journaling Practice

Reflect on the ninth hand position. What was your direct experience of your self-healing treatment? Do you feel a deeper connection to this region of your body? What effect did this self-healing treatment have on your energetic body, especially as it relates to issues of over-extension and responsibilities that may be overwhelming you? Did this analysis lead to any insights for using this hand position in future Reiki healing sessions?

Reiki Exploration Day 23

Daily Intention Review

Take a moment to reflect on your heartfelt intention. Then read it aloud and appreciate your commitment to your healing path.

Reiki Principles Line 4:
"Just for today, I will do my work honestly."

Consider the word "work." For many of us, it has a negative connotation, often invoking images of struggle, endless toil, and burdens we must carry. Now consider the definitions of this word as in appears in the *Oxford Dictionary of English*: "Activity involving mental or physical effort done to achieve a purpose or result" and "a task or tasks to be undertaken, something a person or thing has to do."

Our work isn't limited to how we earn money—it includes any mission or venture undertaken and is not limited to our occupation. Our work can be thought of as our contributions to the world: whether our offerings are great or small, they all matter.

All our endeavors should reflect our personal beliefs and ethics. This notion is essential in the realm of energy healing. The benefits of Reiki should be clearly stated and not misrepresented by making claims of miraculous or spontaneous recovery. Of course, this type of healing may take place but shouldn't be promised or guaranteed. Unless you are licensed in the medical field, never attempt to diagnose an illness or prescribe medication. By honestly representing ourselves, our offerings, and our work, we operate from a place of integrity. The Reiki Principles offers guidance on the ideals associated with living and working ethically.

Reiki Principles: Line 4 Practice

Find a comfortable seated position and settle in for a few moments. Silence your cell phone.

Take a complete inventory of yourself at this moment in time. Notice how you feel physically, emotionally, mentally, and energetically.

Reflect on the fourth line of the Reiki Principles: "Just for today, I will do my work honestly."

Set a timer for five minutes. Use this line of the Reiki Principles as an affirmation, repeating it to yourself or aloud for the duration of your practice.

Sit for a few minutes afterward in contemplation, observing the ripple effects of your practice.

Journaling Practice

Reflect on this line of the Reiki prayer. What does the line mean to you? What role does work play in your life? Do you consider work to be only how you earn money, or can the term be more comprehensive and include other activities? How would your approach to work change if you approached these activities more transparently and ethically? Consider how your personal work ethic relates to your healing path and your Reiki practice. Finally, describe how you might use these insights during future Reiki healing sessions.

Reiki Exploration Day 24

Daily Intention Review

Take a moment to reconnect with your heartfelt intention. As you recite it aloud, picture it in your mind's eye as if it has already happened.

Self-Healing Hand Position 10: Middle Back

The body's middle back is the focus of the tenth hand position in a Reiki self-treatment practice. For this hand placement, place your hands in the center area of your back. If you can't position both hands on this area, try one hand at a time or hover your hands slightly away from your middle back region.

Let's consider how the Reiki energy flows using this hand placement. Your hands cover the middle back region, so the healing energy is channeled into the ribs, lungs, diaphragm, spinal cord, and kidneys. Energetically, the middle back issues may relate to emotions of guilt and remorse as well as regrets about the past.

Conditions that may benefit from this hand placement:

- Back issues
- Poor posture
- Spinal arthritis
- Spinal stenosis
- Herniated disks
- Lung issues
- Asthma
- Kidney issues

- Feelings of guilt
- Dwelling on the past

Characteristics that may be strengthened or balanced with this particular hand placement:

- Back health
- Increased lung capacity
- Release of negative emotions such as guilt
- Ability to move forward in life

Self-Healing Targeted Practice

Settle into a comfortable seated position and take a few deep, centering breaths. Silence your cell phone and set a timer for five minutes.

Begin the flow of Reiki and appreciate its healing power as you are infused with its energy. Self-healing hand position 10 is for the middle back region. Using it with the intention of self-healing with your hands on your middle back, begin your treatment.

Sit in reflection for a few moments after your session, observing any shifts in energy that may have occurred.

Journaling Practice

Reflect on the tenth hand position. What was your direct experience of your targeted self-healing session? Do you feel a deeper connection to your middle back? What effect did this self-healing treatment have on your energetic body, such as the release of negative emotions or past events? What potential do you see for using this hand position in future Reiki healing treatments?

Reiki Exploration Day 25

Daily Intention Review

Connect with your heart by feeling your capacity for love and compassion. From this place of warmth and tenderness, recite your heartfelt intention out loud.

Heart Chakra

The fourth energy center is the heart chakra and focuses on love and compassion not only for others but also for ourselves.

Let's explore your connection to your own heart chakra. Consider these statements:

- "I easily give and release love."
- "I am open to forgive both others and myself."
- "I am often in a peaceful state of being."
- "I love myself without condition."
- "I have compassion for others."
- "I feel that the nature of the universe is one of love."
- "I have compassion for myself."

If you noticed a statement does not feel true at this time, consider paying extra attention to your own heart chakra. In addition to Reiki self-healing sessions and other energetic healing treatments, there are many methods of balancing the heart chakra. Explore the following suggestions of ways to support this energy center.

🪷 Activities

- Explore love, compassion, and forgiveness meditations and practices.
- Volunteer for a cause that is meaningful to you.
- Recite the bija (seed) mantra associated with the heart chakra: YAM (pronounced *yahm*).
- Visualize a vibrant green color.
- Listen to music, read a book, or watch a movie that touches your heart.
- Practice an aerobic activity such as walking, jogging, or swimming.

🪷 Affirmations

- "I love myself unconditionally."
- "I am fully open to giving and receiving love."
- "My heart space is an ocean of tranquility."

You can also purchase metaphysical tools to assist with strengthening your heart center. What follows are some recommendations. Please keep in mind that flower essences are often made with brandy or vodka. If you have issues with alcohol, you may want to find a flower essence made with glycerin, use the flower essence as a room spray, or apply it topically instead of ingesting it.

🪷 Essential Oils

- Jasmine
- Rose
- Pine
- Bergamot

🪷 Crystals

- Rose quartz
- Malachite
- Kunzite

🪷 Flower Essences

- Bleeding Heart assists with compassion for yourself and others
- Sweet Briar Rose assists with all facets of love

Heart Chakra Meditation Practice

Sit in a comfortable position. Take a few deep breaths and bring your awareness to the present moment. Set a timer for five minutes and silence your cell phone.

Using your imagination, picture a vibrant green mist surrounding you. This mist is harmonized with the energetic frequency of the heart chakra associated with love, compassion, self-care, openness, and emotional balance. As you inhale, invite this healing mist into your being. As you exhale, send this healing mist to your heart chakra at the center of your chest. As you continue to send this healing green mist to your heart chakra, see a bright green sphere take shape at your heart center. Imagine this sphere growing brighter and bigger with each breath until you are sitting within a green-colored sphere.

When you have finished your meditation, release the visualization. Sit for a minute or two afterward in observation. Notice any shifts in energy that have occurred.

Journaling Practice

Reflect on your meditation practice. Describe your direct experience of connecting to the energy of the heart chakra. How does your own heart chakra function? Are there opportunities to explore further into the cave of your own heart to see what lies within its depths? Take a moment to draw or sketch your personal cave of your heart and the energies living there. How might these practices of connecting to your heart chakra affect your physical, emotional, mental, and energetic bodies? How might you incorporate your knowledge about the heart chakra into your Reiki healing sessions?

Reiki Exploration Day 26

Daily Intention Review

Begin today by remembering why you embarked on this adventure of Reiki healing and self-discovery. When you are ready, state your heartfelt healing intention aloud.

Gassho Meditation

Gassho (pronounced *GAH-show*) is the hand position held by the recipient of a Reiki attunement during the attunement process. This hand position is also commonly known as the prayer position. In the yogic traditions, it is called Anjali mudra or Atmanjali mudra. To perform the Gassho hand position, place the palms of both hands together at your heart center, the seat of love and compassion for yourself as well as others.

There are energetic benefits to certain hand positions, known as mudras. The benefits of the Gassho hand position include balancing the left and right hemispheres of the brain as well as producing a calming effect on the mind. Once the mind is quiet, clarity can occur. From this place of clarity and mental calmness, we can be a more effective channel of Reiki energy. Every Reiki session should start from a place of focused intention, and the Gassho hand position can help us achieve that state of mind. This hand position can be used during meditation, before a Reiki session, or anytime during a Reiki session to establish a connection to the present moment.

Gassho Meditation Practice

Find a comfortable seated position and settle in for a few moments. Silence your cell phone and set a timer for five minutes. Take a complete inventory of yourself at this moment in time. Without judgment, observe how you feel physically, emotionally, mentally, and energetically.

Your eyes can be opened with a soft gaze or closed. Bring the palms of your hands together in prayer with your thumbs touching your heart center in the Gassho position. Notice the natural flow of your breath without altering it in any way. Bring your awareness to the place where the middle fingers touch. If your mind wanders or drifts, gently invite your focus back to the place of connection of your middle fingers.

Sit for two to three minutes afterward in contemplation, observing the after-effects of your meditation.

Journaling Practice

Journal your direct experience of your meditation practice. Consider your relationship with this hand position. You might feel a religious connection to this hand position, which could bring you a sense of spirituality or a deep connection to the Divine. Alternatively, it may bring up uncomfortable feelings regarding organized religion. Honor your emotional reaction as being neither good nor bad: it just is. Keeping in mind your own internal biases towards this hand position, how did your meditation experience change with the use of this hand placement? What energetic shifts did you notice? How might you use the Gassho hand position during future Reiki healing sessions?

Reiki Exploration Day 27

Daily Intention Review

To connect with your purpose in exploring Reiki energy, read your heartfelt intention aloud.

Self-Healing Hand Position 11: Lower Back

The eleventh hand position focuses on the lower back. Place your hands on your lower back region with your fingers pointing downward.

Let's consider how the Reiki energy flows using this hand placement. When your hands cover the lower back region, the healing energy is channeled into the lower back, spinal column, and large and small intestines. Energetically, the lower back issues may relate to financial concerns and insecurities relating to money matters.

This hand placement may benefit the following conditions:

- Back issues
- Poor posture
- Lordosis (curvature of the lower spine)
- Spinal arthritis
- Spinal stenosis
- Herniated disks
- Large intestine issues
- Small intestine issues
- Financial issues

This hand placement may benefit or strengthen the following:

- Back health
- Digestive health
- Financial health

Self-Healing Targeted Practice

Settle into a comfortable seated position and take a few deep, centering breaths. Silence your cell phone and set a timer for five minutes.

Begin the flow of Reiki and appreciate its healing power as you are infused with its energy. Using the hand position with hands on your lower back, begin your Reiki self-healing treatment.

Sit in reflection for a few moments after your self-healing session, taking note of any subtle energy shifts that may have occurred.

Journaling Practice

Reflect on the eleventh hand position. What did you experience during your self-healing treatment? Did you experience any random thoughts or emotions while performing your

Reiki self-healing treatment? If so, what were they? Do you feel a deeper connection to this region of your body? What effect did this self-healing treatment have on your energetic body? What did your analysis inform you of the potential for healing using this hand position? How might you use these insights during future Reiki healing sessions?

Reiki Exploration Day 28

Daily Intention Review

Take a few deep, cleansing breaths to anchor yourself in this present moment. From this place of inner stillness, read out loud your heartfelt intention as a reminder of your healing journey .

Reiki Principle Line 5: "Just for today, I will be kind to all living creatures."

Kindness is our ability to be warm, open, friendly, and giving. Kindness can be a way to approach life—not only guiding our actions but also our thoughts.

This concept isn't unique to Reiki. In the Gospel of Luke (6:31), Jesus is reported to have said "Do to others as you would have them do unto you." The concept can also be viewed through the lens of karma, as you eventually receive everything you put out into the universe, positive and negative. In Wicca, neo-Paganism, and certain occult traditions is a belief that whatever you send out into the world returns to you threefold.

There are several ways to invoke the quality of kindness, even in the most difficult of situations. Here are some suggestions for your consideration:

- Practice random acts of kindness. Opportunities to help others, including animals and the planet, are everywhere. Try to do one kind, selfless act for someone daily.

- Volunteer for a worthy cause that is close to your heart.

- Recite the following affirmation, especially during times when being kind and generous is difficult. "My heart is overflowing with kindness and compassion for others."

Reiki Principle Affirmation Practice

Find a comfortable seated position and settle in for a few moments. Silence your cell phone and set a timer for five minutes. Take a complete inventory of yourself at this moment in time. Observe how you feel physically, emotionally, mentally, and energetically.

Reflect on the last line of the Reiki Principle: "Just for today, I will be kind to all living creatures." Use this line as an affirmation, repeating it to yourself or out loud for the duration of the practice.

Sit for a few minutes afterward in reflection, observing the ripple effects of your practice.

Journaling Practice

Reflect on this line of the Reiki Principle: "Just for today, I will be kind to all living creatures." What does this line mean to you? How do you currently show your kindness for all living things? Is there a subset of all living things for whom you could dedicate more time or energy assisting in some way? How do you show kindness and generosity toward yourself? How might you use these insights during your Reiki healing sessions?

Reiki Exploration Day 29

Daily Intention Review

Pause and consider your authentic voice. There is power in the way you express yourself in the world. From this place of authenticity, recite your heartfelt intention aloud.

Throat Chakra

The fifth energy center is the throat chakra, which focuses on communication, self-expression, and the ability to speak your truth.

Let's explore your connection to your own throat chakra. Consider these statements:

- "I easily speak my truth."
- "I am an effective communicator."
- "I can express myself honestly and sincerely."
- "I feel safe and secure."
- "I am an effective listener."
- "Authenticity is important to me."
- "I deserve to be heard and understood."

If you feel one of these statements is not true for you today, consider spending extra attention on your own throat chakra. In addition to Reiki self-healing sessions and other energetic healing treatments, there are many methods of balancing your throat chakra. Explore the suggestions here for ways to support this energy center.

Activities

- Sing, chant, or hum.
- Listen to music.
- Recite the bija (seed) mantra associated with the throat chakra: HAM (pronounced *hahm*).
- Visualize a bright blue color.
- Write in a journal or explore other forms of communication both written and spoken.
- Drink a throat soothing beverage such as herbal tea.

Affirmations

- "I am able to speak my truth with ease and confidence."
- "My voice is heard."
- "I am an effective listener."

Explore the various metaphysical tools available to assist you with connecting to your throat chakra. Below are some recommendations. Please keep in mind that flower essences are often made with brandy or vodka. If you have issues with alcohol, you may want to find a flower essence made with glycerin, use the flower essences as a room spray, or apply it topically instead of ingesting it.

❀ Essential Oils

- Blue chamomile
- Rosemary
- Eucalyptus

❀ Crystals

- Turquoise
- Aquamarine
- Lapis lazuli

❀ Flower Essence

- Cosmos for aid in all types of communication

Throat Chakra Meditation Practice

Sit in a comfortable position. Silence your cell phone. Take a few deep breaths and bring your awareness to the present moment. Set a timer for five minutes.

Using your imagination, picture a bright blue mist surrounding you. This mist is harmonized with the energetic frequency of the throat chakra and associated with communication, self-expression, and effective listening. As you inhale, invite this healing mist into your being. As you exhale, send this healing mist to your throat chakra located at the center of your throat. As you continue to send this healing blue mist to your throat chakra, see a vibrant blue sphere take shape at your throat. Imagine this sphere growing more vibrant and larger with each breath until you sit within a blue-colored sphere.

When you have finished your meditation, release the visualization. Sit for a minute or two afterward in observation, noticing any shifts in energy that have occurred.

Journaling Practice

Reflect on your meditation experience. How is your throat chakra functioning? How might these practices of connecting to your throat chakra affect your physical, emotional, mental, and energetic bodies? How might balancing this energy center affect your daily life, relationships, and job? How might you incorporate your knowledge about the throat chakra in your Reiki healing sessions?

Reiki Exploration Day 30

Daily Intention Review

You are thirty days into your Reiki immersion experience! Congratulate yourself on the progress you are making on your healing path. Take a moment to reflect on your heartfelt intention. Does it still resonate with you? Give yourself permission to modify the wording of your intention so that it reflects your current vision, and then read it aloud to reaffirm your commitment to your Reiki path.

Self-Healing Hand Position 12: Sacrum

The body's sacrum (tailbone) is the focus of the twelfth hand position in a Reiki self-treatment practice. For this hand placement, place your hands on your sacrum almost as if you were sitting on your hands.

Let's consider how the Reiki energy flows using this hand placement.

Your hands cover the base of your spine so the healing energy would be channeled into the sacrum, sacroiliac joint (SI joint), pelvis, and sex organs.

Energetically, the sacrum is related to the root chakra governing survival, vitality, stability, and security.

This hand placement may benefit the following conditions:

- Sacroiliac Joint Dysfunction (SI joint pain)
- Low back pain
- Pelvis issues
- Pelvic floor dysfunction
- Sexual health issues
- Constipation
- Hemorrhoids
- Low vitality
- Insecurity
- Fear
- Financial difficulties

This hand placement may strengthen the following characteristics or attributes:

- Sexual health
- Proper elimination
- Vitality
- Stability
- Sense of safety and security
- Financial health

Self-Healing Targeted Practice

Settle into a comfortable seated position and take a few deep, centering breaths. Silence your cell phone and set a timer for five minutes.

Begin the flow of Reiki and appreciate its healing power as you are infused with its energy. Self-healing hand position twelve is for the sacrum. Place your hands on your sacrum at the very base of your spine.

Sit in reflection for a few moments after your self-healing session, observing any changes in energy that may have occurred.

Journaling Practice

Reflect on the twelfth hand position. What was your direct experience of your self-healing treatment? Do you feel a deeper connection to this region of your body? What effect did this self-healing treatment have on your energetic body, especially related to the characteristics of the root chakra concerning safety, security, stability, and financial health? What did this analysis inform you of the potential for Reiki healing using this hand position? How might you incorporate these insights into future Reiki healing sessions?

Reiki Exploration Day 31

Daily Intention Review

Take a few deep breaths and draw your attention inward. Pause to consider your progress along your healing path and the insights you have gained thus far on your personal journey. When you are ready, state out loud your heartfelt intention.

The Flow of Reiki Energy

The universal healing energy of Reiki is ever-present. Its origin is divine, and the name you call this Source may be tailored to your personal belief system: the Universe, God, the Source, the Goddess, or whatever name resonates with you.

Once you received your first Reiki attunement, you began to access this pure, high-vibrational, healing energy. Consider how you "turn on" the flow of Reiki. You may start the flow of Reiki energy by stating your intention to access Reiki for the purpose of healing. Alternatively, you could visualize the flow of Reiki beginning. Images such as a light switch, a power button, or a radio dial might resonate with you. Experiment with what method makes the connection to Reiki more powerful.

When you start the flow of Reiki, Reiki energy is channeled from the divine source through the crown chakra at the top of your head. This energy travels throughout your body along the pathways called nadis or meridians. As you begin to channel Reiki energy, you may experience warmth or tingling throughout your body or only in your hands. It's just as likely that you may not experience any physical responses at all, but it doesn't mean that Reiki energy isn't flowing. Honor your experience without judgment and release any expectations of how Reiki energy "should" feel. The more you practice accessing Reiki energy, the more powerful your connection will become.

Remember to turn off Reiki at the close of your Reiki session using the same method you employed to start the process.

Reiki Affirmation Practice

Find a comfortable seated position and settle in for a few moments. Silence your cell phone and set a timer for five minutes. Take a complete inventory of yourself at this moment in time. Notice how you feel physically, emotionally, mentally, and energetically.

Connect with the sentence, "The universal healing energy of Reiki flows through me effortlessly." What thoughts and feelings come up for you as you state this phrase aloud? For the duration of your practice, silently repeat the affirmation: "The universal healing energy of Reiki flows through me effortlessly."

Sit for a few minutes afterward in contemplation, observing the ripple effects of your affirmation practice.

Journaling Practice

Repeating affirmations can have a powerful effect on the physical, emotional, mental, and energetic bodies. What was your direct experience of your affirmation practice?

Visualize how you are connected to Reiki energy and the image of Reiki energy flowing throughout your being. How does this image appear to you? Next, take a moment to sketch your vision of your own connection to Reiki energy. How might these insights be helpful in future Reiki healing sessions?

Reiki Exploration Day 32

Daily Intention Review

Pause and consider your inner vision. Our inner vision is a valuable tool when crafting the life we want to live. In your mind's eye, picture yourself in perfect health and with a deep understanding of Reiki's healing power. Then, recite your heartfelt intention aloud connected to the future you are creating.

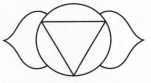

Brow Chakra

The sixth energy center is the brow or third eye chakra, located slightly above the space between your eyebrows. It is related to inner vision, imagination, intuition, and psychic abilities.

Let's explore your connection to your own brow chakra. Consider the following statements:

- "I see situations clearly for what they truly are."
- "I trust my insights and inner guidance."
- "My imagination is an integral part of my true self."
- "I am open to receiving information from my psychic senses."
- "I see with both my physical eyes and my inner vision."
- "I have a clear vision for my life and who I am."
- "I remember my dreams."

If you noticed a statement does not feel true for you now, consider paying extra attention to your brow chakra. In addition to Reiki self-healing sessions and other energetic healing treatments, there are many methods of balancing your brow chakra. The suggestions that follow offer ways to support this energy center:

⚜ Activities

- Practicing meditation
- Journaling your dreams
- Developing your psychic senses
- Reciting the bija (seed) mantra associated with the brow chakra: Om (pronounced *aum*)
- Visualizing the color indigo

⚜ Affirmations

- "I have unlimited possibilities."
- "I see every situation with perfect clarity."
- "I effortlessly trust my intuition."

There are many options such as crystals, essential oils, or flower essences to balance your brow chakra. Please keep in mind that flower essences are often made with brandy or vodka. If you have issues with alcohol, you may want to find a flower essence made with glycerin or use it as a room spray or apply it topically instead of ingesting it.

⚜ Essential Oils

- Clary sage
- Lavender
- Thyme

⚜ Crystals

- Labradorite
- Sodalite
- Sapphire

🪷 *Flower Essences*

- Cerato assists with accessing and trusting your intuition
- White Chestnut assists with anxiety and soothes the mind

Brow Chakra Meditation Practice

Sit in a comfortable position. Silence your cell phone and set a timer for five minutes. Take a few deep breaths and bring your awareness to the present moment.

Picture a rich indigo mist surrounding you. This mist is harmonized with the energetic frequency of the brow chakra and is associated with intuition, creativity, and a balanced mind. As you inhale, invite this healing mist into your being. And as you exhale, send this healing mist to your brow chakra, slightly above your eyebrows. As you continue to send this healing indigo mist to your brow chakra, see a dynamic indigo sphere take shape at your third eye center. Imagine this sphere growing more vibrant and larger with each breath until you sit within an indigo-colored sphere.

When you have finished your meditation, release the visualization. Sit for a minute or two afterward in observation, noticing any shifts in energy that have occurred.

Journaling Practice

Reflect on your meditation experience. How is your brow chakra functioning? Are you able to access your intuition and trust your inner wisdom? Are you connected to your imagination in a healthy, productive way? Do you have vivid dreams and the ability to access the dream world easily? How might these practices of connecting to your brow chakra affect your physical, emotional, mental, and energetic bodies? How might balancing this energy center affect your daily life? How might you incorporate your knowledge about the brow chakra into your Reiki healing sessions?

Reiki Exploration Day 33

Daily Intention Review

Settle in for a moment, noticing how you are showing up today. Then, honoring who you are at this moment, state your heartfelt intention out loud.

Self-Healing Hand Position 13: Knees

The thirteenth hand position in a Reiki self-treatment is focused on the knees. For this hand placement, place your hands on each kneecap. Consider how the Reiki energy flows using this hand placement: your hands are covering your knee caps, so the healing energy would be channeled into the legs and knees. Energetically, the knees are associated with excessive pride, an overactive ego, and stubbornness.

Conditions that may benefit from this hand placement:

- Knee pain
- Issues with walking or balance
- Bursitis
- Arthritis
- ACL injury
- Nighttime leg cramps
- Restless leg syndrome
- Varicose veins
- Torn meniscus
- Shin splints
- Issues concerning pride
- Ego-related issues
- Stubbornness
- Inflexibility

Characteristics that may be strengthened or balanced with this particular hand placement:

- Knee and leg health
- Altruism
- Ability to compromise
- Mental flexibility

Self-Healing Targeted Practice

This hand position is for knees and legs. First, prepare for your self-healing session by silencing your cell phone, settling into a comfortable seated position for a few moments, and setting a timer for five minutes. Then, with your hands on your kneecaps, begin your Reiki self-healing treatment.

Sit in reflection for a few moments after your self-healing session and observe any shifts in energy that may have occurred.

Journaling Practice

Reflect on the thirteenth hand position. What was your direct experience of your self-healing treatment? Do you feel a deeper connection to your knees? What effect did this self-healing treatment have on your energetic body, especially related to stubbornness, the ego, and inflexibility? What does this analysis inform you of the potential for Reiki healing using this hand position? How can you use these insights during future Reiki healing sessions?

Reiki Exploration Day 34

Daily Intention Review

Take a few cleansing breaths and connect to your intuition. From this place of inner wisdom and understanding, recite out loud your heartfelt intention.

Sacred Intuition

Sacred intuition is a gift granted to all of us from the moment of our birth. You might know it as a gut feeling, inner knowing, or the sixth sense. It's a form of knowing not born from the rational mind. Unfortunately, society has diminished the role that intuition can play in our daily lives by valuing the logical at the expense of the intuitive. In reality, we operate most effectually when our rational, analytical mind and intuitive nature are in harmonious balance.

It is vital to develop your intuitive skills as your Reiki journey progresses. Intuitive guidance can come in many forms, such as an image in your mind's eye, a sudden thought or inspiration, a word heard in your inner ear, or a simple sense of knowing. When you simply listen to your gut and inner voice, your intuition will naturally develop over time.

Sacred Intuition and Self-Healing Practice

Find a comfortable seated position and settle in for a few moments. Silence your cell phone.

Take a complete inventory of yourself at this moment in time. Notice how you feel physically, emotionally, mentally, and energetically.

Turn on Reiki using your unique method of connection and feel the infusion of Reiki energy into your being.

Set an intention to connect with your inner guidance and allow yourself to receive all information without judgment or expectation. Pause a few moments, allow yourself to sit with the intention, and remain present for any guidance you receive. As you receive intuitive feedback, place your hands guided by your inner wisdom and hold the hand positions until you feel that body part is full of healing energy. Be patient with yourself—these skills take time to develop.

Sit for two to three minutes afterward in contemplation, observing the after-effects of your Reiki treatment.

Journaling Practice

Journal your direct experience of this practice. Then, consider what role intuition plays in your life.

Do you habitually listen to your gut feelings? How do you receive your intuitive feedback: physical sensations, inner visions, or flashes of insight? Are there opportunities to strengthen your intuition more in your daily life?

How might you use your intuition during future Reiki healing sessions?

Reiki Exploration Day 35

Daily Intention Review

Take a moment to consider your connection to the Divine. From this place of personal spirituality, recite your heartfelt intention aloud.

Crown Chakra

The seventh energy center is the crown chakra located at the top of your head. This energy center governs our connection to the Divine, our ability to understand, our thoughts, and our higher consciousness.

Let's explore your connection to your own crown chakra. Consider these statements:

- "I am connected to the Divine."
- "I am open-minded."
- "I am connected to all that is."
- "I experience bliss in everyday life."
- "I am open to receiving wisdom from my higher self."
- "I feel blessed."
- "I am at peace with myself and others."

If you noticed a statement that does not feel true for you now, consider paying extra attention to your crown chakra. In addition to Reiki self-healing sessions and other energetic healing treatments, there are many methods of balancing the crown chakra. The suggestions that follow include ways to support this energy center.

✿ Activities

- Meditation
- Prayer
- Fast for brief periods of time
- Read a spiritual book
- Visualize a violet or white light

✿ Affirmations

- "I am connected to my higher self."
- "I honor the divine aspect of myself."
- "I am in unity with all there is."

Consider the options that follow to help balance your crown chakra. Please keep in mind that flower essences are often made with brandy or vodka. If you have issues with alcohol, you may want to find a flower essence made with glycerin, use the flower essences as a room spray, or apply it topically instead of ingesting it.

❀ *Essential Oils*

- Neroli
- Frankincense
- Myrrh

❀ *Crystals*

- Amethyst
- Lepidolite
- Purple fluorite

❀ *Flower Essences*

- Star of Bethlehem to assist with connection to the Divine
- Trillium to assist with connection to all things

Crown Chakra Meditation Practice

Sit in a comfortable position. Take a few deep breaths and bring your awareness to the present moment. Silence your cell phone. Set a timer for five minutes. Using your imagination, picture a violet mist surrounding you. This mist is harmonized with the energetic frequency of the crown chakra associated with the connection to the Divine, understanding, and consciousness. As you inhale, invite this healing mist into your being, and as you exhale, send this healing mist to your crown chakra located at the top of your head. As you continue to send this healing violet mist to your crown chakra, see a brilliant violet sphere take shape at your crown. Imagine this sphere growing more vibrant and larger with each breath until you sit within a violet-colored sphere.

When you have finished your meditation, release the visualization. Sit for a minute or two afterward in observation, noticing any shifts in energy that have occurred.

Journaling Practice

Reflect on your meditation experience. How is your crown chakra functioning? Are you able to feel your connection to both the Divine and humanity? Are you cultivating a deeper understanding of the world and your place in it? Are feelings of serenity and tranquility a part of your daily life? How might these practices of connecting to your crown chakra affect your physical, emotional, mental, and energetic bodies? How might balancing this energy center affect your daily life? How might you incorporate knowledge about the crown chakra in your Reiki healing sessions?

Reiki Exploration Day 36

Daily Intention Review

Consider the progress you've made on your healing journey. Take a moment to be grateful for your hard work and dedication. When you are ready, state your heartfelt healing intention aloud.

Self-Healing Hand Position 14: Ankles and Feet

The body's feet are the focus of the fourteenth and final hand position in a Reiki self-treatment practice. Traditionally, the hands are placed over the ankles and the tops of the feet. A variation of the fourteenth hand position is to place one hand over the ankle and the other hand on the sole of the foot. When finished, you would repeat the hand position on the other foot.

Consider how the Reiki energy flows using this hand placement. Your hands cover the ankles and feet so that the healing energy would be channeled into the foot, ankle, and toes.

Energetically, there are minor chakras located at the soles of the feet, assisting with grounding and connection to the earth.

This hand placement may benefit the following conditions:

- Foot issues
- Bunions
- Plantar fascitis
- Heel spurs
- Gout
- Diabetic neuropathy
- Arthritis
- Ankle issues

- Lack of grounding
- Loss of connection to the earth

This hand placement may strengthen or balance the following characteristics:

- Foot health
- Ankle health
- Connection to the earth
- Sense of grounding, stability, and security

Self-Healing Targeted Practice

Settle into a comfortable seated position and take a few deep centering breaths. Silence your cell phone and set a timer for five minutes.

Begin the flow of Reiki and acknowledge its healing power as you are filled with its energy. Use the fourteenth hand position for self-healing with your hands over the top of the ankles and feet to begin your self-healing session.

Sit in reflection for a few moments after your self-healing session, observing any shifts in energy that may have occurred.

Journaling Practice

Reflect on the fourteenth hand position. What was your direct experience of your self-healing treatment? Do you feel a deeper connection to your feet? What effect did this self-healing treatment have on your energetic body? Pay special attention to feelings of connection to the earth and a sense of being in a grounded state. What did your analysis reveal about the potential for Reiki healing using this hand position? How might you use these insights during future Reiki healing sessions?

Reiki Exploration Day 37

Daily Intention Review

Spend a few moments in quiet reflection focusing on your healing journey to date. When you feel ready, state out loud your heartfelt intention.

Maintaining Chakra Health

You are in a constant state of flux, from your thoughts to your emotions, to your energy levels, to the very cells within your physical body. This concept also applies to your energetic body. The energy that once flowed smoothly through the chakras can become stagnant and even blocked.

Although chakras can become blocked or misaligned for an infinite number of reasons, energetic imbalances are quite common in the following situations:

- Illness
- Trauma
- Stress
- Marriage
- Death of a loved one
- Abuse
- Change in employment
- Financial difficulties
- Relationship issues
- Change in diet
- Birth of a child
- Poor habits
- Exhaustion

As we encounter life's challenges and daily stresses, maintaining our energetic balance is an essential tool for a healthy lifestyle. We can help retain our energetic equilibrium and thrive by assessing our chakras periodically.

Chakra Meditation Practice

Find a comfortable seated position and settle in for a few moments. Silence your cell phone.

Take a complete inventory of yourself at this moment in time. Notice how you feel physically, emotionally, mentally, and energetically. Pay attention to any energetic blocks or stagnant energy you may be experiencing.

Now, take a journey through your chakras. At your root chakra, picture a red spinning disk at your tailbone. Imagine this disk rotating clockwise, revitalizing your root chakra, the energy center associated with security, stability, and financial health.

When your root chakra feels balanced, move up to your sacral chakra located a few inches below your belly button. Here, picture an orange spinning disk restoring balance to this energy center, which is responsible for your emotions and creativity.

When you have a sense of completion, move upward to your solar plexus chakra located at your core. In your mind's eye, imagine a yellow spinning disk rotating in a clockwise direction revitalizing this energy center associated with personal power and vitality.

When this energy center feels renewed, continue moving up to your heart chakra located at the center of your chest. Picture a green spinning disk moving in a clockwise direction that heals the energy vortex associated with love and compassion.

After you intuitively feel that this energy center is balanced, move up to the throat chakra, your place of authentic communication. Picture a blue spinning disk rotating in a clockwise direction revitalizing this energy center.

Once you are ready to move on, draw your attention upward to the brow chakra located slightly above your eyebrows. At this energy center, imagine an indigo spinning disk rotating clockwise, balancing the energy center associated with your intuition and insight.

When you have a sense of completion, move to the last primary chakra, the crown chakra, located at the top of the head. Picture a violet spinning disk moving in a clockwise direction at your crown balancing this energy center, which is associated with your connection to all things, including the Divine.

Once you feel your seven main chakras are harmoniously balanced, end the meditation.

Pause for a few moments to observe the after-effects of your meditation.

Journaling Practice

Journal your direct experience of this practice. Did you perceive any energy blockages or stagnant energy before your meditation practice? Consider what life events may be present that triggered these blocks or energy imbalances to occur. Did you notice any subtle shifts or changes during or after your meditation—physically, emotionally, mentally, or energetically? Draw a quick sketch showing your chakra system before and after your meditation. How might you use these insights in your Reiki healing sessions?

Reiki Exploration Day 38

Daily Intention Review

Take a few deep breaths and consider those individuals who have assisted you along your healing path. Then, from this place of gratitude and connection, read out loud your heartfelt intention.

Hawayo Takata

Hawayo Takata is the mother of Reiki healing in the West. Through her teachings, the Usui Reiki lineage has grown into a worldwide healing modality.

Born on December 24, 1900, on the island of Kauai in Hawaii, Hawayo Kawamura was the daughter of Japanese immigrants. She married Saichi Takata and had two daughters. After the death of her husband, the stress and physical toll of supporting her family precipitated her decline in health. Diagnosed with multiple health issues, she was told that she needed surgery. Instead, she went to Dr. Hayashi's clinic in Tokyo for treatment in 1935.

Impressed with her remarkable recovery, Hawayo Takata became a student of Dr. Hayashi. In 1937, Hawayo Takata received permission from Dr. Hayashi to open a Reiki healing clinic in Hawaii. She opened several clinics throughout the islands of Hawaii. In addition, she traveled to the mainland of the United States, Canada, and Europe to teach others the art of Reiki and perform healing sessions.

By the time of her death on December 11, 1980, Hawayo Takata had trained hundreds of Reiki practitioners and elevated twenty-two Reiki practitioners to the level of Reiki Masters. Consequently, these twenty-two Reiki Masters shared their teachings with countless others facilitating the spread of Reiki worldwide.

Hawaya Takata Meditation Practice

For this meditation, you'll need an image of Hawayo Takata (many are available online). Please remember that when we meditate on a picture of a person, we aren't worshipping them. Instead, we are honoring the individual and focusing our attention on the qualities in them that we wish to cultivate within ourselves.

Before you begin, place a picture of Hawayo Takata where you can view it without straining your neck. Set a timer for five minutes, sit in a comfortable position, and silence your cell phone.

With a soft gaze, look upon the image of Hawayo Takata and allow yourself to connect with her healing energy. Actively cultivate a connection with this prolific healer by meditating on her picture.

Sit for a few moments afterward in contemplation and gratitude for the contributions of Hawayo Takata.

Journaling Practice

Consider the contributions of Hawayo Takata to the world of energy healing. What elements of her life story resonate with you? What attributes would you like to emulate? Compose a thank you letter to her for her many gifts to the world of healing and for the way her contributions have impacted your personal healing journey. Finally, how might you make use of your knowledge of Hawayo Takata in future Reiki healing sessions?

Reiki Exploration Day 39

Daily Intention Review

To help set the tone for today, take a moment to reconnect with your heartfelt intention and recommit to your healing path by reciting it aloud.

Experiencing the Benefits of Reiki

At this point on your journey through the foundational concepts of Reiki, you've experienced all the key hand positions for a self-healing Reiki treatment. Self-healing is a crucial component of Reiki. By performing self-healing treatments, you actively participate in your own healing process. Self-healing treatments can be done anytime, anywhere, and for any amount of time. Self-treatments can either be full-body treatments using the fourteen hand placements, spot treatments on areas that need specific healing, or an intuitively guided session that uses a blend of both. The benefits of these treatments affect all elements of your being: physical, emotional, mental, energetic, and spiritual.

Since your forty-day immersion experience began, you may have experienced one or more of the following:

- Stress reduction
- Pain relief
- Assistance with preventative care

- Improvement with overall well-being
- Relaxation
- Greater mind-body-spirit connection
- Energetic balance

The more often you perform Reiki on yourself, the more significant healing benefits you'll experience.

Full-Body Self-Healing Session

Settle into a comfortable seated position and take a few deep, centering breaths. Silence your cell phone and set a timer for the amount of time you can dedicate to your Reiki self-treatment.

Begin the flow of Reiki and appreciate its healing power as you are infused with its energy and proceed through the fourteen hand positions to give yourself a full Reiki treatment. Use your intuition to determine the amount of time spent on each body part.

At the end of your healing session, spend a few moments in silence observing the effects of your Reiki treatment.

Journaling Practice

Journal about your direct experience of your Reiki session. Did you sense any physical sensations? How did your Reiki session impact your emotional, mental, and energetic bodies? What benefits did you experience using the Reiki healing treatments over the last thirty-eight days? How might these insights be used to deepen your understanding of Reiki and the benefits of Reiki healing? How might you use these insights during future Reiki healing sessions?

Reiki Exploration Day 40

Daily Intention Review

With a thankful heart for all the progress you have made along your healing path, recommit to your healing goals by stating out loud your heartfelt intention.

Integration

In the hustle and bustle of life, we often don't have time to integrate what we have learned. Integration is the process of bringing together different elements into a cohesive whole. It takes time to understand the fundamentals of Reiki and incorporate them into our daily lives. Be patient with yourself during this process.

Daily practices to consider to reinforce your Reiki knowledge include the following:

- Reiki self-healing treatments
- Recital of the five Reiki Principles
- Scanning your physical, emotional, mental, and energetic bodies
- Chakra meditations
- Reading books on Reiki and the chakra system
- Performing Reiki on family and friends

Integration Affirmation Practice

Find a comfortable seated position and settle in for a few moments. Silence your cell phone.

Take a complete inventory of yourself at this moment in time. Pay attention to how you feel physically, emotionally, mentally, and energetically.

Connect with the phrase, "I have built a strong Reiki foundation upon which I can expand my healing abilities to benefit both myself and others." Consider the thoughts and feelings that come up for you as you state this phrase aloud.

Set a timer for five minutes and silently or aloud repeat the affirmation for its duration: "I have built a strong Reiki foundation upon which I can expand my healing abilities to benefit both myself and others."

Sit for a few minutes afterward in contemplation, observing the ripple effects of your affirmation practice.

Journaling Practice

Consider your forty-day Reiki immersion experience. What have been your experiences over the last forty days? What have you learned about yourself during this process? What areas of Reiki would you like to explore further? What practices might you use daily to reinforce and integrate the foundational concepts of Reiki? How has your connection to Reiki energy shifted over this immersion experience? How could this knowledge make you a more effective Reiki healer?

Part 3

Beyond the Basics: Reiki Level Two

Chapter 8

What Is Reiki Level Two?

Reiki Level Two increases the power and effectiveness of your Reiki healing by introducing three Reiki symbols. Techniques for sending Reiki energy across time and space to heal situations in the past as well as the future are taught. Additionally, methods of sending Reiki energy to animals, plants, and objects are also presented.

As your personal energetic frequency changes, your spiritual gifts, including your psychic senses, may present themselves as your connection to the Divine is strengthened. You may become aware of your spirit guides and the alliance of healing deities available to assist you along your healing path. Typically, these topics are reviewed, in detail, during the Reiki Level Two training.

Why Advance to Reiki Level Two?

There are many reasons you may want to extend your Reiki training to this next level. Personal reflection regarding your intention to pursue this training is a valuable part of your personal evolution as an individual and a healer. Some common reasons for following this path include the following:

- To become a professional Reiki healer.
- To increase the effectiveness of your Reiki healing sessions.
- To actively raise your personal vibration to a higher frequency.
- To develop your intuition and psychic senses.
- To perform distance healing sessions.
- To heal situations in the past or the future.

- To heal past lives and karma associated with your family lineage.
- To send healing to your ancestors.

When Are You Ready to Advance to Reiki Level Two?

There are no definitive rules regarding the length of time you should wait between Reiki Levels One and Level Two; the decision is personal, and only you should make it. At a minimum, you may want to complete the twenty-one-day self-healing practice allowing your energetic body to become accustomed to Reiki energy before receiving your next attunement. However, I recommend you take the time to integrate all the concepts of Level One before proceeding to Level Two. This proficiency can be obtained by completing the forty-day immersion experience in part two of this text. When you are ready to take this step, trust your intuition that you are prepared to proceed.

Reiki Level Two Attunement Process

Similar to the Reiki Level One process, you will be attuned to the three Reiki symbols in the Reiki Level Two attunement. Once you receive this attunement, the power and effectiveness of your Reiki healing abilities will dramatically increase. After your attunement, you should practice Reiki self-healing for a minimum of twenty-one days and engage in daily meditation. Keeping a Reiki journal to track your progress and record your insights is highly recommended.

After your Reiki Level Two attunement, you may experience any of the following:

- Shifts in relationships: as your personal energy changes, you might find new relationships forming and older, unhealthy relationships falling away.
- Changes in eating and drinking habits: you may be drawn to eating more organic, healthier foods.
- Changes in energy levels
- Change in sleep patterns, including vivid dreams
- Desire to act in a more ethical manner
- A deeper connection to the Divine
- Awareness of psychic senses
- Awareness of your spirit guides

You may consider expanding your healing services to become a professional Reiki healer at the completion of this level.

Chapter 9

The Reiki Symbols

Consider what a symbol is at its core. A symbol is both a form or a shape as well as a force or the power behind it.[5] Symbols are not two-dimensional images. Instead, picture them as three-dimensional entities with dynamic energies. You can engage with these energies for your own healing and personal development. There are innumerable ways that the energies of the Reiki symbols can be used in situations requiring healing, strength, purification, and balance.

The three Reiki symbols were received by Dr. Usui during his spiritual retreat on Mount Kurama outside Kyoto, Japan. These sacred symbols have traditionally been kept secret and only presented to students during Reiki training. As a result, there are variations on what is considered the correct way to draw the symbols. If you received a version of the Reiki symbols during your Reiki training that differ from those presented in this text, feel free to experiment to see which version resonates with you.

I have made a conscious decision to include the images of the Reiki symbols in this book for two reasons. The first is due to the accessibility of these symbols on the internet and in other Reiki books. The second is that I believe those individuals who approach the topic of Reiki sincerely (such as healers who opt to purchase this book) should have the symbols readily available for reference. Still, the power behind these symbols is only available to those who have been attuned to its energy by a Reiki Master-Teacher. Therefore, whether or not you choose to display Reiki symbols or share the images with others is a personal choice.

The Reiki symbols should be memorized so they can be drawn accurately during Reiki healing sessions.

---

5. W. E. Butler, *The Magician: His Training and Work* (North Hollywood, CA: Melvin Powers Wilshire Book Company, 1969), 41.

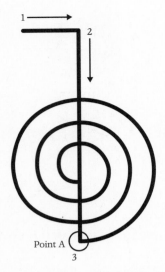

Symbol One: Cho Ku Rei

Cho Ku Rei (pronounced *cho-koo-ray*), also known as the Power Symbol, is the only Reiki symbol that can be used by itself. The purpose of this symbol is to increase and focus the power of Reiki energy. The name of this symbol translates to "straight, direct, or correct spirit," providing us with the insight that Reiki connects us to our higher self, the inner nature of our being.[6] Another standard translation is "placing all the power of the universe here."[7] This alternate interpretation provides us with an awareness of how this symbol can be used to direct and intensify Reiki's energy.

Cho Ku Rei is used for empowering, cleansing, and protecting. Your intention determines how the power of this symbol will be manifested. When used in conjunction with others symbols, Cho Ku Rei activates the other symbols and increases the overall energy of the healing session.

Initially, I was taught to draw the Cho Ku Rei symbol in the counter-clockwise direction. However, during the course of my studies, I discovered that traditionally the symbol is drawn in a clockwise direction. Experiment to see which version of the Cho Ku Rei symbol best aligns with your connection to Reiki energy.

---

6. Frans Steine, *The Inner Heart of Reiki: Rediscovering Your True Self* (Winchester, UK: Ayni Books, 2015), 64.

7. Lisa Powers, *Reiki Level I, II and Master Manual* (Self-published, 2016), 96.

The activation of the Cho Ku Rei symbol occurs during your attunement process. To use Cho Ku Rei in healing sessions, draw the character while silently stating "Cho Ku Rei" three times. Experiment with different methods of drawing this symbol:

- Draw the symbol with your pointer finger or both your pointer and middle fingers.
- Draw the symbol with your outstretched hand.
- Draw the symbol with your eyes.
- Draw the symbol on the roof of your mouth with your tongue.

Suggested uses for the Cho Ku Rei symbol are listed below, but the real opportunities to utilize this symbol are only limited by your imagination.

- Healing of the physical body
- Activating additional Reiki symbols
- Purifying of food and drink
- Promoting energetic balance
- Healing of careers and work situations
- Energetic cleansing of physical spaces such as homes and offices

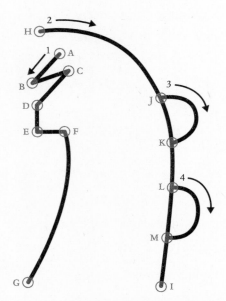

Symbol Two: Sei He Ki

Sei He Ki (pronounced *say-hey-kee*), the Harmony Symbol or sometimes called the Mental and Emotional symbol, is associated with bringing balance and returning the object of the healing to a state of equilibrium. A translation of the name of this symbol is "God and man coming together."[8] The purpose of this symbol is to cultivate inner harmony by balancing both the emotions and the mind. Your intention determines how the power of this symbol will manifest.

Many physical imbalances and illnesses have emotional or mental root causes. A perfect example is chronic stress and anxiety, which can directly lead to multiple health concerns such as mental health problems, cardiovascular disease, eating disorders, and digestion problems. The Sei He Ki symbol is a valuable tool to assist with healing the mental and emotional causes of these physical manifestations.

However, this symbol can't stand alone. It is empowered by the Cho Ku Rei symbol and activated by silently intoning the symbol's name three times. For example, to use Sei He Ki, follow this method:

---

8. Stein, *Essential Reiki*, 59.

1. Draw the Cho Ku Rei symbol and intone "Cho Ku Rei" three times.
2. Draw the Sei He Ki symbol and intone "Sei He Ki" three times.
3. Draw the Cho Ku Rei symbol and intone "Cho Ku Rei" three times.

Suggested uses for the Sei He Ki symbol are listed here, but experiment and use your intuition to find the appropriate application of the Harmony Symbol:

- Healing of the mental and emotional bodies
- Reducing/eliminating stress, anxiety, or nervousness
- Balancing the left and right hemispheres of the brain
- Healing relationship issues
- Assisting with forgiveness
- Assisting with memory issues
- Facilitating the grieving process
- Releasing addictive behaviors
- Balancing the energies of your home or work environment
- Facilitating creative expression
- Diffusing arguments or tense situations

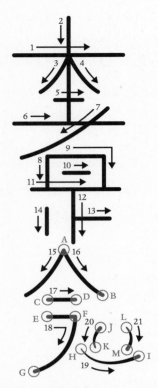

Symbol Three: Hon Sha Ze Sho Nen

Hon Sha Ze Sho Nen (pronounced *hone-shah-zay-show-nen*) is known as the Distance symbol for distant or remote healing. It is also called the Connection symbol. A translation of the name of this symbol is "No past, no present, no future."[9] As with the other Reiki symbols, your intention determines how the power of this symbol will be used. There are several variations of this symbol, so please use the version that resonates with you.

The power of this symbol isn't limited to physical distance—it can also be used to send Reiki energy across time and space. Additionally, this symbol can be a gateway for accessing the Akashic Records, also known as the Book of Life, in which the soul's history has been documented across lifetimes. By accessing the Akashic Records, a person's familial lineage karma (that is, the karma inherited from one's family) can be healed, positively affecting the individual's current life. Please note that the karma you accrue

---

9. Stein, *Essential Reiki*, 60

based on your actions in this lifetime is best corrected by performing good works and assisting others.

As with the Sei He Ki symbol, the Hon Sha Ze Sho Nen symbol should not be used alone. It is empowered by the Cho Ku Rei symbol and activated by intoning the symbol's name three times. To use Hon Sha Ze Sho Nen, follow this method:

1. Draw the Cho Ku Rei symbol and say "Cho Ku Rei" three times.
2. Draw the Hon Sha Ze Sho Nen symbol and say "Hon Sha Ze Sho Nen" three times.
3. Draw the Cho Ku Rei symbol and say "Cho Ku Rei" three times.

Suggested uses for the Hon Sha Ze Sho Nen symbol appear here, but experiment and use your intuition to find the appropriate use of the Connection Symbol.

- Distance healing in the present
- Healing of past issues, including relationships, traumas, and grief
- Past life healing
- Karmic related issues
- Healing for a group of people
- Healing for a specific situation or event
- Healing the planet
- Spiritual healing
- Ancestral healing
- Inner child healing
- Deep roots diseases
- Future events

Using the Three Symbols In a Reiki Session

The Reiki symbols can be used at the beginning of your Reiki session or any point during the treatment. For example, they can be stacked together in a "Reiki sandwich" using the following method:

1. Draw the Cho Ku Rei symbol and say "Cho Ku Rei" three times.
2. Draw the Sei He Ki symbol and say "Sei He Ki" three times.

3. Draw the Cho Ku Rei symbol and say "Cho Ku Rei" three times.

4. Draw the Hon Sha Ze Sho Nen symbol and say "Hon Sha Ze Sho Nen" three times.

5. Draw the Cho Ku Rei symbol and say "Cho Ku Rei" three times.

Using your intuition or based on your evaluation of your healing participant's chakras, you may use a specific symbol or combination of symbols on a particular body part or energy center. Consider drawing the character, or combination of symbols, over the selected area and then hovering your hand palm down over the symbol; imagine pressing the image into your healing participant without physically touching their body. Alternatively, you could draw the character and then tap it in using your pointer and index fingers.

Consider the example of a healing participant who has been through the ending of a significant relationship. When you evaluate this individual's chakras, you feel an intense heaviness at the heart center, representing the capacity for love and compassion, and the sacral chakra, indicating intimacy issues. At the beginning of the session, use all three symbols and proceed using the standard hand placements. When you reach the heart chakra, draw the Cho Ku Rei symbol with your finger and then energetically press the symbol into your healing participant. Next, draw the Sei He Ki for emotionally healing, and with your palm facing down, imagine pushing the symbol into your healing participant. Finally, draw the Cho Ku Rei symbol and follow the same practice of pressing the symbol into the heart center. Continue with your hand placements until you reach the sacral chakra area and repeat the same technique of pushing the characters of Cho Ku Rei, Sei He Ki, and Cho Ku Rei into the energy center. Complete the healing session as your intuition guides you.

Chapter 10

Distance Healing

After your Reiki Level Two attunement, you will have the ability to perform distance healing. This powerful tool allows you to send Reiki energy across distance, time, and space. Several methods can be used when sending Reiki energy remotely. Experiment to see what approach best resonates with you or develop your unique way of performing distance healing.

No matter your method, the Hon Sha Ze Sho Nen symbol should be used for all distance healings.

Consider using the entire Reiki symbol sandwich method, outlined here:

1. Draw the Cho Ku Rei symbol and say "Cho Ku Rei" three times.
2. Draw the Sei He Ki symbol and say "Sei He Ki" three times.
3. Draw the Cho Ku Rei symbol and say "Cho Ku Rei" three times.
4. Draw the Hon Sha Ze Sho Nen symbol and say "Hon Sha Ze Sho Nen" three times.
5. Draw the Cho Ku Rei symbol and say "Cho Ku Rei" three times.

Alternatively, you can focus on just the Hon Sha Ze Sho Nen symbol using the method below:

1. Draw the Cho Ku Rei symbol and say "Cho Ku Rei" three times.
2. Draw the Hon Sha Ze Sho Nen symbol and say "Hon Sha Ze Sho Nen" three times.
3. Draw the Cho Ku Rei symbol and say "Cho Ku Rei" three times.

Sending Reiki Energy Across Distance

A correspondence is a close correlation or equivalence. Humanity has a rich history using correspondences. The following are examples for your consideration:

- Letters of the alphabet correspond to certain vocalized sounds.
- Sign language uses hand gestures to correspond to words.
- Churches across the world feature a cross as a representation of Jesus Christ.

The purpose of using correspondence in a distance Reiki healing session is to help keep the Reiki practitioner's focus on a representation of the object of the Reiki healing. This method is also known as the surrogate method. If we lose our focus or attention during a Reiki session, we are no longer in the present moment. Without focus, we may not be able to regulate our own energy levels and can become ungrounded.

There are several ways to employ the correspondence or surrogate method. What follows are some examples you may want to try:

- A teddy bear or doll: Using a teddy bear or doll to represent the focus of your Reiki healing, you can perform the same hand placements as you would in a typical Reiki healing session. Although the teddy bear or doll may appear to be receiving the healing energy, the energy is actually being sent remotely to the object of your healing intention.
- A photograph or image: By using a picture or photo of the person or object for whom you are sending Reiki energy, you keep your awareness on the actual person or object. Unlike the teddy bear method, you are not using different hand positions; instead, you can focus the Reiki energy on one body part at a time using the power of your intention. If you wish, you can place the image between the palms of your hands as you send Reiki healing to it. Alternatively, you can imagine Reiki energy surrounding the entire image or photograph at one time; in essence, Reiki energy surrounds the person in a Reiki bubble of healing energy. If you do not have a picture of your healing participant, you can draw one. Your drawing doesn't have to be an exact likeness of the individual but a simple guide to keep your focus.
- Yourself: You can use your own body, or a part of your body, to represent the person to whom you are sending Reiki energy. The difference between this method and a Reiki self-healing treatment is the power of your intention.

The inner healing temple method uses your imagination to create your unique healing temple where you perform your Reiki healing session. To conduct a Reiki healing session using the inner healing temple method, picture in your mind's eye a sacred healing space. Once this image is formed in as much detail as possible, visualize your healing participant lying on your Reiki table in your inner healing temple. Now, picture yourself within your inner healing temple and begin to perform a Reiki healing session as if you were both there in person.

This method doesn't require anything except your own sacred imagination, the consent of your healing participant, and your ability to keep your focus for the duration of the healing session.

Sending Reiki Healing Across Time and Space

Since Reiki energy is ever-present, it can be used effectively to heal situations that happened in the past and events that may occur in the future.

Sending Reiki Energy to the Past

Since Reiki's energy isn't limited to the present moment, consider how you could use this healing modality to release past trauma. Here are some common examples:

- Interpersonal conflicts
- Traumatic events
- Loss of a loved one or pet
- Past lives
- Ancestors

You can modify the correspondence method or the inner healing temple method to send Reiki energy to the past. For example, you could use the correspondence method if you have a picture or you can make a drawing representing a past event or trauma. If you do not want to use an image, you could write down the event on a piece of paper as the focus of your healing session. Alternatively, you could use your sacred imagination to picture the event as you send Reiki energy to the past.

Sending Reiki Energy to a Future Event

Worrying about the future can cause anxiety and stress. By sending Reiki healing to a future event, we can prepare for the unfolding of the future to be in alignment with our higher self and the Divine. Some examples of how you could employ Reiki healing in future events include:

- Successful completion of a project
- Meeting new friends or embarking on a new relationship
- Attainment of goals
- Development of new talents or abilities
- Creation of new sources of income
- Life events such as a child's birth, marriage, etc.

As with sending energy to the past, you can use either the correspondence method or the inner healing temple method for sending Reiki energy to a future event. You could choose the correspondence method if you have a picture or make a drawing of a future event. If you do not want to use an image, you could write down the event on a piece of paper as the focus of your healing. Alternatively, you could use your sacred imagination to picture the event as you send Reiki energy to the future.

Chapter 11

Non-Human Reiki Healings

Reiki energy is not limited to healing humans. Since all beings and objects are made of energy, Reiki healing can be applied in a limitless number of situations.

Pets/Animals

Reiki healing can be sent to pets and animals with the following benefits:

- Increases health and well-being
- Reduces stress and anxiety
- Assists with recuperation after injury or surgery
- Alleviates depression

You can use the hands-on method to perform Reiki directly on a pet or hover your hands around your pet. Your pet may inform you when it has received enough Reiki energy by moving away from you or leaving the room. You can also let your intuition guide you when the healing session should be completed.

To perform Reiki on an animal that is not your pet, you can beam the Reiki energy from your hands or perform distance healing.

Food/Drink/Medicines/Vitamins

Reiki healing can be performed on your food and drink for purification and to increase the effectiveness of the nutrients you will be receiving. Additionally, your vitamins and medications can also be strengthened by using Reiki energy. Consider drawing the Cho Ku Rei symbol over your food, drinks, vitamins, and medications to purify these items and increase their effectiveness.

Plants/Gardens/Trees

Reiki healing can be sent to plants, gardens, and trees. Plants are living beings and benefit from Reiki energy. The benefits of sending Reiki energy to plants, gardens, and trees can assist with growth and health maintenance. Examples of how Reiki healing can be used on vegetation include the following:

- Before planting, hold seeds in your hands and send Reiki energy to them.
- To perform Reiki on a house plant, hold the container in your hands while performing Reiki or gently lay your hands on the leaves of the plant.
- To perform Reiki on your garden, you can work directly with each plant by placing your hands on the leaves or letting your hands hover over the garden, moving slowly from plant to plant.
- To perform Reiki on a tree, place your hands directly on the tree's bark.

Home

Your home environment can benefit from Reiki. For example, the energy in your home may feel unbalanced, such as after a disagreement or a large gathering. In that case, you can draw the Cho Ku Rei symbol in each corner of your room to purify the energy of the space and remove any negativity from your environment. Additionally, drawing the Cho Ku Rei symbol at the entrance of your home can add an element of protection. Your intention determines how the force behind the symbol will be directed.

Work/Office

Reiki energy can also be beneficial in your work environment. Here are some suggestions on how you can use Reiki healing at work:

- Consider drawing the Cho Ku Rei symbol in your office space to clear out stale, stagnant, or negative energies.
- Inviting Reiki energy to flow as you perform your work can bring a sense of calm and peace to your work environment.

- Sending Reiki energy to all your office equipment such as your computer, your chair, your pens, your phone, and your paper to remove negative energy and increase your productivity.
- Drawing the Distance symbol while talking on the phone to allow communication to flow smoothly and for the benefit of all may assist with clarity of ideas and improved communication.

There are many possibilities, so experiment to see what works best for you.

Objects

Inanimate objects are also made of energy. Therefore, Reiki energy can be sent to any object to increase its performance, add extra healing to the item, or remove negative energies. For example, you could:

- Send Reiki energy to your car before a trip.
- Cleanse your crystals with Reiki energy.
- Charge a gift with Reiki energy before giving it to a friend or family member.
- Send Reiki energy to your bed before sleep.
- Charge your vision board with Reiki energy.
- Send Reiki energy into your bathwater before bathing to assist with cleansing and strengthening your auric field.

Finances

Reiki energy can be sent to assist us with our finances. Consider sending Reiki energy to your wallet to help with financial healing. Additionally, when planning your budget, you can ask the Reiki energy to flow to assist while making financial decisions that align with your higher self.

Creative Endeavors

Since Reiki energy can remove energetic blocks and stagnant energies, allowing Reiki energy to flow during any creative process enhances our ability to expand beyond our current limitations, open our minds to new possibilities, and improve problem-solving skills. Reiki energy can assist with opening ourselves to the potential of our imagination.

The possibilities to employ Reiki healing in everyday life are endless. Experiment with the suggestions in this chapter but don't limit yourself to them. Your personal experience is your best teacher, so as opportunities and challenges present themselves, take a few moments to reflect on how Reiki energy can assist you. The more you use Reiki in your everyday life, the more opportunities you will find to use this versatile, healing modality.

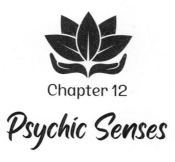

Chapter 12

Psychic Senses

As you develop your Reiki skills, your intuition, gut feeling, or sixth sense will strengthen, and you may begin to access your psychic senses. Our psychic senses are specific manifestations born from our intuition. Psychic senses are often referred to as "clair-" senses. The psychic senses we will be exploring in detail are found here:

Clairvoyance: Clear seeing, related to the sense of sight

Clairaudience: Clear hearing, associated with the sense of hearing

Claircognizance: Clear knowing, related to thought

Clairempathy: Clear feeling, related to our emotions

Clairsentience: Clear sensing

Clairalience: Clear smelling, related to smell

Clairtangency: Clear touching, related to physically touching objects or people

Clairgustance: Clear tasting, associated with the sense of taste

You may gravitate strongly toward one or two of these senses, but keep an open mind to learn how you can develop all of them.

Clairvoyance

Clairvoyance through your physical eyes can occur in two ways. The first is seeing an object or person that doesn't physically exist in the material plane. If this happens, the object or person may appear less dense or more translucent than the physical objects surrounding it. These images may disappear suddenly or disperse over time. The second way clairvoyance occurs through the physical eyes is seeing signs in your environment that have significance for you. Examples include seeing a message on a signpost or billboard, repeatedly seeing the same number, or sighting a specific animal numerous times.

Clairvoyance through your mind's eye is the receiving of a specific vision or series of pictures. These images are often vibrant, clear, and experienced as if you were within the scene itself. In addition, signs and symbols may be a part of this experience. Although there are many books that contain interpretations of signs and symbols, check in with your intuition first for figuring out what a symbol means to you.

Clairvoyance can also come in the form of dreams and daydreams. If you are prone to vivid dreams, consider keeping a dream journal to track and analyze your dreams. However, don't discount your daydreams. Daydreams can contain intuitive messages. If you daydream, spend a few moments exploring your experience for more profound messages or insights.

Clairaudience

The clairaudient sense is related to hearing. Your physical ears may perceive it as sounds from outside, or you may experience clairaudience as inner hearing. A person with solid clairaudience connections receives information through auditory methods.

Clairaudience is associated with a balanced throat chakra. The color associated with this chakra is blue, located at the throat's center. For more details about the throat chakra, refer to Day 29 of the Immersion Experience in part two.

Clairaudience may be experienced through the physical ears, although the source of the sound vibration does not necessarily have a source in the physical world. Although there are an infinite number of sounds that can be experienced, typical examples of sounds that may be heard through your clairaudient sense are as follows:

- Music or musical instruments
- Humming or buzzing
- Whispers, chanting, prayers, or singing
- Animal noises
- Doors opening or closing

Alternatively, these sounds may be heard inside your head. This type of clairaudience may be challenging to distinguish from the regular mind chatter of your own inner dialogue. Nevertheless, pay attention to these voices; with some discernment, you will begin to recognize authentic clairaudient experiences.

One of my most profound clairaudient experiences occurred while driving with my two young sons in my car traveling down a busy stretch of I-95 North between Rhode Island and Massachusetts. My car was in the middle lane when suddenly, my front tire sheared off from the car and bounced across the highway's median. An authoritative voice spoke clearly to me, saying, "Don't step on the breaks. Put on the hazard lights and ease up on the gas. Turn on your blinker and move into the slow lane after the next car passes. Now move into the breakdown lane and stop." I followed the instructions step by step. If I had stepped on my breaks at that high level of speed, my car would have flipped. I credit this clairaudient experience for saving my life and my sons' lives.

Claircognizance

Claircognizance is related to knowing. This psychic sense may be experienced as a download of information directly into your brain without any extra method of receiving the information. A person with strong claircognizance connections often has an active mind and may learn best through reading and writing.

Claircognizance is associated with a balanced solar plexus chakra and balanced brow chakra. For more details about the solar plexus chakra, refer to Day 18 of the Immersion Experience in part two. If you are interested in refreshing your knowledge about the brow chakra, explore Day 32 of the Immersion Experience in part two.

A personal example of claircognizance is my uncanny ability to know which crystals would be appropriate for a Reiki session without having prior knowledge of the individual or their reason for requesting the appointment.

Often, it's only when we reflect upon a past situation that we know we had a claircognitive experience.

Clairempathy

Clairempathy is related to empathy, or the capacity to share in the feelings of another. This psychic sense often manifests as experiencing another person's emotions as if they are your own.

Clairempathy is associated with the sacral chakra. The color associated with the sacral chakra is orange, and it's located a few inches below your navel. For more details about the sacral chakra, refer to Day 13 of the Immersion Experience in part two.

Clairempathy is a psychic sense that I've experienced since childhood. I would absorb all the emotional baggage of others which led to anxiety, emotional stress, and feeling overwhelmed. Now knowing how this sense functions, I strongly suggest clearing energy whenever you are in crowds, have interactions with negative people, or are involved in challenging situations. For tips on energy clearing, please refer to Day 20 of the Immersion Experience in part two.

Although clairempathy can be challenging, it is a valuable tool for Reiki healers. This sense can assist with understanding our healing participants' issues, provided we as healers use consistent energy clearing techniques.

Clairsentience

Clairsentience is the ability to sense the energetic signature or vibe of another person, object, or place. Unlike clairempathy, which is associated with taking on the emotions of others, clairsentience is knowing information regarding the way something or someone feels. For example, clairsentience may be experienced when entering a building that just doesn't "feel right" or meeting someone who feels "off" in some way.

Like clairempathy, clairsentience is associated with the sacral chakra. The color associated with the sacral chakra is orange, and it is located a few inches below your navel. For more details about the sacral chakra, refer to Day 13 of the Immersion Experience in part two.

Clairsentience is a valuable tool when going to new places and meeting new people. In situations where you don't like the vibe, trust your intuition and take the appropriate action.

Clairalience

Clairalience is related to the physical sense of smell. Our sense of smell is linked to memory, behavior, and emotions, making clairalience a powerful psychic sense. Clairalience can happen by smelling scents with your physical nose that are not present or by your mind perceiving a smell even though the source of the aroma isn't there.

Clairalience is associated with the throat chakra. The color associated with this chakra is blue, located at the throat's center. For more details about the throat chakra, refer to Day 29 of the Immersion Experience in part two.

A few typical aromas you may experience using your psychic sense of smell are perfume, flowers, smoke, chemicals, food, freshly cut grass, and decay.

Clairgustance

The clairgustance psychic sense is related to the physical sense of taste. Clairgustance occurs when you taste something in your mouth that isn't there. You perceive this information through your psychic sense of taste.

Like clairalience, clairgustance is associated with the throat chakra. The color associated with this chakra is blue, located at the throat's center. For more details about the throat chakra, refer to Day 29 of part two's Immersion Experience.

Typical tastes that you may experience are food, cigarettes, metal, chemicals, and blood.

Clairtangency

The clairtangency psychic sense is related to the physical sense of touch. Therefore, clairtangency is receiving previously unknown information by touching a person or object.

Clairtangency is associated with the root chakra, the chakra related to our physical body. The color associated with this chakra is red, located at the base of the spine. For more details about the root chakra, refer to Day 4 of part two's Immersion Experience.

Common clairtangency experiences include the following:

- Touching a person and knowing information about them.
- Holding an object and knowing information about its history.
- Petting an animal and receiving impressions about its health or its mood.

Chapter 13

Spirit Guides For Reiki and More

As you progress along your healing path and your intuition strengthens, you may become aware of your spirit guides and other divine beings of light who are there to help and support you. From the time of your birth, you have a core spirit team assigned to assist you. Some guides come into and out of your life to help with specific goals and areas of interest. Additionally, you can call upon angels and other healing deities to provide additional insights, protection, and assistance with your Reiki healing skills.

A Personal Story

My first direct encounter with a spirit guide dedicated to healing occurred shortly after my Reiki Level Two attunement. It was a spontaneous and humbling experience. Since that initial encounter, my spirit healing team has grown and changed over the years. In addition to my personal healing guides, a few of my constant spirit team companions for Reiki sessions and my personal healing practices include the Archangels, especially Archangel Raphael, for overall healing, and Archangel Michael, for protection and increased vitality. Chiron, the wise centaur from Greek mythology who taught knowledge of healing to Asclepius, the Greek god of medicine, has supported me over the years. Due to my chronic issues with celiac disease, I have a personal affinity with the Roman goddess Carna, who is helpful with all types of physical healing, especially with the absorption of nutrients from food, an issue for those diagnosed with celiac disease. Consider researching healing deities to broaden your knowledge about the vast world of divine support available to you.

You never know what form your spirit guides may take or how they might communicate with you. It's best to allow the process of meeting with and working with your spirit guides to unfold without judgment or expectation. Most importantly, trust your personal experience of meeting and interacting with your spirit guides.

Types of Spirit Guides

A variety of enlightened beings of light in the spirit realm can be called up to provide us with support and guidance. Below are some examples you may wish to explore as you continue along your journey through life.

Personal Spirit Guides: These beings of pure light are divine in origin. Their mission is to assist you along your life path. They may act as teachers, providing you with wisdom, insights, and knowledge. Others may work as protectors who provide you guidance on safety and health topics. Guides can also assist with cultivating joy in life, and others help with creative endeavors.

Reiki Spirit Guides: A specific type of spirit guide that begins to work with you when you receive your first Reiki attunement and assists with Reiki healings. The connection with this guide grows stronger as you continue to study and use Reiki energy.

Animal Spirit Guides: These guides exist as animals and can share gifts of knowledge and medicine that are unique to their animal characteristics.

Ancestors: Your ancestors are a powerful group of spiritual allies who once lived on Earth. Your ancestors aren't limited to those of your own bloodline. Examples of types of ancestors that may be assisting you include the following:

- Ancestors related to you directly through your paternal and maternal lines.
- Ancestors related to you via adoption or foster care.
- Ancestors related to you through marriage or partnership.
- Ancestors of the land on which you live.
- Ancestors of your religious or spiritual affiliation.
- Ancestors of your profession, your creative pursuits, and your hobbies.

Angels: Angels are divine beings who have never been incarnated in human form. Angels can be called upon at any time to assist with every aspect of life, including healing, personal growth, problem resolution, protection, creative projects, and abundance.

Ascended Masters: This is a group of spiritually enlightened beings that are connected to the evolution of humanity and the planet.

Saints and Mystics: Saints and mystics were once human and have obtained divine grace through significant spiritual development. They can be called up for assistance with healing, abundance, protection, and a multitude of other topics.

Healing Deities, Gods, and Goddesses: There are a host of divine healing deities across all the religions of the world that can assist with health and healing.

Communicating with Your Spirit Guides

Your spirit guides may communicate with you through various means, including your physical and psychic senses. Signs that a spirit guide is communicating could include:

- Seeing an animal, a feather, a number multiple times or in an unusual context.
- Hearing a voice in your mind that provides you with guidance or instruction.
- Sensing a message intuitively, such as a gut feeling, or experiencing an inner knowing.
- Receiving information in the form of dreams.
- Receiving information directly through channeling or meditation.

For you to communicate with your spirit team, state your intention to connect with your guide(s) and ask for assistance, guidance, and support.

Embrace Your Free Will

As human beings, we have the gift of free will. Although we may receive guidance from our spirit allies, we do not need to act on their instructions. The choice is ours alone in how we walk our chosen path.

The Importance of Boundaries

You are responsible for your boundaries—both in your relationships in the physical and spirit worlds. If you aren't in the right frame of mind to receive divine guidance or if a spirit ally is making their presence known at an inconvenient time, you can direct the spirit guide to leave—at least for the present moment.

Our spirit team is a vast resource of guidance and support. Open your awareness to their presence and remain watchful for their signs. Don't limit yourself with preconceived notions regarding how spirit guides "should" appear; allow the process of discovering your spirit team to unfold organically.

Chapter 14

Setting Your New Healing Intention

Let's go deeper into our self-exploration. We'll develop a new intention for our next forty-day immersion experience based on your unique goals and areas of interest. Before beginning to craft your new healing intention, let's consider the material presented during Reiki Level Two.

By exploring our likes and dislikes, we can learn more about ourselves and discover biases that we may never knew existed.

In your Reiki journal, list five main Reiki concepts that resonate with you the most.

_____

_____

_____

_____

In your Reiki journal, list five Reiki concepts that you feel neutral about or do not connect with at this time.

_____

_____

_____

_____

Now consider your goals, hopes, and wishes for your upcoming forty-day immersion experience and list them in your Reiki journal.

You are now ready to craft your personal intention for the next forty days based on your unique aims. For example, you may wish to develop a deeper understanding of the topics that interest you the most, or perhaps you may want to connect more with topics that did not resonate with you at this time. As a reminder, intention setting assists us with providing clarity and vision, aligning our daily actions with longer-term goals. We will connect with your intention daily to remind you of your commitment to yourself and your healing journey.

Sample Heartfelt Intention

I, [your name], agree to follow the daily practices in these pages, including meditation, journaling, and self-healing, for a minimum of forty days. I will be open to developing a deeper understanding of the core concepts relating to the three Reiki symbols and how to use these powerful symbols. Although I do not currently connect with the concept of working with spirit guides, I am open to this experience and wish to learn through my personal experience how I can make this connection. I will say *yes* to activities, choices, and thoughts that align with my goals of learning the tools and techniques to heal myself and others on physical, emotional, mental, energetic, and spiritual levels.

Today, with a grateful heart for my unique journey, I am ready to commit myself to my study of Reiki healing and integrate Reiki energy into my daily life.

Signed: _____

Date: _____

Craft your heartfelt intention in your Reiki journal.

Part 4

Reiki Forty-Day Immersion Experience: Beyond the Basics

Reiki Exploration Day 1

Daily Intention Review

As a reminder of why you've embarked on this journey of healing, read your heartfelt intention out loud.

Cho Ku Rei: The Power Symbol (Focus on Form)

What comes to mind when you think of a symbol? Characters such as the Reiki symbols contain a force when activated. In this way, they are both a form (the physical drawing of the symbol) and a force (the energy that is released and directed to perform a particular function).[10]

When you reflect on the Cho Ku Rei symbol, what does the form resemble to you? Drawing from my personal experiences, I associate the vertical line of the Cho Ku Rei symbol with divine will or my own connection with the Divine. I associate the horizontal line with my personal will and my actions. The spiral is a universal symbol used throughout the ages and across cultures to represent various concepts, including the following: force; continuity, a vortex of energy, the cosmos, cycles of time such as the seasons, and the process of birth, death, and rebirth.

The Cho Ku Rei symbol has been drawn using a clockwise and counterclockwise spiral. I have found that a clockwise spiral increases energy, and I primarily use this method of drawing the symbol of Cho Ku Rei. However, your experience may differ, so experiment to find which way works most effectively for you.

Cho Ku Rei Meditation Practice: Focus on Form

To begin our journey to form a deep understanding of the power of the Cho Ku Rei symbol, we will consider the character's shape. Set the intention to develop a deep connection to the power of the Cho Ku Rei symbol. Then, draw the Cho Ku Rei symbol seven times as accurately as possible.

Scan the images you created and pick the one you are most drawn to working with for your meditation. Next, consider the image you have drawn. Does this image speak to you in some way?

---

10. Butler, *The Magician*, 41.

Begin your meditation practice by silencing your cell phone, setting a five-minute timer, and finding a comfortable seated position. Then take a few centering breaths and, with a soft gaze on the Cho Ku Rei image, invite your mind to focus on the symbol. If your mind wanders during this practice, simply re-focus your attention back to the Cho Ku Rei symbol.

After your meditation, sit for a moment or two in quiet reflection.

Journaling Practice

Journal your direct experience of your meditation. Did drawing the symbol multiple times awaken any new insights? How did you feel during this part of the practice? Did it stir up emotions or random thoughts? What insights, if any, did you receive during your meditation? How might you use this more profound awareness of the Power symbol in your Reiki healing sessions?

Reiki Exploration Day 2

Daily Intention Review

Take a moment to reflect on your heartfelt intention. Then, read it aloud and appreciate your dedication to your healing path.

Cho Ku Rei: The Power Symbol (Focus on Force)

As a reminder, the Reiki symbols' force or dynamic energy is initially activated during the Reiki attunement process. It is turned on, so to speak, when you draw the character and recite its name, "Cho Ku Rei," three times silently or out loud.

Consider the nature of the force behind the Cho Ku Rei symbol, which is empowering, grounding, purifying, and protecting. This dynamic energy is directed based on your intention and focus.

Reflect on the various ways you might use the different aspects of the energy of the Cho Ku Rei symbol.

❀ *For empowerment*

- To increase your personal power, determination, and drive
- To increase your confidence level

- To add strength to a goal
- To strengthen the potency of medications and vitamins

❧ *For grounding*

- To reduce stress and anxiety
- To increase focus
- To release excess energy

❧ *For purification*

- To cleanse your personal auric field
- To purify food and drink
- To clear the energy of a room or space

❧ *For protection*

- Your physical body
- Your home
- Your belongings
- Your family and pets

The opportunities to use the Cho Ku Rei symbol every day are limitless.

Cho Ku Rei Chanting Practice

Continuing our journey to form a deep connection to the power of the Cho Ku Rei symbol, we will use the power of intonation or vibration. By chanting the name of the character, Cho Ku Rei, we can tap into the essence of the symbol and begin to experience the potential of the symbol's power.

Begin your chanting practice by setting a five-minute timer, silencing your cell phone, and finding a comfortable seated position. Set the intention to connect to the energy of the Cho Ku Rei symbol. Spend a minute centering yourself by taking a few deep breaths. Slowly and mindfully, repeat the phrase "Cho Ku Rei" aloud.

At the end of your chanting practice, sit for a few moments observing any aftereffects you may experience.

Journaling Practice

Describe your direct experience of your chanting practice. What effects did this practice have on you physically, emotionally, mentally, and energetically? What, if any, shifts in energy occurred in your physical location? Consider the force of the Cho Ku Rei symbol. How might you use this symbol in your daily life for empowerment, protection, purification, and grounding? And how might you include these insights during your Reiki healing sessions?

Reiki Exploration Day 3

Daily Intention Review

Take several cleansing breaths and connect to your inquisitive nature. Then, from this place of curiosity, read your heartfelt intention aloud.

The Power of Curiosity and the Cho Ku Rei Symbol

I remember when I realized that I had lost my sense of curiosity. I was attending a yoga class and was going through the motions. The teacher prompted us to be curious about what was happening right now. A light bulb suddenly went off in my mind. I realized that I hadn't been curious about anything in a long, long time. Instead, I have been living my life in an endless cycle of work, caring for my children, cleaning my house, and occasionally finding time to attend yoga classes. That unhealthy and unfulfilling cycle was broken in an instant.

I've come to appreciate and cultivate my curious nature. I am always asking *why*, *how*, and *what will happen if I try something new*? From this inquisitive state of mind, I embarked on my own healing journey, which led me to Reiki and all the gifts that Reiki has provided me.

Curiosity, in a healer, can lead to unique insights and new interpretations of old methods. With the aid of a curious mind, we can eliminate assumptions and expectations we might have. As you approach your exploration into the Reiki symbols, stay curious. Be open to new experiences as you use these symbols in your healing sessions. Cho Ku Rei can not only help with healing on a physical level and add power to your Reiki healing session but also help you step into your own power as a healer.

Cho Ku Rei Self-Healing Practice

Find a comfortable seated position and settle in for a few moments. Set a timer for five minutes, the duration of your targeted self-healing session today.

Take a complete inventory of yourself at this moment in time. Notice how you feel physically, emotionally, mentally, and energetically.

Turn on Reiki using your unique method of connection and feel the infusion of Reiki energy into your being. Set your personal healing intention and cultivate a sense of curiosity. Release any expectations you may have about the Cho Ku Rei symbol and allow your experience to unfold.

Since Cho Ku Rei is associated with healing the physical body and adding increased power to the healing session, scan your physical body looking for any areas that may need extra healing and would benefit from the energy of the Cho Ku Rei symbol. Then, begin your Reiki healing session using your intuition or the standard self-healing hand positions. Use the Cho Ku Rei symbol during your healing session whenever you are intuitively drawn to do so.

After your healing session, take a few moments to scan your body and observe any subtle shifts of energy that may have occurred.

Journaling Practice

Journal your direct experience of your self-healing session. What was your experience using only the Cho Ku Rei symbol during your self-healing practice? Did you notice any energetic shifts that occurred during your healing session?

What is your relationship with curiosity? Is there an opportunity to be more curious as you approach your development as a Reiki healer?

How might this information be helpful in future Reiki healing sessions?

Reiki Exploration Day 4

Daily Intention Review

As you read aloud your heartfelt intention, take a moment to connect with the meaning of the words you selected.

Sei He Ki: The Harmony Symbol (Focus on Form)

Sei He Ki, also known as the Mental and Emotional symbol and the Harmony symbol, is associated with returning the object of the healing session to a state of equilibrium and balance. The purpose of this symbol is to cultivate inner harmony by balancing both the emotions and the mind. Your intention determines how the power of this symbol will manifest.

What comes to mind when you look at the Sei He Ki symbol? The first line reminds me of the changing nature of our thoughts and emotions. Sometimes, they can be sharp and edgy. Other times, my thought and feelings are smooth and flowing. The second line reminds me of a camel's back with two humps. Camel's humps store fat and nutrients, which I relate to our own emotional reserves that nurture us and which we need to replenish often.

Fortunately, Reiki can assist with replenishing our energy and building up our emotional and mental bandwidths, allowing us the resiliency and balance to move forward in our life's journey.

Sei He Ki Meditation Practice

To begin our journey to form a deep understanding of the power of the Sei He Ki symbol, we will consider the shape of the character. Set the intention to create a deep connection to the power of the Sei He Ki symbol. Then, draw the Sei He Ki symbol seven times as accurately as you can.

Scan the images you created and pick the one you are most drawn to working with for your meditation. Next, consider the shape of the image you have drawn. Does this image speak to you in some way?

Begin your meditation practice by setting a five-minute timer, silencing your cell phone, and finding a comfortable seated position. Then, take a few centering breaths, and with a soft gaze on the Sei He Ki image, invite your mind to focus on the symbol. If your mind wanders during this practice, simply re-focus your attention back to the Sei He Ki symbol.

At the conclusion of your meditation, sit for a moment or two to absorb the benefits of the practice.

Journaling Practice

Journal your direct experience of your meditation. Did drawing the Sei He Ki symbol multiple times awaken any new insights? How did you feel during this part of the practice? Did you notice any emotions surfacing or random thoughts appearing? What insights, if any, did you receive during your meditation? How might you use this deeper awareness of the Sei He Ki symbol during your Reiki healing sessions?

Reiki Exploration Day 5

Daily Intention Review

Take a moment to cultivate a state of equilibrium and inner harmony. From this place of balance, state your heartfelt intention aloud.

Sei He Ki: The Harmony Symbol (Focus on Force)

Just like the Cho Ku Rei symbol, the force of the Sei He Ki symbol is awakened during the Reiki attunement process. It is then activated when you draw the symbol, Cho Ku Rei, and recite its name "Cho Ku Rei" three times and then draw the symbol, Sei He Ki, and recite its name "Sei He Ki" three times. To increase the power behind the Sei He Ki symbol, repeat the drawing of the Cho Ku Rei symbol and repeat "Cho Ku Rei" three times.

The force behind the Sei He Ki symbol is of a higher vibration than the Cho Ku Rei symbol. Please remember that "higher" doesn't mean "better." The higher frequency of the symbol corresponds to the emotional nature of the symbol. The force behind the Sei He Ki symbol is balancing and releasing. This dynamic energy is directed based on your intention and focus.

Reflect on the various ways you might use the different aspects of the energy of the Sei He Ki symbol.

❀ For balancing

- Restoring balance to the emotional body
- Calming and focusing the mind
- Enhancing the balance between the left (analytical) and right (creative) hemispheres of the brain
- Creating a harmonious home or work environment

For releasing

- Healing relationship issues
- Releasing harmful or toxic thought patterns
- Assisting with forgiveness
- Facilitating the grieving process
- Releasing addictive behaviors
- Diffusing arguments or tense situations

Sei He Ki Chanting Practice

Continuing our exploration of the power of the Sei He Ki symbol, we will use the tool of vibration. By chanting "Sei He Ki," we can tap into the essence of the symbol and begin to experience the potential of the symbol's power.

To begin your chanting practice, find a comfortable seated position, silence your cell phone, and set a timer for five minutes. Set the intention to connect to the energy of the Sei He Ki symbol. Spend a minute centering yourself by taking a few deep breaths. When you are ready, slowly and mindfully, begin repeating "Sei He Ki" aloud.

At the end of your chanting practice, sit for a few moments observing any after-effects you may experience.

Journaling Practice

Describe your direct experience of your chanting practice. What effects did this practice have on you physically, emotionally, mentally, and energetically? Did any emotions surface? What thought patterns emerged during your session? Did your energy shift during your chanting practice? If so, what were the changes? What is your understanding of the force behind the Sei He Ki symbol? How might you use these insights during your Reiki healing sessions?

Reiki Exploration Day 6

Daily Intention Review

Take a moment to connect with what nurtures you. Then, from this place of self-reflection, read out loud your heartfelt intention.

The Power of Self-Care and the Sei He Ki Symbol

Healers often prioritize the health and welfare of others while sacrificing their own self-care. When we neglect ourselves, imbalances can occur that may lead to disharmony in our outer and inner lives. The impact of these imbalances might be reflected in declining physical health, relationship issues, anxiety, depression, difficulties maintaining energy levels, sleep disorders, and spiritual crisis. It's not selfish to spend time caring for yourself—it's an act of love.

Remember that you, as much as anyone on the planet, is deserving of your own love, care, attention, and healing efforts. Following are some suggestions for improving your self-care routine.

Physical Body

- Engaging in a regular exercise practice
- Eating healthy, nourishing foods
- Maintaining a regular sleep schedule

Mental Body

- Practicing meditation
- Reading
- Journaling
- Completing puzzles or other mind engaging experiences

Emotional Body

- Engaging in creative pursuits
- Spending time with friends and loved ones
- Listening to music
- Writing or reading poetry

Energetic Body

- Taking baths with sea salt or essential oils
- Attending sound baths or meditating with singing bowls
- Spending time in nature

🪷 *Spiritual Body*

- Praying
- Spending time in nature
- Reading spiritual books or scriptures
- Meditating on the Divine

Performing daily Reiki self-healing sessions is an effective way of giving care and attention to all aspects of yourself.

If you are (or want to be) a professional Reiki healer, it's essential to determine how many healing sessions you can do a day without sacrificing your own well-being. By maintaining our self-care practices, we put ourselves in a better position to continue contributing to our communities and the larger world.

Sei He Ki Self-Healing Practice

Find a comfortable seated position and settle in for a few moments. Silence your cell phone and set a timer for five minutes, the duration of today's targeted self-healing session.

Turn on Reiki using your unique method of connection and feel the infusion of Reiki energy into your being. Set your personal healing intent and cultivate a sense of curiosity. Release your expectations about the Sei He Ki symbol and allow your experience to unfold.

Since the Sei He Ki symbol is associated with healing mental and emotional bodies, scan your mind and your heart center briefly. Then, begin your Reiki healing session using your intuition or the standard self-healing hand positions. Be sure to utilize the Cho Ku Rei and Sei He Ki symbols during your Reiki session.

After your healing session, take a few moments to scan your body and observe any subtle shifts of energy that may have occurred.

Journaling Practice

Journal your direct experience of your self-healing session. For example, what was your experience using only the Cho Ku Rei and Sei He Ki symbols during your self-healing practice? How did your self-healing session affect you physically, emotionally, mentally, and energetically?

What priority do you give to your own self-care? Is there an opportunity to develop a self-care practice that aligns with your daily needs and supports your long-term goals?

Did you gain insights regarding using the Sei He Ki symbol and the importance of self-care that may be helpful in future Reiki healing sessions?

Reiki Exploration Day 7

Daily Intention Review

Take a moment to reflect on your heartfelt intention. Then, read it aloud and appreciate your dedication to your healing path.

Hon Sha Ze Sho Nen: The Distance Symbol (Focus on Form)

Hon Sha Ze Sho Nen is the symbol for distant or remote healing. It is also called the Connection symbol. First, consider the shape of the symbol. What does it resemble to you? I connect with Diane Stein's description of this symbol resembling a tall structure such as a pagoda or stupa, a Tantric Buddhist representation of the chakras or five elements in a statuary or architectural form.[11]

I used the pagoda or stupa as inspiration for my analysis of the Hon Sha Ze Sho Nen symbol. The character's shape can reflect Reiki's power to assist with our spiritual growth and development moving from the mundane, physical world to higher realms. It may also reflect Reiki's ability to transform and transmute lower vibrational energy to a higher frequency as we move up the levels of the structure. Finally, it speaks to me about the limitless quality of Reiki energy transcending time, space, and distance.

Hon Sha Ze Sho Nen Meditation Practice

To start exploring our connection to the Hon Sha Ze Sho Nen symbol, think about the shape of the character. Set the intention to create a deep connection to the power of the Hon Sha Ze Sho Nen symbol. Then, draw the Hon Sha Ze Sho Nen symbol seven times as accurately as you can.

Scan the images you created and pick the one you are most drawn to working with for your meditation. Now, consider the symbol you have drawn. Does this image speak to you in some way? Does it stir up any emotions, memories, or random thoughts?

---

11. Stein, *Essential Reiki*, 60.

Begin your meditation practice by silencing your cell phone and finding a comfortable seated position. Then, set your timer for five minutes and take a few centering breaths. Next, gently focus your gaze on the Hon Sha Ze Sho Nen symbol, and invite your mind to focus on the image. If your mind wanders during this practice, simply refocus your attention on the symbol.

After your meditation, sit for a moment or two to absorb the benefits of the practice.

Journaling Practice

Journal your direct experience of your meditation. What does the shape of the Hon Sha Ze Sho Nen symbol resemble for you? Did drawing the symbol multiple times awaken any new insights? How did you feel during this part of the practice? Did you notice any random sensations or thoughts emerging? What insights did you receive during your meditation? How might you use this deeper connection to the Hon Sha Ze Sho Nen symbol during your Reiki healing sessions?

Reiki Exploration Day 8

Daily Intention Review

Begin today by remembering why you embarked on this adventure of self-healing and discovery. Then, when you are ready, state your heartfelt healing intention aloud.

Hon Sha Ze Sho Nen: The Distance Symbol (Focus on Force)

Just like the previous two symbols, the force of the Hon Sha Ze Sho Nen symbol is awakened during the Reiki attunement process. It is then activated when you draw the symbol Cho Ku Rei, recite its name three times, and then draw the symbol Hon Sha Ze Sho Nen followed by reciting its name three times. To increase the power behind the Hon Sha Ze Sho Nen symbol, repeat the drawing of the Cho Ku Rei symbol and repeat "Cho Ku Rei" three times.

The force behind the Hon Sha Ze Sho Nen is of a higher vibration than both the Cho Ku Rei and Sei He Ki symbols. Please remember that "higher" doesn't mean "better"—the higher frequency of the character corresponds to the spiritual nature of the healing energy. The force behind the Hon Sha Ze Sho Nen symbol is transforming, unifying, and transcending. This dynamic energy is directed based on your intention and focus.

Reflect on the various ways you might use the different aspects of the energy of the Hon Sha Ze Sho Nen symbol.

For transforming

- Healing of past issues, including relationships, traumas, and grief
- Healing for a specific situation or event in the present
- Ancestral healing
- Healing of deep-rooted diseases
- Healing energy sent to future events

For unifying

- Spiritual healing
- Healing the planet

For transcending

- Karmic related issues
- Past-life healing
- Distance healing in the present

Hon Sha Ze Sho Nen Chanting Practice

Continuing our journey to form a deep connection to the power of the Hon Sha Ze Sho Nen symbol, we will use the power of the spoken word. When we chant the name of the character, Hon Sha Ze Sho Nen (pronounced *hone-sha-zay-show-nehn*), we can tap into the essence of the symbol and begin to experience the potential of the symbol's power.

Begin your chanting practice by silencing your cell phone, setting a five-minute timer, and finding a comfortable seated position. Set the intention to connect more deeply to the energy of the Hon Sha Ze Sho Nen symbol. Spend a minute centering yourself by taking a few deep breaths. When you are ready, begin slowly, mindfully repeating "Hon Sha Ze Sho Nen" aloud.

At the end of your chanting practice, sit for a few moments observing any after-effects that you may experience.

Journaling Practice

Describe your direct experience of your chanting practice. What effects did this practice have on you physically, emotionally, mentally, and energetically? Did any emotions surface? What thought patterns emerged during your practice? How did your energy shift during your chanting session? Describe your understanding of the power behind the Hon Sha Ze Sho Nen symbol. How might you use these insights regarding the Hon Sha Ze Sho Nen symbol during your Reiki healing sessions?

Reiki Exploration Day 9

Daily Intention Review

Take a few deep, clearing, breaths to anchor yourself in this present moment. From this place of presence, read out loud your heartfelt intention as a reminder of your healing journey.

Connection and The Hon Sha Ze Sho Nen Symbol

Consider what elements compose your physical body, such as oxygen, hydrogen, nitrogen, carbon, and calcium. These elements aren't unique just to our planet—they are the building blocks of the entire universe. In essence, you are made up of the same elements as stars, planets, rocks, hummingbirds, etc. We can break this concept down further to the atomic and sub-atomic levels. At our very essence, we are connected to all things both living and inanimate.

Through this connection, we can explore the Hon Sha Ze Sho Nen symbol. The Hon Sha Ze Sho Nen symbol is often called the Connection symbol and is used in distance healing as well as healing through time to past and future events. We are already connected to the person or object of our healing: whether that object or person is in the room with us, across the country, in the past, or in the future. Of course, we can enhance this connection through visualization and intention, but the basis for the link already exists.

Hon Sha Ze Sho Nen Self-Healing Practice

Find a comfortable seated position, settle in for a few moments, silence your cell phone and set a timer for five minutes, the duration of your targeted self-healing session today.

Take a complete inventory of yourself at this moment in time. Notice how you feel physically, emotionally, mentally, energetically, and spiritually. Since Hon Sha Ze Sho Nen is associated with healing the spiritual body, spend a moment contemplating your connection to the Divine.

Turn on Reiki using your unique method of connection and feel the infusion of Reiki energy into your being. Set your personal healing intention. Release your expectations about the Hon Sha Ze Sho Nen symbol and allow your experience to unfold. Remember to use the Cho Ku Rei symbol before and after the Hon Sha Ze Sho Nen symbol. Then, begin your Reiki healing session using your intuition or the traditional self-healing hand positions.

After your healing session, take a few moments to scan your body and observe any subtle shifts of energy that may have occurred.

Journaling Practice

Journal your direct experience of your self-healing session. What was your experience using only the Cho Ku Rei and Hon Sha Ze Sho Nen symbols during your self-healing practice?

What is your relationship to the Divine? Is there an opportunity to further explore your spirituality? How might you establish a daily practice to deepen this connection?

Did you gain any insights regarding using this combination of symbols that may be helpful during Reiki healing sessions? What role might your personal spiritual journey play in your future Reiki sessions?

Reiki Exploration Day 10

Daily Intention Review

You are ten days into your second healing immersion. Congratulations! Take a moment to connect with your heartfelt intention. Read it aloud. Does it still resonate with you? Does it still reflect your goals for your Reiki journey? If it feels appropriate, feel free to modify or re-word your intention.

Distance Healing: Surrogate Method

The surrogate or correspondence method of distance healing uses a substitute in place of your healing participant. The purpose of the surrogate is to keep your focus during the distance healing session. It's essential to consider your ability to maintain concentration as well as your personal preferences when deciding which distance method best suits your healing work. Reflect on your initial reaction to these options without judgment or self-criticism.

If you prefer to use hand placements when performing Reiki healing, using a teddy bear or a doll as a substitute for your healing participant may be the most appropriate option for you. However, some individuals might find this practice silly or distracting. If that's the case, consider using your own body as a stand-in for your healing participant.

If you do not wish to use hand placements to channel the Reiki energy, consider using a photograph or an image of the person to whom you will send Reiki energy. However, you might not have access to a photo or image of your healing participant. In that case, you can simply write down the name and any information you have regarding your healing participant on a piece of paper and use the paper as the surrogate for the individual.

By knowing ourselves and our preferences, we can become more effective and efficient channelers of Reiki energy. Feel free to experiment with the different correspondence healing methods to see which one(s) resonates with you and your healing style.

Distance Reiki Healing Session: The Correspondence Method

Before you begin, select a person you wish to use as your Reiki healing recipient. Then, please obtain permission for Reiki healing from this person if you don't already have it. Consent is vital since we shouldn't impose our will on others, and the individual must be willing to receive the Reiki energy.

Decide which correspondence method you want to explore today.

Set the stage for your Reiki practice by finding a quiet place free of distractions and silence your cell phone.

Set your timer for five minutes and take a comfortable seated position.

Turn on Reiki using your unique method of connection and feel the infusion of Reiki energy into your being. Set your intention to send Reiki healing energy to the person you selected. Remember to use the Distance symbol, Hon Sha Ze Sho Nen, which must first be activated with the Cho Ku Rei symbol. When you feel ready, begin to send Reiki energy using the correspondence method you selected.

At the close of your Reiki healing session, pause for a few moments in quiet reflection.

Journaling Practice

Journal your direct experience of sending Reiki energy using your selected correspondence method. Which method did you select? Why did you choose this particular approach? Were you able to connect to the recipient of your Reiki healing? Were you able to keep your focus during the session? What changes, if any, would you make for future distant healing sessions? What feelings, thoughts, emotions, and insights came up for you?

How might you use your insights regarding sending healing energy using this particular correspondence method in future Reiki healings?

Consider experimenting with the other correspondence methods during future distance healing sessions.

Reiki Exploration Day 11

Daily Intention Review

Take a few deep, cleansing breaths and connect with the power of your creative mind. From this place of imagination, read out loud your heartfelt intention as a reminder of your healing journey.

Distance Healing: Inner Healing Temple Method

Your sacred imagination is a powerful tool; with this distance healing method, we can unleash our creative power. For this method, we will create our inner healing space, a temple, to perform distance healing. Your healing temple can take any shape or size and is limited only by your imagination.

Build it from the ground up. What does the floor look like? A grass meadow? Marble or wood? Does your inner healing temple have walls or perhaps standing Greek marble columns? Maybe it looks like a Native American tipi or a Gothic cathedral? Form a picture of the outside of your inner healing temple now.

Next, consider the interior of your healing temple. What do you want to see? Are there crystals or statues present? Are candles or incense burning? Are there columns or a fountain in your inner temple? Are any trees or flowers present? Please take a moment and design the interior of your inner temple. Once you have created your inner healing temple, place a beautiful healing table in the center of it.

Within this inner healing temple, you can envision yourself performing Reiki healing on another. Your inner healing temple isn't a static creation. It can grow and change over time as you continue to develop as a Reiki healer.

Distance Reiki Healing Session: The Inner Healing Temple Method

Before you begin, select a person you wish to use as your Reiki recipient. Then, please obtain consent for Reiki healing from this person if you don't already have it. Permission is crucial since we shouldn't impose our will on others, and the individual must be willing to accept the Reiki energy.

Set the stage for your Reiki practice by finding a quiet place free of distractions and silence your cell phone.

Set your timer for five minutes and take a comfortable seated position.

Turn on Reiki using your unique method of connection and feel the infusion of Reiki energy into your being. Set your intention to send Reiki healing energy to the person you selected. Remember to use the Distance symbol, Hon Sha Ze Sho Nen, which is first activated by the Cho Ku Rei symbol. Call to mind your inner healing temple. Picture it as clearly as possible. Imagine yourself inside the healing temple. In your mind's eye, picture the person to whom you are sending Reiki energy lying on the healing table in the center of your healing temple. When you feel ready, begin to send Reiki energy as you imagine yourself performing an in-person, hands-on Reiki treatment.

At the close of your Reiki healing session, pause for a few moments in quiet reflection.

Journaling Practice

Journal your direct experience sending Reiki energy using the inner healing temple method. Were you able to visualize your inner healing temple? If so, describe in detail the appearance of your healing temple.

Were you able to connect to your Reiki recipient? Were you able to keep your focus during the session? What changes, if any, would you make for future distant healing sessions using the inner healing temple method? What feelings, thoughts, emotions, and insights came up for you?

How might you use your insights regarding sending healing energy using the inner healing temple method in future Reiki healings?

Reiki Exploration Day 12

Daily Intention Review

Take a few moments to appreciate how far you've progressed as a Reiki healer. When you are ready, read your heartfelt intention aloud.

Sending Reiki to an Object

A practical way to use Reiki healing is to send Reiki energy to objects we use every day. Just because these objects don't have consciousness as we understand our own, they are still composed of energy and can benefit from Reiki healing.

Consider the items you use every day, such as your cell phone, computer, television, and car. Next, think about your hobbies and the things used during those pursuits, for example, a kayak, bicycle, tennis racket, rollerblades, paints, cooking utensils, or woodworking equipment. Then consider appliances that make our lives easier: washing machines, dishwashers, refrigerators, and air conditioners. Finally, consider the objects you use at work, which would vary based on your chosen profession.

I've routinely performed Reiki healing on the crystals I use during Reiki sessions and the singing bowls used during sound healings. I've found that using the Cho Ku Rei symbol keeps the energy of the objects clear and assists with increasing their overall effectiveness.

Experiment using Reiki healing on various objects you use every day and be open to how Reiki healing can assist with their performance.

Sending Reiki Healing to an Object Exercise

Select an object to use for this Reiki healing session and be sure to have that object with you for this exercise. Set the stage for your Reiki practice by finding a quiet place free of distractions and silence your cell phone.

Set your timer for five minutes and take a comfortable seated position.

Turn on Reiki using your unique method of connection and feel the infusion of Reiki energy into your being. Set your intention to send Reiki healing energy to your chosen object. When you feel ready, send Reiki energy to the object using the Cho Ku Rei symbol to clear the object of any negative or stagnant energies and to increase the object's effectiveness.

At the close of your Reiki healing session, pause for a few moments in quiet reflection.

Journaling Practice

Journal your direct experience of sending Reiki energy to an object. What object did you select and why did you make this choice? Were you able to develop a connection to the object? What feelings, thoughts, emotions, and insights came up for you?

How might you use your insights regarding sending healing energy to an object in future Reiki healings?

Reiki Exploration Day 13

Daily Intention Review

To connect with goals of healing and personal growth, read your heartfelt intention aloud.

Psychic Senses Overview and Personal Bias

Our intuition, gut feeling, or sixth sense, is a sacred gift given to all of us. Our psychic senses are specific manifestations born from our intuition. Our psychic senses mimic our physical senses. The psychic sense we will be exploring in detail are found here:

Clairvoyance: clear seeing, related to the sense of sight

Clairaudience: clear hearing, associated with the sense of hearing

Claircognizance: clear knowing, related to thought

Clairempathy: clear emotions, related to our emotions

Clairsentience: clear sensing in our physical bodies

Clairalience: clear smelling, related to smell

Clairtangency: clear touching and is related to physically touching objects or people

Clairgustance: clear tasting and is associated with the sense of taste

Although we may be more inclined toward one or two of these psychic senses, it is possible to develop all of them using specific techniques. Before we dive deeper, we should consider our biases regarding our psychic senses.

For our purposes here, you can think of a bias as an inclination toward or against a thought, object, person, or idea. Our biases can reflect our personal preferences, family patterns, religious beliefs or upbringing, peer group, and society. Any of these combinations of factors can contribute to the blocking of our psychic senses. As we work to unravel these thought patterns consciously and deliberately open ourselves to explore our physics senses, these skills will begin to unfold in a manner unique to each of us.

Do any of the following statements resonate with you?

- "I am very concerned about what other people think about me."
- "I am reluctant to explore my latent psychic abilities because I was taught that they are 'evil' or 'bad.'"
- "I often hide my authentic self to please others."
- "I often ignore information gained from my psychic senses because I don't understand or trust the insights I receive."

If you feel any of the above statements are true, you may want to create an affirmation to assist in removing any preconceived notions that you might have about your psychic senses. Here's an example of this type of affirmation: "I confidently embrace my intuitive nature and trust insights I receive from my psychic senses."

Self-Inquiry Meditation Practice

Begin your meditation practice by silencing your cell phone and finding a comfortable seated position. Set your timer for five minutes and take a few centering breaths. Next, ask yourself, "What is blocking the development of my psychic senses?" Pause a moment to see what thoughts and emotions arise. Then, repeat the question and pause again. Repeat the inquiry process throughout the five minutes. If your mind wanders during this practice, simply re-focus your attention on the question.

After your meditation, sit for a moment or two in quiet reflection.

Journaling Practice

Consider your psychic senses. Which psychic senses appeal to you the most? Which ones don't resonate with you at this time? Which ones do you feel you want to develop consciously?

Now, reflect on your own biases towards psychic abilities. What do you think are the causes of these biases? How might you work on changing these attitudes toward your psychic skills?

How might you use your insights regarding your internal biases during your Reiki healing sessions and for personal growth?

Reiki Exploration Day 14

Daily Intention Review

Take a few deep breaths and connect to the energies of Mother Earth. From this place of groundedness, state aloud your heartfelt intention.

Healing the Earth

In my opinion, we are all blessed to be living on this amazing planet. Earth provides us with everything we need to survive: water, oxygen, water, food, and so many more gifts. In addition, the earth provides us with beautiful landscapes, incredible sunsets, and varieties of plant and animal life. Unfortunately, we often receive these gifts with ambivalence or take Mother Earth's precious resources for granted.

Human civilization has caused damage to our earth's fragile ecosystem. Depleting the ozone layer, pollution of our bodies of water, unchecked mining operations, and a host of other human activities have caused damage to Earth's environment over the centuries.

Whether or not you believe that planet Earth is a living being, she is still in need of your healing energies. It's a beautiful gratitude practice to send Reiki energy to the earth.

Healing the Earth: Distance Healing Practice

Set the stage for your meditation by finding a quiet place free of distractions and silence your cell phone. Set your timer for five to ten minutes and sit comfortably. Turn on Reiki using your unique method of connection, and feel the infusion of Reiki energy into your being. Set your intention to provide the earth with healing Reiki energy. Picture the earth clearly in front of you. Then use the following symbols: Cho Ku Rei, Sei He Ki, Cho Ku Rei, Hon Sha Ze Sho Nen, and Cho Ku Rei to send healing energy to the planet. For this practice, you may choose to have your hand facing down toward the earth. Focus on sending the Reiki energy to heal the planet and pay attention to any impressions, feelings, thoughts, and insights you might receive.

At the close of your Reiki healing session, send a little extra gratitude to the earth and pause for a few moments in quiet reflection.

Journaling Practice

Journal your direct experience of sending Reiki energy to Earth. Were you able to feel a connection to the world? If so, describe the connection. What feelings, thoughts, and sensations did you experience during the healing session? Did you receive any insights from the planet itself?

How might you use your insights on distance healing in future Reiki healing sessions?

Reiki Exploration Day 15

Daily Intention Review

Take a few deep, cleansing breaths, anchoring yourself in this present moment. From this place of inner stillness, read out loud your heartfelt intention.

Clairvoyance

The clairvoyant psychic sense is related to vision and is one of the most widely known of the psychic senses. This second sight may be perceived through the mind's eye in the form of inner visions or observed through the physical eyes. A person with strong clairvoyant connections often best receives information through visual methods.

Please review the statements below for the clairvoyance self-assessment and rate your response as never, sometimes, or always.

- "I learn best through visual methods."
- "I have seen orbs or balls of light."
- "I often see signs such as feathers, animals, or other omens in my physical environment."
- "I often experience vivid dreams."
- "I have seen shadows manifest without a physical cause."
- "I have experienced a prophetic dream."

- "I often find myself daydreaming."
- "I can visualize easily."
- "I see repeating numbers such as on a clock, a license plate, or by other means."
- "I see images running through my mind similar to a movie or TV show."
- "I have seen a spirit, apparition, or ghost."
- "I have seen colors surrounding people—either in my mind's eye or with my physical eyes."

Even if you only had one or two "sometimes" or "always" responses, you may be clairvoyantly gifted. No matter your natural inclination toward clairvoyance, you can develop and strengthen this ability with dedication and practice. Here's an affirmation to evolve your clairvoyant abilities: "I am open to receive the wisdom and insights of my inner sight."

Clairvoyance Meditation for Developing Inner Sight

This meditation will help develop your inner sight. Don't stress or become anxious if you have problems creating the image in your mind's eye. Skill development takes time. My advice when these difficulties occur is to imagine what it would be like if you *could* see these images. Simply relax and allow the process to unfold. Release judgment and expectation. Trust that this skill will develop in time as long as you actively cultivate your inner sight.

Set the stage for your meditation: find a quiet place free of distractions, silence your cell phone, and set a five-minute timer. After finding a comfortable seated position, take a few centering breaths and close your eyes. Imagine a clear sky in front of you as clearly as possible in your imagination. In this clear sky, we are going to build a rainbow. Imagine the rainbow forming by picturing a red arc across the sky. Once that image develops in your mind's eye, visualize the second arc of orange appearing above the red one. Once that image takes shape, focus on a yellow arc of color appearing above the orange arch. Now, form the image of a green arc forming above the yellow one. When that image appears, begin to picture a blue arc forming over the green one. When this vision is clear, imagine an indigo color arch forming over the blue arc. Finally, picture a violet arch forming over the indigo arc, completing your rainbow. Hold the visualization until the meditation time expires.

After your meditation, sit for a moment or two in quiet reflection.

Journaling Practice

Journal your direct experience of this meditation. For example, how easy or difficult was it to picture the rainbow in your mind's eye? Were there any colors that were less challenging to visualize than others? What role does clairvoyance currently play in your day-to-day life? Are there opportunities to develop and grow your "seeing" abilities? How might you use your insights regarding your psychic sense of clairvoyance during your Reiki healing sessions?

Reiki Exploration Day 16

Daily Intention Review

Settle in for a moment, noticing how you are showing up today. Then, honoring who you are at this moment, state your heartfelt intention out loud.

Healing Food and Drink

Remember the adage, "you are what you eat"? There is deep wisdom found in that simple saying. The act of consuming food and drink is an intimate one. When we eat, we are nourishing our body and our energy field. We are literally consuming the energetic frequency of the food and drink we intake. The quality of food and drink is directly related to our sense of physical, emotional, mental, and energetic health.

We can take simple steps to eat healthy by buying organic and locally sourced food. We can reduce or eliminate genetically modified food, artificial preservatives, and processed food. We can avoid high sodium and high sugar food and drink options. These are all effective ways to create a healthy diet, but have you considered the energetic quality of your food?

The energetic quality of food and drink can be related to the physical food and the way the food is prepared. First, consider the energy of a chicken raised in a tiny, confined pen for its entire life without sunlight or the opportunity to move freely. What might the energy of this chicken feel like? What might happen to you energetically when you consume this chicken's meat?

Additionally, consider the energy of the person preparing your meal. For example, contrast the loving energy of a grandmother preparing a home-cooked meal for her grandchildren with a meal served in a restaurant where a fight occurred between the chef and the waitstaff. One meal would contain the energetic vibration of love, and the other would have the energetic frequency of tension and anger. As we ingest our food, these vibrations are absorbed into our personal energy field with positive or negative results.

Just as we can make wise decisions regarding the quality of the food we consume, we can also elevate the energy of our food and drink by performing Reiki because Reiki can help transmute the energetic vibration of food and drink. Performing Reiki on our food and drink contributes to our energetic health and strengthens our auric field.

Healing Food and Drink Reiki Practice

Set the stage for your meditation by having a snack or a drink available and finding a quiet place free of distractions. Silence your cell phone and set your timer for five minutes. Take a comfortable seated position.

Turn on Reiki using your unique method of connection and feel the infusion of Reiki energy into your being. Set your intention to send Reiki energy to your food or drink. Intuitively select what Reiki symbols you will be using, if any, and begin to send healing energy to your snack or drink.

At the close of your Reiki healing session, send a little extra gratitude to your food or drink for all the sustenance it will provide you, and pause for a few moments in quiet reflection. Then, feel free to eat or drink your Reiki-infused item.

Journaling Practice

Journal your direct experience of sending Reiki energy to your snack or drink. Were you able to feel a connection to the food item? If so, describe the connection. What feelings, thoughts, and sensations did you experience during the healing session? Did you receive any insights as you ate or drank the Reiki-infused item?

How might you use your insights to broaden your use of Reiki healing in the future?

Reiki Exploration Day 17

Daily Intention Review

With a thankful heart for all the progress you have made along your healing path, recommit to your healing goals by stating out loud your heartfelt intention.

Reiki Healing for a Pet/Animal

Pets play a vital role in both in our homes and the community at large. They provide companionship, entertainment, unconditional love, and emotional support during trying times. They encourage us to exercise and remind us to enjoy ourselves. However, pets often absorb their owners' emotional pain and stress.

Animals do not have to be pets to add value to the world. Consider the plight of some of the beautiful creatures that are endangered either because their natural habitat is compromised or because they have been hunted to the point of extinction. For example, think about the bumblebee, which plays a vital role in maintaining the health of our ecological system by pollinating our crops. Yet, the Center for Biological Diversity, a nonprofit organization in the United States, reports that the American bumblebee population has declined by ninety percent. These animals need healing energy to assist with their very survival.

Animals readily absorb the healing benefits of Reiki, and sending Reiki to an animal is a gift of love.

Pet/Animal Healing Session

If you have a pet, this is an opportunity to send healing energy to your pet. Please have your pet near you for this Reiki session. If you don't have a pet, find an image of an endangered species and use that image as the focus of your Reiki healing session.

Set the stage for your Reiki practice by finding a quiet place free of distractions and silence your cell phone. Set your timer for five minutes and take a comfortable seated position. If your pet is larger, you may find it more comfortable to stand during this Reiki treatment.

Turn on Reiki using your unique method of connection and feel the infusion of Reiki energy into your being. Set your intention to send Reiki healing energy to your pet or the endangered animal. If your pet is next to you, use your intuition to determine the appropriate hand placements. When considering what Reiki symbols to use, please remember that if you send the healing energy remotely to the endangered animal, you will need to use the Distance symbol, which must first be activated by the Power symbol. When you feel ready, send Reiki energy to the pet or endangered animal.

Journaling Practice

Journal your direct experience sending Reiki energy to your pet or endangered animal. What pet or endangered animal did you select? Why did you make this choice? What sensations, thoughts, and emotions did you have as you performed Reiki healing? Did you receive any insights regarding your pet or the endangered animal?

How might you use your insights regarding the healing of an animal in future Reiki healings?

Reiki Exploration Day 18

Daily Intention Review

Appreciate all the progress you are making on your Reiki journey and recite aloud your heartfelt intention.

Clairaudience

The clairaudient psychic sense is related to hearing. It may be perceived by your physical ears as sounds from outside yourself or you may experience clairaudience as inner hearing. A person with strong clairaudience connections receives information through auditory means.

Please review these statements for the clairaudience self-assessment, rating your response as never, sometimes, or always.

- "I learn best through auditory methods."
- "I have heard footsteps when no one was present."
- "I have heard unexplained whispers, humming, or other human sounds."
- "I have heard voices in my head that were not my own."
- "I have heard music, bells, or other musical instruments when none were playing."
- "I have heard unexplained animal noises such as barking, growling, or chirping."
- "I have heard doors closing or opening without a rational cause."
- "I have received messages and insights through my inner hearing."

Reflect on your responses. Even if you only answered one or two "sometimes" or "always," you may have a natural affinity with clairaudience. No matter your natural ability, you can develop and strengthen your clairaudient skills with dedication and practice. Here's an affirmation to develop your clairaudient abilities: "I am open to receive the wisdom and insights of my inner hearing."

Clairaudient Meditation for Developing Inner Hearing

This meditation will help develop your inner hearing by focusing on your outer hearing. Release judgment and expectation, and trust that this skill will unfold for you in time as long as you actively cultivate your inner hearing.

Set the stage for your meditation by finding a quiet place free of distractions and silence your cell phone. Begin your practice by setting a five-minute timer and sitting in a comfortable position. Take a few centering breaths and close your eyes. Begin to focus on your sense of hearing. Can you hear the noises in the building that you are in? Pause and listen. Now, narrow your focus and listen to the noises in the room that you are in. Pause and listen. Again, narrow the focus to your physical body. Can you hear your own breath? Pause and listen. Finally, release your conscious control of the experience and simply listen.

At the conclusion of your meditation, sit for a moment or two in reflection.

Journaling Practice

Journal your direct experience of this meditation. What sounds did you hear from your outer environment? What sounds did you hear when you tuned into your body? Did you perceive any sounds with your inner ears?

What role does clairaudience currently play in your day-to-day life? Are there opportunities to develop and grow your inner hearing abilities? How might you use your insights regarding your psychic sense of clairaudience during your Reiki healing sessions?

Reiki Exploration Day 19

Daily Intention Review

Reflect on your development as a Reiki healer, and when ready, read your heartfelt intention out loud.

Healing the Past

The past is one of our greatest teachers. Through exploring our personal history, we can gain insights into our habits, preferences, behaviors, and belief system. This contemplation is a beneficial practice that can lead to personal growth. However, when we start obsessing over past mistakes, childhood traumas, missed opportunities, or failed relationships, we can fall into a negative pattern that can lead to mental health issues such as depression. Depression is associated with various physical health issues including heart disease, diabetes, respiratory problems, and addiction to drugs or alcohol. Depression can also negatively affect job performance as well as personal and professional relationships.

Since Reiki's energy is not limited to our concepts of time and space, we can send Reiki healing to any past situation still affecting us today. Although this type of energy work can't change the outcome of past events, it can help heal the emotional and energetic wounds that are still present. When these wounds are healed and the lessons learned, we can successfully move forward on our life path without excess emotional baggage.

Healing the Past Reiki Practice

Set the stage for your Reiki practice: find a quiet place free of distractions, take a comfortable seated position, silence your cell phone, and set a timer for five minutes.

Bring to mind a past event that caused you pain or sadness; a situation that you still think about today and are ready to heal.

Turn on Reiki using your unique method of connection and feel the infusion of Reiki energy into your being. Set your intention to send Reiki energy to that past event. Be sure to utilize the Distance symbol, which must first be activated by the Power symbol as you intuitively select which Reiki symbols you will use, and begin to send healing energy to the past event by clearly picturing it in your mind. Imagine the Reiki energy permeating the entire event, transmuting the situation's energy into one of healing.

At the close of your Reiki healing session, pause for a few moments taking notice of your session's ripple effects.

Journaling Practice

Journal your direct experience of sending Reiki energy to a past situation. What past situation did you select and why did you make this choice? Energetically, what did you experience during the healing session? What sensations, thoughts, and emotions did you have? Did you gain any insights or feelings of closure regarding this past event?

How might you use your insights regarding healing past events in future Reiki healings?

Reiki Exploration Day 20

Daily Intention Review

Congratulations on reaching the twentieth day of your Reiki immersion experience! Reflect for a few moments on your growth as a Reiki healer. When you are ready, recite aloud your heartfelt intention.

Reiki and Your Personal Goals

What are your aspirations, your dreams, your hopes, and wishes? Developing a set of goals can turn wishes into reality. Goals serve as a map to help us navigate our daily life with focus, eliminating unnecessary distractions. Goals can help us change habits, learn new skills, and live life in alignment with our higher purpose.

Consider breaking larger goals down into more manageable pieces. Set your daily and weekly objectives and work toward these goals while keeping your eye on fulfilling your dreams. When you feel overwhelmed or lose your focus, Reiki can help. The Cho Ku Rei symbol can bring extra power toward reaching your goals be they large or small.

Reiki healing can provide strength and energy to assist you with achieving your goals and realizing your dreams—simply draw the Cho Ku Rei symbol over your written goal and silently intoning "Cho Ku Rei" three times.

Cho Ku Rei to Power Your Personal Goals

Find a comfortable seated position and settle in for a few moments. On a piece of paper, write down a dream you are ready to manifest. State your ultimate goal and then break it down into a series of more manageable steps. Consider adding expected completion dates for each step toward your ultimate goal. Silence your cell phone and set a timer for five minutes.

Turn on Reiki using your unique method of connection and feel the infusion of Reiki energy into your being. Set your intention to use the Cho Ku Rei symbol to increase the power of your goal-setting process and to provide you with the strength and determination to realize your dream.

Begin your Reiki healing session by drawing the Cho Ku Rei symbol over your handwritten goal and silently intoning "Cho Ku Rei" to yourself three times. Next, place your hands over the sheet of paper and beam Reiki energy toward it. In your mind's eye, picture yourself easily achieving each step of your ultimate goal until your dream is realized.

After your Reiki session, take a few moments in quiet reflection.

Journaling Practice

Journal your direct experience of your Reiki-infused goal-setting session. What was your goal and what were the steps you outlined for achieving it? What was your experience using the Cho Ku Rei symbol to provide power and strength to your goal? Did you notice any physical, emotional, mental, or energetic shifts? Did you gain any insights regarding using Cho Ku Rei to assist with your goal-setting process? How might this information be useful in future Reiki healing sessions?

Reiki Exploration Day 21

Daily Intention Review

Take a deep inhalation, retain the breath for a moment, and then exhale completely. Now, with clarity of mind, state aloud your heartfelt intention.

Claircognizance

Claircognizance is related to knowing. This psychic sense may be experienced as a download of information directly into the brain without any additional method of receiving the information. A person with solid claircognizance connections often has an active mind and may learn best through reading and writing.

Review the statements below for the claircognizance self-assessment and rate your response as "never," "sometimes," or "always."

- "I learn best through reading and writing methods."
- "I have known who calling me without the aid of caller ID."
- "I knew what someone was going to say before they said it."
- "I had known when someone wasn't telling the truth."

- "I have known the right choice to make and what the result of my action will be."

- "I have known the solution to a problem without any background or relevant information."

- "I knew not to trust someone even though they appeared very nice and friendly."

- "I knew to take a different route to work and avoided a major accident as a result."

Review your responses. You might be a naturally gifted claircognizant even if you rated only a few statements as "sometimes" or "always." No matter your level of natural claircognizant ability, you can develop and strengthen it with dedication and practice.

An affirmation to develop your claircognizance abilities is as follows: "My mind is open to receive the wisdom of the universe."

Claircognizance Exercise for Developing Inner Knowing

Automatic writing is a way of developing your claircognative abilities. Automatic writing is the process of putting pen to paper without the involvement of the rational, thinking mind. As you approach this exercise, please release all judgment and expectations. Trust that this skill will unfold to you in time as long as you actively cultivate your inner knowing.

Set the stage for this exercise: find a quiet place free of distractions and silence your cell phone. Set a timer for ten to fifteen minutes.

Take a piece of paper, notebook, or journal. At the top, write a question. State this question aloud to the universe. Take a few cleansing breaths and begin to write as you allow your mind to relax into a meditative state. Don't focus on the question or if you are doing this exercise correctly. Just write and write, and write some more.

After your automatic writing exercise, sit for a moment or two in reflection before examining what you wrote.

Journaling Practice

Journal your direct experience of this practice. Was it challenging to release judgment and allow the process to unfold? Were you surprised by any of the words or phrases in your writing?

What role does claircognizance currently play in your day-to-day life? Are there opportunities to develop and grow your "knowing" abilities?

How might you use your insights regarding your psychic sense of claircognizance during your Reiki healing sessions?

Reiki Exploration Day 22

Daily Intention Review

Take a few cleansing breaths to anchor yourself in the present moment. Then, when you are centered, recite your heartfelt intention out loud.

Healing a Future Event

The future contains the potential for limitless possibilities and potential outcomes. Unfortunately, we may become fixated on possible negative results that haven't happened yet or may never happen. This focus on the future and potential adverse effects can lead to feelings of helplessness, worry, and overall anxiety. In addition, prolonged stress has serious health consequences, such as high blood pressure, heart disease, digestive issues, decreased immune function, and sleep disorders.

Since Reiki's energy transcends time and space, we can send Reiki healing to any future situation. By sending healing power to a future event, we can be assured that the event or situation will unfold in a way that serves the greater good. These practices might not necessarily provide us with the outcome we desire most but can help the event unfold in a way that serves us in some way—either as a blessing or an opportunity for growth.

Healing a Future Event Exercise

Set the stage for your Reiki practice by finding a quiet place free of distractions. Silence your cell phone and set a timer for five minutes.

Bring to mind a future event that is causing you anxiety or concern. Turn on Reiki using your unique method of connection and feel the infusion of Reiki energy into your being. Set your intention to send Reiki energy to that future event. Using the Distance symbol, which must first be activated by the Power symbol, and other intuitively selected symbols, begin to send healing energy to the future event by clearly picturing it in your mind. Imagine the Reiki energy permeating the entire event, transmuting the situation's energy into one of healing.

At the close of your Reiki healing session, pause for a few moments, noticing your treatment's ripple effects.

Journaling Practice

Journal your direct experience of sending Reiki energy to a future situation. What future event did you select for your healing session and why? Energetically, what did you experience? What sensations, thoughts, and emotions did you have? Did you gain any insights or feelings regarding this future event? If so, how might you use these insights in future Reiki healings?

Reiki Exploration Day 23

Daily Intention Review

Begin today by remembering why you embarked on this adventure of self-healing and discovery. When you are ready, state your heartfelt healing intention aloud.

Reiki for Protection

We all need to feel safe and secure to perform at our best. Internally, our sense of safety is related to our root chakra, located at the base of our spine. When this chakra is balanced and functioning optimally, we are free from fear and have a sense of being protected physically and emotionally.

Externally, protection involves keeping us from harm. The source of this harm can take various forms depending on the circumstances. Our homes and cars should be places where we are safe, but that isn't always the case. Traveling can increase our exposure to harmful or unstable forces.

Reiki can assist us with our internal sense of safety and provide us with additional protection from our external environment. Using the Cho Ku Rei symbol and the intention to create protective boundaries, we can increase our overall sense of safety and security.

There are infinite ways we can use the Cho Ku Rei symbol for protection. Here are some examples:

- Draw the Cho Ku Rei symbol on the doorways and/or windows of your home or office
- Draw the Cho Ku Rei symbol on your car before driving
- Draw the Cho Ku Rei symbol on your luggage before a trip
- Draw the Cho Ku Rei symbol during self-healing sessions for strengthening your root chakra
- Draw the Cho Ku Rei symbol in front of you to establish, protect, and strengthen your personal boundaries

Experiment with the various uses of the Cho Ku Rei symbol for protection. The possibilities are endless, and you are only limited by your own imagination.

Cho Ku Rei for Protection Healing Session

Find a comfortable seated position and settle in for a few moments. Silence your cell phone and set a timer for five minutes.

Take a complete inventory of yourself at this moment in time. Notice how you feel physically, emotionally, mentally, energetically, and spiritually.

Turn on Reiki using your unique method of connection and feel the infusion of Reiki energy into your being. Set your intention to use the Cho Ku Rei symbol to increase your personal sense of safety and security.

Begin your Reiki healing session by drawing the Cho Ku Rei symbol and silently intoning "Cho Ku Rei" three times. Let your intuition guide you to self-healing hand positions that resonate with you, but spend time healing your root chakra located at your tailbone.

After your healing session, take a few moments to scan your body and observe any subtle shifts of energy that may have occurred.

Journaling Practice

Journal your direct experience of your self-healing session. Consider the role that protection plays in your life. What is your relationship with the feelings of safety and security? What in your life needs more protection?

What was your experience using the Cho Ku Rei symbol for protection? Did you notice any energy shifts physically, emotionally, mentally, or energetically? Did you gain any insights regarding the use of Cho Ku Rei for protection?

How might this information be helpful in future Reiki healing sessions?

Reiki Exploration Day 24

Daily Intention Review

Pause and honor the emotions that you are feeling at this moment. Don't judge, accept what is. From this place of feeling, recite your heartfelt intention out loud.

Clairempathy

This psychic sense is related to empathy, the capacity to share in another's feelings. This sense often manifests as experiencing another person's emotions as if they were your own feelings.

Please review the following statements for the clairempathy self-assessment and rate your response as never, sometimes, or always.

- "I have experienced overwhelming emotions when I'm in a crowd."
- "I find it challenging to establish and maintain my boundaries."
- "I have felt when someone is not being truthful."
- "I have experienced emotions that appear out of the blue with no rational cause."
- "I need time alone to recharge and replenish my energy."
- "I have intensely experienced the emotions of others as if they were my own feelings."
- "I can always tell what others feel, even if they conceal their genuine emotions."
- "Animals gravitate to me, and I have a natural affinity with the animal kingdom."

Reflect on the results of your self-assessment. Even if you only rated a few statements as "sometimes" or "always," you may be a naturally gifted clairempath. No matter your natural ability for clairempathy, you can develop and strengthen it with dedication and practice.

An affirmation to develop your clairempathy is as follows: "I embrace my empathic nature while maintaining my energetic boundaries."

Clairempathy Meditation

This meditation will help develop your ability to sense the emotions of others by understanding your own emotional landscape.

Set the stage for your meditation by finding a quiet place free of distractions and silence your cell phone. Take a comfortable seated position, take a few cleansing breaths, and turn your focus inward. Call to mind a time you felt deep happiness. Invite the feeling of joy to fill your being and notice how you experience the emotion of joy. Sit within this feeling for a minute or two. When you are ready to move on, remember a time when you felt profound sadness. Allow the feeling of sadness to wash over you and stay with this emotion for a few minutes to notice how you experience this difficult emotion. When you intuitively know that it's time to continue, cultivate the emotion of peace and harmony. Sit with this emotion and take note of how you experience it. When you feel a sense of completion, call to mind a time when you felt anger. Sit with this emotion, observing how you personally experience it. Finally, bring to mind a time when you felt pure pleasure. Notice how you experience this emotion. When you are ready, release all emotions and take a few grounding breaths.

At the conclusion of your meditation, sit for a moment or two in reflection.

Journaling Practice

Journal your direct experience of this practice. Did you find connecting with your different emotions a challenging or relatively easy endeavor? Which emotion was easiest to cultivate? Which feeling was the most difficult to foster? Did you feel the emotions express themselves physically, emotionally, mentally, energetically, or in a combination of ways? How might knowledge of your own feelings assist you with developing clairempathy?

What role does clairempathy currently play in your day-to-day life? Are there opportunities to develop and grow your "feeling" abilities? If your clairempathy skills are already strong, is there an opportunity to do more energy clearing practices to assist with your energetic health?

How might you use your insights regarding your psychic sense of clairempathy during your Reiki healing sessions?

Reiki Exploration Day 25

Daily Intention Review

Consider the progress you've made on your healing journey. Take a moment to be grateful for your hard work and dedication. Then, when you are ready, state your heartfelt healing intention aloud.

Healing a World Disaster

In our current climate, world disasters and large-scale tragedies occur with staggering frequency. Just turn on the news, and a multitude of images of war, mass shootings, regional uprisings, and natural disasters fill the screen. Many of us feel helpless and want to provide support, but distance and other practical concerns may prevent us from being able to provide direct assistance. This inability to help may cause profound feelings of helplessness or powerlessness.

In addition to sending "thoughts and prayers," we, as Reiki healers, are empowered to do more. We can provide Reiki healing as a gift to those in need. The power of sending thoughts, prayers, and Reiki energy can be immensely effective in contributing to the recovery of the situation and easing the suffering of the affected population. By sending healing to the damaged region affected by the tragedy, you are contributing to the overall recovery of the planet, which indirectly benefits us all.

World Disaster Healing Session

Set the stage for your Reiki practice by finding a quiet place free of distractions and silence your cell phone.

Consider a recent world disaster or large-scale tragic event that pulls at your heartstrings. From that place of emotional connection, set your intention to provide distance healing to the affected region of the globe.

Set your timer for five minutes and take a comfortable seated position.

Turn on Reiki using your unique method of connection and feel the infusion of Reiki energy into your being. Then, using the distance healing method of your choice, begin to send healing energy to that crisis. Finally, imagine the Reiki energy permeating the entire region, transmuting the energy of the situation into one of healing.

At the close of your Reiki healing session, pause for a few moments in quiet reflection.

Journaling Practice

Journal your direct experience of sending Reiki energy to a world crisis. What world crisis did you select and why did you make this choice? Were you able to connect on an emotional level to the tragic event? What energetically did you experience? What sensations, thoughts, and emotions did you have as you performed Reiki healing? What insights did you receive during and after the healing session?

How might you use your insights regarding healing world tragedies in future Reiki healings sessions?

Reiki Exploration Day 26

Daily Intention Review

To connect with your purpose in exploring Reiki energy, read your heartfelt intention aloud.

Reiki and the Power of Affirmations

During our previous immersion experiences, we experienced the power of affirmations. As a reminder, affirmations are personal, positive statements drafted in the first person. Affirmations are best when crafted as if the statement were already true. An example would be "I am open to both giving and receiving love" or "I am connected to my own inner wisdom."

Affirmations can be repeated silently throughout the day whenever you have a few spare moments. Additionally, you could develop a structured affirmation practice over a period of time to give your affirmation more power. Of course, the number of times you repeat the affirmation is a personal choice, but you may want to consider the inherent power of the number you select to repeat your affirmation. Different teachings assign various correspondences to numbers.

Below are some examples for your consideration from Godwin's *Cabalistic Encyclopedia*:

- The number 13 corresponds to both unity and love.[12]
- The number 23 corresponds to life and living things.[13]
- The number 28 corresponds to a union with God and one's beloved.[14]

---

12. Godwin, *Godwin's Cabalistic Encyclopedia*, 491.

13. Ibid., 494.

14. Godwin, *Godwin's Cabalistic Encyclopedia*, 495.

An additional resource is the *Dictionary of Symbols,* which also ascribes meanings to various numbers. Below are several examples from this resource:

- The number 10 corresponds to completion and endings.[15]
- The number 21 corresponds to maturity and wisdom.[16]
- The number 36 corresponds to cosmic unity.[17]

The Cho Ku Rei symbol can be used to supercharge your affirmations, giving them extra power.

Cho Ku Rei to Power Your Affirmation Practice

Craft your personal affirmation. For example, "I am a clear and open channel for Reiki energy." Write your affirmation on a piece of paper as a way of giving it physical form.

Decide on the number of times you will repeat your affirmation. You may want to consider the symbolism of the number, or you may select the number based on your intuition.

Find a comfortable seated position and settle in for a few moments.

Turn on Reiki using your unique method of connection and feel the infusion of Reiki energy into your being. Set your intention to use the Cho Ku Rei symbol to increase the power and effectiveness of your affirmation.

To begin your Reiki healing session, draw the Cho Ku Rei symbol on the piece of paper over your affirmation and silently intone "Cho Ku Rei" to yourself three times. Place your hands over the affirmation, and you repeat your affirmation for your chosen number of times.

After your Reiki session, take a few moments in quiet reflection.

Journaling Practice

Journal your direct experience of the Reiki-infused affirmation session. What was your chosen affirmation? Why did you make this selection?

What was your experience using the Cho Ku Rei symbol to super-charge your affirmation? Did you notice any energy shifts physically, emotionally, mentally, or energetically?

---

15. Chevalier and Gheerbrant, *The Penguin Dictionary of Symbols*, 981.
16. Ibid., 1045.
17. Ibid., 989.

Did you gain any insights regarding using Cho Ku Rei to add power to your affirmation practice?

How might this information be helpful in future Reiki healing sessions?

Reiki Exploration Day 27

Daily Intention Review

Take a few cleansing breaths and notice how you are showing up today. Then, from this place of self-acceptance, state your heartfelt intention out loud.

Clairsentience

The clairsentient psychic sense is sensing the energetic signature or "vibe" of another person, object, or place. Unlike clairempathy, which is associated with taking on the emotions of others, clairsentience is about receiving information regarding the way something or someone feels. For example, the feeling of a place or a person being "off" are both clairsentient experiences.

Review the statements below for the clairsentient self-assessment and rate your response as never, sometimes, or always.

- "I can easily sense the energy of the people around me."
- "My physical environment profoundly influences me."
- "I have experienced sensing a room's energy or 'vibe' as soon as I enter it."
- "I have experienced sensations of overwhelm and exhaustion when engaging with a large number of people."
- "As a child, I was told that I was overly sensitive."
- "I have sensed the energy signature of a building—either positive and welcoming or negative and unfriendly."
- "I have sensed the energy of inanimate objects such as crystals and rocks."
- "Spending time in nature recharges me."

Consider your responses to the self-assessment. Even if you only rated a few statements as "sometimes" or "always," you may still be naturally gifted in this area. No matter your natural level of ability, you can develop and strengthen your clairsentient psychic sense with desire, dedication, and practice.

Here's an example of an affirmation to develop your clairsentient abilities: "I honor all the sensory data I receive and intuitively understand the energetic messages."

Clairsentience Meditation

This meditation will help develop your ability to sense the energy of a room. Take your meditation practice to a new area of your home or even outside.

Set the stage for your meditation by finding a quiet place free of distractions and silence your cell phone.

Settle into a comfortable seated position and take a few cleansing breaths. Close your eyes and simply be in the space that you are in. Sense the vibe of the area: Does the energy seem calmer or active? What emotions would you associate with the energy in this space? If the energy had a color, what color would it be? Be open to the experience and sense the energetic frequency as it unfolds for you.

After your meditation, sit for a moment or two in reflection.

Journaling Practice

Journal your direct experience of this practice. For example, what was your experience of sensing the vibe of the room? Describe the energy of your space? What color would you associate with this energy? When focusing on the energy of the room, did you experience any physical, emotional, mental, or energetic sensations? If so, describe them.

What role does clairsentience currently play in your day-to-day life? Are there opportunities to develop and grow your "sensing" abilities?

How might you use your insights regarding your psychic sense of clairsentience during your Reiki healing sessions?

Reiki Exploration Day 28

Daily Intention Review

Take a few moments in quiet reflection focusing on your healing journey to date. When you feel ready, state your heartfelt intention out loud.

Healing a Plant

Plants are indeed friends of humanity. Through their process of photosynthesis, they create the oxygen that we breathe. Their beauty and calming presence add to our enjoyment when spending time outdoors. Certain plants are edible and add to our food supply. Other plants have medicinal properties and assist us when we are ill. Considering all that plants do for us, what can we do for them in return?

By sending Reiki energy to plants or seeds, we can assist our plant allies with their overall health and well-being. This gift of Reiki can be performed on house plants, gardens, and trees. You can also consider sending Reiki to water before watering plants and the soil before planting seeds. Experiment with different variations of sending Reiki to plants and see the amazing results for yourself.

Healing a Plant Reiki Treatment

For this exercise, you'll need a plant. If you don't have a houseplant, consider doing this practice outside and finding a garden, tree, or even grass as the focal point of your Reiki.

Set the stage for your Reiki practice by finding a quiet place free of distractions and silencing your cell phone. Set your timer for five minutes and take a comfortable seated position.

Turn on Reiki using your unique method of connection and feel the infusion of Reiki energy into your being. Spend a moment to connect with your plant's energy. Intuitively select the Reiki symbols appropriate for healing this particular plant and begin to send it healing energy. Imagine the Reiki energy permeating every cell of the plant.

At the close of your Reiki healing session, pause for a few moments in quiet reflection.

Journaling Practice

Journal your direct experience of sending Reiki energy to a plant. What plant did you select and why? What sensations, thoughts, and emotions did you have as you performed Reiki healing? Did you receive any insights regarding the health or history of the plant?

How might you use your insights regarding healing a plant in future Reiki healings?

Reiki Exploration Day 29

Daily Intention Review

Take a few deep breaths. Consider your heritage and how previous generations have impacted your life. Then, from this place of reflection, recite out loud your heartfelt intention.

Reiki for the Ancestors

Our ancestors are powerful allies in the spirit world. Ancestors, like your grandparents and great-grandparents, are related to you by your maternal and paternal lines back through generations. If you are adopted or raised by a family not biologically related you, you have access to the ancestors of the family who nurtured you. You also have ancestors of the land on which you live. One more ancestor type is the ancestors of a specific affinity or interest, such as Reiki healing, painting, writing, or gardening.

These ancestors are powerful helpers that can assist us in various ways from the spirit world. They can act as guides and provide blessings, inspiration, insights, and protection. A beautiful gesture in recognition of our connection to our ancestors is to send them Reiki healing. This healing can directly assist them with their evolutionary and healing process.

Ancestor Reiki Healing Session

Set the stage for your Reiki practice by finding a quiet place free of distractions and silence your cell phone.

Decide which ancestor or group of ancestors to whom you will send Reiki healing. To assist with focus, write down the name of the ancestors or group of ancestors on a piece of paper. Set your timer for five minutes and take a comfortable seated position.

Turn on Reiki using your unique method of connection and feel the infusion of Reiki energy into your being. Set your intention to send Reiki healing energy to your ancestor(s). While holding the piece of paper in one hand, trace the Reiki symbols while intoning the symbol's names three times: Cho Ku Rei, Sei He Ki, Cho Ku Rei, Hon Sha Ze Sho Nen, Cho Ku Rei. Hold the paper between your hands and send your ancestors Reiki energy.

At the close of your Reiki healing session, pause for a few moments in quiet reflection.

Journaling Practice

Journal your direct experience of sending Reiki energy to your ancestors. Which ancestors did you select to receive Reiki healing? Why did you make this choice? What sensations, thoughts, and emotions did you have as you performed Reiki healing? Did you receive any insights regarding your ancestors and how they may, in turn, provide you with assistance?

How might you use your insights regarding ancestor healing in future Reiki healings?

Reiki Exploration Day 30

Daily Intention Review

With a grateful heart for all the progress you've already made, recommit to your healing goals by stating out loud your heartfelt intention.

Clairalience

The clairalience psychic sense is related to the physical sense of smell. Our sense of smell is linked to memory, behavior, and even our emotions, making clairalience a very powerful psychic sense. Clairalience can describe the experience of physically smelling scents that are not present when the mind perceives a smell even though the source of the aroma isn't there.

Please review the statements below for the clairalience self-assessment and rate your response as never, sometimes, or always.

- "My sense of smell is highly developed."
- "I have smelled an unexplained scent such as perfume, cigar smoke, food, or the ocean."
- "Certain scents trigger an emotional response from me."
- "I am sensitive to essential oils and incense."
- "I have noticed an unpleasant odor when I am near someone ill."
- "I have noticed a smell that no one else can perceive."
- "I have noticed unusual, unexplained smells that I can't identify."

Reflect on your responses to the clairalience self-assessment. Even if you only rated a few statements as "sometimes" or "always," you may still be naturally gifted in this area. No matter your natural level of ability, you can develop and strengthen your clairalience psychic sense with dedication and practice.

Here's an affirmation to develop your clairalience abilities: "I embrace my sense of smell, and I am open to receiving its guidance."

Clairalience Meditation

This meditation will help develop your clairalient ability by focusing on your physical sense of smell. You will need an essential oil, incense, or a flower. Set the stage for your meditation by finding a quiet place free of distractions and silence your cell phone.

Settle into a comfortable seated position and take a few cleansing breaths. Set a timer for five minutes. Close your eyes and begin to connect with the object of your meditation using your sense of smell. Take a few deep breaths, inhaling the aroma of your chosen item. Now feel your breath's natural flow as you continue to inhale the scent. Notice any memories and emotions that may appear. If your mind wanders during the five-minute interval, simply invite your mind to connect again with your sense of smell. After your meditation, sit for a moment or two in reflection.

Journaling Practice

Journal your direct experience of this practice. What was the object of your meditation and why did you select this object? What was your experience focusing on your sense of smell? What memories and/or emotions came up for you? Next, consider trying this meditation again with a different scent and compare the results.

What role does clairalience currently play in your day-to-day life? Are there opportunities to develop and grow your smelling abilities?

How might you use your insights regarding your psychic sense of clairalience during your Reiki healing sessions?

Reiki Exploration Day 31

Daily Intention Review

Take a few deep breaths and bring to mind the childlike qualities within yourself: joy, curiosity, and playfulness. Then, from this place of connection to your inner child, read out loud your heartfelt intention.

Inner Child Healing

I was attending a yoga workshop where we were discussing the inner child. A young woman took a picture out of her wallet. It was a picture of an adorable two-year-old girl wearing a sundress and a huge smile. She explained to the group that she always carried this picture of herself as a young child as a reminder of her true nature: one of unbridled love, joy, and innocence. This practice was her unique way of connecting to her inner child. I was so impressed with her story that I asked her if I could share it with others, and she enthusiastically gave her permission.

We all have an inner child, the childlike aspect of ourselves that is innocent, fun-loving, and creative. However, our natural, childlike tendencies are often stifled due to childhood trauma and emotional wounding, even if we do not consciously remember the cause. When we work with our inner child with compassion and love, we can heal old wounds and restore a sense of playfulness, joy, and love.

Because Reiki is not limited by time or space, we can send healing Reiki energy to our inner child to help heal childhood wounds we have carried with us into adulthood. Reiki can also help us restore our natural inclinations toward play, fun, creativity, and pure love.

Inner Child Reiki Treatment

Set the stage for your Reiki practice by finding a quiet place free of distractions and silence your cell phone. Set your timer for five minutes and take a comfortable seated position.

Turn on Reiki using your unique method of connection and feel the infusion of Reiki energy into your being. Connect with your inner child by envisioning an image of yourself from childhood. With that vision firmly in place, use the Reiki symbols Cho Ku Rei, Sei He Ki, Cho Ku Rei, Hon Sha Ze Sho Nen, and Cho Ku Rei for your Reiki healing session.

At the close of your Reiki healing session, pause for a few moments in quiet reflection.

Journaling Practice

Journal your direct experience of sending Reiki energy to your inner child. What are your inner child's characteristics? What sensations, thoughts, and emotions did you have as you performed Reiki healing on your inner child? Did you receive any insights regarding the health of your inner child and any next steps you could take to align yourself with your own childlike innocence and joy? How might you use your insights regarding inner child healing in future Reiki healings?

Reiki Exploration Day 32

Daily Intention Review

Take a moment to notice the energy of the room you are in and how your environment is affecting you. Then, from this place of connection, state aloud your heartfelt intention.

Creating Sacred Space

A sacred space is a place we create ourselves. It is an oasis away from the mundane concerns of our daily lives and the world at large. It is a space that feels safe and secure, clear of negative energy. From this peaceful space, we can connect to and co-create with the Divine.

There are many ways to incorporate sacred space in your practices. Before engaging in a creative pursuit such as writing, painting, or drawing, create a sacred space to act as a container to deepen your connection to your inspiration or muse. Before prayer or meditation, you could create a sacred space to enhance your connection to the Divine or the collective consciousness. Consider creating a sacred space prior to a Reiki healing session to promote an atmosphere of peace and tranquility compatible with healing.

The Cho Ku Rei symbol can assist with creating sacred space. By drawing this symbol at every corner of the room, we can facilitate the release of any negative energies in the room, and with the power of our intention, create an environment of sacred space.

Creation of Sacred Space Using Reiki

Pick the room you will use to create your sacred space and silence your cell phone.

Sit for a moment and feel the energy of the room. Does it feel open or closed? Does it feel positive or negative? Does the energy feel stagnant or oppressive? Does it feel energetically clean or dirty? Don't attach judgment: just observe your impressions.

Turn on Reiki using your unique method of connection and feel the infusion of Reiki energy into your being. Set your intention to create sacred space using the Cho Ku Rei symbol. Walk to each corner of the room and draw the Cho Ku Rei symbol while silently intoning Cho Ku Rei three times.

Once completed, set your timer for five minutes and sit comfortably. Notice the energy of the room in which you are seated. Take a few cleansing breaths and sit while feeling the energy of the room. Has the energy shifted in some way? Notice any thoughts, emotions, or physical sensations that might occur as you sit in your scared space. Simply observe the atmosphere of your room as your meditation's focal point. At the close of your meditation, pause for a few moments in quiet reflection.

Journaling Practice

Journal your direct experience of sending Reiki energy to create sacred space. First, describe the environment of the room before your Reiki session. Next, describe the environment after your Reiki session. Were you able to sense a shift in energy after you performed your Reiki healing to the energy of the room? What feelings, thoughts, emotions, and insights came up for you? How might you use your insights regarding sending Reiki energy to create sacred space in future Reiki healing sessions?

Reiki Exploration Day 33

Daily Intention Review

Take a few centering breaths and bring to mind why you embarked on this path of inner exploration and healing. From this place of connection to your goals, recite your heartfelt intention aloud.

Clairgustance

Clairgustance is related to the physical sense of taste. This psychic sense is experienced when we taste something in our mouth that isn't there.

Review the following statements for the clairgustance self-assessment. Rate your responses as never, sometimes, or always.

- "My sense of taste is highly developed."
- "I have experienced an unexpected or unexplained taste in my mouth."
- "Particular tastes trigger an emotional response from me."
- "I have remembered experiencing the sense of taste in a dream."
- "I have a powerful emotional connection to food."
- "I have experienced an unexplained taste in my mouth when thinking about a particular person."
- "I have noticed an unusual, unexplained taste in my mouth when meditating."

Consider your responses to the clairgustance self-assessment. Even if you only rated a few statements as "sometimes" or "always," you may still be naturally gifted in this area. No matter the level of your natural clairgustance ability, you can develop and strengthen this psychic sense with dedication and practice. Here's an affirmation to develop your clairgustance abilities: "I easily perceive taste through my psychic senses, and I am open to receive its guidance."

Clairgustance Meditation

This meditation will help develop your clairgustance ability by focusing on your physical sense of taste. Set the stage for your meditation by finding a quiet place free of distractions and silencing your cell phone. Set a timer for five minutes and settle into a comfortable seated position.

Take a few cleansing breaths. Close your eyes and call to mind the memory of tasting something sweet. Cultivate awareness in your mouth and your tongue as you focus on your sense of taste. Pause for a minute, attempting to taste the sweetness. Now call to mind a memory of tasting something sour. Bring awareness to your mouth and tongue as you actively try to recreate the sensation of sourness. Fixate your attention on that flavor for a minute. Finally, bring to mind a salty food that you have tasted. Focusing on your mouth and tongue, try to recreate that taste in your mouth. At the conclusion of your meditation, sit for a moment or two in reflection.

Journaling Practice

Journal your direct experience of this practice. What was the experience focusing on your sense of taste? What memories and/or emotions came up for you? Consider trying this meditation again using savory and bitter taste sensations.

What role does clairgustance currently play in your day-to-day life? Are there opportunities to develop and grow your "tasting" abilities? How might you use your insights regarding clairgustance in future Reiki healing sessions?

Reiki Exploration Day 34

Daily Intention Review

Take a few deep, cleansing breaths to center yourself. Then, when you are ready, recommit to your Reiki path by stating out loud your heartfelt intention.

Reiki Healing for Skill/Talent/Ability Development

Personal growth and development can be a lifelong transformative journey as we explore our potential. Carved upon the Greek temple of Apollo at Delphi are the words "Know Thyself," an adage that can be applied to this inner exploration. We are born with innate talents and abilities and develop others through perseverance and dedication. We can continue to hone our skills through the learning process with practice, practice, and more practice.

Reiki healing can also be used to power up a talent, ability, or skill. Specifically, the Cho Ku Rei symbol can assist with accelerating the development of a chosen talent or skill. We can effectively and efficiently explore our potential by using Reiki in this manner.

Consider how you might benefit from increasing your healing abilities, your psychic skills, artistic abilities, or communication skills, for example. By enhancing your natural talents and developing skills that interest you, you can further yourself along your life path and explore your true potential.

Psychic Sense Healing Session

Decide which psychic sense you wish to develop. Consider where in your body that psychic sense is most strongly felt—that area will be part of the focus of your Reiki healing session today. Also, consider which chakras might be able to assist with this psychic skill development. These energy centers should also receive Reiki healing energy.

Set the stage for your Reiki practice by finding a quiet place free of distractions and silence your cell phone. Set your timer for five minutes and take a comfortable seated position.

Turn on Reiki using your unique method of connection and feel the infusion of Reiki energy in your being. Set your intention to send Reiki healing energy to develop the psychic sense of your choice. When you feel ready, send Reiki energy to yourself to develop your psychic skill using the Cho Ku Rei symbol. At the close of your Reiki healing session, pause for a few moments in quiet reflection.

Journaling Practice

Journal your direct experience sending Reiki energy to a specific ability, specifically with the development of a psychic sense. Which psychic sense did you select, and what drew you towards picking that particular psychic sense? What shifts physically, emotionally, mentally, and energetically occurred during your Reiki self-healing treatment? Did you receive any random feelings, thoughts, or insights during your Reiki session? If so, what were they? Did you receive any guidance or insights regarding developing this psychic gift? How might you use your insights regarding sending healing energy to develop a specific skill or talent in future Reiki healing sessions?

Reiki Exploration Day 35

Daily Intention Review

As a reminder of your healing path, read aloud your heartfelt intention.

Reiki and Past Lives Healing

The concept of past lives and reincarnation is a controversial one. If you don't ascribe to this belief, please keep an open mind as you approach this section. You'll see an alternate approach to this practice that may be more aligned with your current belief structure.

Reincarnation is the belief that an eternal soul of a person or animal can be reborn and live multiple lives. Throughout these numerous lifetimes, particular traits, habits, oaths, and traumas can appear in the current life, causing potential roadblocks to realizing our dreams. For example, in a past life, you may have taken a vow of poverty that could manifest as continual financial difficulties in this lifetime.

If you don't believe in past lives, consider the traumas of your family lineage. All families have behavioral patterns that may have served a purpose once but are now constricting and limiting your potential and growth. For example, suppose your grandparents or great-grandparents lived through the Great Depression. In that case, you may still feel the effects of the feelings of scarcity, which may contribute to a fear of losing money or a scarcity mindset that could manifest as hoarding. Likewise, if domestic violence is a part of your family lineage, there may be a pattern of abuse or lack of self-worth that may be present. Consider exploring your family's history or your intuition regarding your past lives for clues about cycles of behavior that you wish to change.

Past Life Healing Session

Find a comfortable seated position and settle in for a few moments. Set a timer for five minutes, the duration of your targeted self-healing session today.

Consider a pattern of behavior or a condition in your current life that may have roots in a past life event or family lineage trauma. Set your intention to heal this trauma from the past using Reiki energy.

Turn on Reiki using your unique method of connection and feel the infusion of Reiki energy into your being. Begin your Reiki session utilizing all three Reiki symbols in the following way: Cho Ku Rei, Sei He Ki, Cho Ku Rei, Hon Sha Ze Sho Nen, and Cho Ku Rei, silently intoning the name of the symbol three times as you draw it. Then allow your intuition to guide your hand positions as you perform Reiki healing on yourself to address past life issues or family lineage concerns.

After your Reiki session, take a few moments in quiet reflection.

Journaling Practice

Journal your direct experience of using Reiki to heal past life or family lineage issues. What past life or family lineage pattern did you select for your healing session? How has this cycle of behavior caused problems in your life? Did you notice any physical, emotional, or mental shifts in your energy as you performed Reiki healing to your past life or family lineage issues? Did you gain any insights regarding Reiki's use to address current problems or patterns of behavior that may have roots in past lives or your family lineage? How might this information be helpful in future Reiki healing sessions?

Reiki Exploration Day 36

Daily Intention Review

Take a moment to reflect on your heartfelt intention. Then, read it aloud to renew your dedication to your healing path.

Clairtangency

Clairtangency is related to the physical sense of touch. When someone has a clairtangent experience, they are receiving previously unknown information by touching a person or object.

Please review the statements below for the clairtangency self-assessment and rate your response as never, sometimes, or always.

- "My skin is very sensitive, and my clothing can be irritating."
- "I have difficulty sleeping in a different bed because I can perceive the energy of the other individuals who have slept on it."
- "I have picked up an object and sensed information about its history or previous owner."
- "I have picked up a crystal or essential oil and knew how to best use its healing properties."
- "I can touch people and know information about them, such as their health, mood, or personal history."

- "I cannot wear second-hand clothes because they energetically feel 'off.'"
- "I have received impressions about an animal's health or mood as I pet it."

Consider your responses. Even if you only rated a few statements as "sometimes" or "always," you may be naturally gifted in this area. No matter your natural inclination toward clairtangency, this psychic sense can blossom with your focus, dedication, and practice. Here's an example of an affirmation to develop your clairtangent abilities: "I am open to receive psychic information through my sense of touch."

Clairtangency Meditation

This meditation will help develop your clairtangent ability by focusing on your sense of touch. You will need a crystal or a simple stone.

Set the stage for your meditation by finding a quiet place free of distractions and silence your cell phone. Set your timer for five minutes and take a comfortable seated position. Take the crystal or stone in your non-dominant hand. (If you are right-handed, place the crystal in your left hand.) Squeeze it and rub your fingers along the surface of the crystal or rock. Set an intention for receiving information about the object. You may receive information about the crystal or stone's history. You may get a message about how the crystal or stone can help you in some way. Visualize a line of energy connecting your heart center to the crystal. With a sense of curiosity, stay open to any insights or messages you may receive.

At the conclusion of your meditation, sit for a moment or two in reflection.

Journaling Practice

Journal your direct experience of this practice. For example, what was the experience focusing on your connection to your crystal or stone? Did you receive any insights? If not, don't close yourself off to the experience. This practice is a meditation to be explored repeatedly to heighten your clairtangent abilities.

What role does clairtangency currently play in your day-to-day life? Are there opportunities to develop and grow your connection to your sense of touch to access your clairtangent ability?

How might you use your insights regarding your psychic sense of clairtangency during your Reiki healing sessions?

Reiki Exploration Day 37

Daily Intention Review

Take a few deep breaths and draw your attention inward. Consider your progress along your healing path and the insights you have gained on your personal journey. Then, when you are ready, state out loud your heartfelt intention.

Spirit Guides

Reiki healing with the aid of your spirit guides is an exciting and deeply personal experience. A spirit guide is an evolved, non-physical being who exists in the spirit realm. The role of a spirit guide is to protect and assist with our personal evolutionary process.

When you received your first Reiki attunement, you acquired a specific type of spirit guide to assist you with your Reiki healings. Your Reiki spirit guide plays many roles and can assist you with various topics and tasks, including:

Physician/Doctor: assists with overall health encompassing physical, emotional, mental, energetic, and spiritual well-being

Teacher: assists with learning the tools and techniques of Reiki healing

Messenger: helps with receiving and understanding the needs of your healing participant

Protector: helps with dispelling negative energies

Your Reiki guide is always available to you. You may want to develop your own ritual to call in your Reiki guide at the beginning of a healing session. You can also ask for support or insights from your guide at any time during your Reiki treatment. You may wish to develop a relationship with your guide by meditating to communicate with this powerful ally. Be open to the messengers you may receive from your Reiki guide, which may appear through any of your psychic senses and in your dreams.

Please keep in mind that you are always in control. If you sense unpleasant energy or a guide that doesn't resonate with you, you can command that the energy leave by either stating this aloud or waving an arm in dismal.

Spirit Guide Meditation

Set the stage for your meditation by finding a quiet place free of distractions and silence your cell phone. Set your timer for five to ten minutes and sit comfortably.

Picture in your mind's eye a curtain in front of you. This curtain can be any fabric and color that appeals to you. Set your intention to meet a spirit guide that can assist you with Reiki and develop your skills as a healer. Take a deep breath and open the curtain.

As you open the curtain, imagine a large field of grass. Begin walking through the meadow towards a large willow tree with a beautiful two-person bench underneath its generous branches. Sit on the bench and ask for your Reiki spirit guide to join you and provide you with guidance and insights regarding your healing path.

Allow the experience to unfold without expectation or judgment. Notice what images may appear, what feelings you experience, what thoughts pop into your mind, and what sensations you experience.

At the close of your meditation, thank the spirit guides for the assistance and spend a few moments in quiet reflection.

Journaling Practice

Journal your direct experience of your spirit guide meditation. What sensations, thoughts, or feelings did you experience? Did you experience a vision of your spirit guide? If so, what form did your spirit guide take? Did your spirit guide have a message for you? What insights, if any, did you receive? How might you consider further developing your relationship with your spirit guides?

How might you use your insights regarding your spirit guides during your Reiki healing sessions?

Reiki Exploration Day 38

Daily Intention Review

Pause and consider all the support that you have, both seen and unseen, on your life path. From this place of appreciation, state out loud your heartfelt intention.

Angels

Angels are distinct spiritual beings separate from spirit guides. They are intermediaries directly from the divine source, God, or Goddess—whatever version of the Divine that resonates with you. Angels have never been incarnate humans, with two notable exceptions: Metatron, who was the prophet Enoch, and Sandalphon, who was the prophet, Elijah. Angels serve the Divine and can help humans, especially when called upon for assistance. There are four archangels in particular you may wish to call on for assistance during healing sessions.

Archangel Michael: Angel of Protection

The color associated with Archangel Michael is red, and the elemental association is fire. Archangel Michael may be depicted holding a sword.

Areas of assistance:

- Protection
- Boundaries
- Releasing energetic cords and attachments
- Releasing emotions associated with fear and self-doubt

Archangel Raphael: Angel of Healing

The color of Archangel Raphael is yellow, and the elemental association is air.

Raphael may be pictured holding a caduceus, a winged staff entwined by two snakes.

Areas of assistance:

- Healing of the body, mind, and spirit
- World healing
- Animal healing
- Learning the study of medicine or any healing modality
- Communication

Archangel Gabriel: Angel of Guidance

The color associated with Archangel Gabriel is blue, and the elemental association is water.

Gabriel may be pictured holding a chalice or a lily.

Areas of assistance:

- Healing of the emotional body
- Forgiveness

- Love
- Development of intuition

Archangel Uriel (or Auriel): Angel of Peace

The color associated with Archangel Uriel is deep green, and the elemental association is earth.

Uriel may be pictured holding a book, pentacle (five-pointed star within a circle,) or a cornucopia.

Areas of assistance:

- Financial healing
- Divination
- Connection to the physical body

Another mighty angel that you may wish to work with specifically for using crystals and crystal grids during your healing sessions is Archangel Metatron, the angel of sacred geometry.

Angel Letter and Meditation

Set the stage for your meditation by finding a quiet place free of distractions and silence your cell phone.

Decide on your specific healing request and select an angel whom you wish to ask for assistance with that intention. Compose a letter to the angel asking for guidance, healing, and insights. You may want to add why you are making this request and be sure to express gratitude for all you already have.

Place the letter in front of you, set your timer for five minutes, and sit comfortably. State your intention to connect with the angel of your choice concerning your specific intention. You may wish to draw the Cho Ku Rei symbol over the letter to increase the power of your words. Then sit in silent meditation, noticing any sensations, feelings, thoughts, visions, or insights you might receive. At the close of your meditation, thank the angel for the assistance and spend a few moments in quiet reflection.

Journaling Practice

Journal your direct experience of your letter writing and angel meditation. What sensations, thoughts, or feelings did you experience? Did you experience a vision of the angel? If so, what form did the angel take? What insights, if any, did you receive?

How might you use your insights regarding angels during your Reiki healing sessions?

Reiki Exploration Day 39

Daily Intention Review

Take a moment to reflect on your heartfelt intention. Then, read it aloud and appreciate your dedication to your healing path.

Secrecy and the Reiki Symbols

Historically, the Reiki symbols were kept secret until a Reiki practitioner reached Level Two. The role of secrecy, especially regarding sacred teachings, is not unique to Reiki; it appears across religions, magical traditions, and esoteric organizations. Only those individuals who have proven their dedication to a chosen path were gifted with these secrets.

Initially, the Reiki symbols were passed down to students orally, not in print. Students were required to memorize the characters during class. And after completing the training, students were required to destroy any printed copies of the symbols to protect the symbols' secrecy. This practice may be why the variations of the Reiki symbols exist today.

At some point, information previously kept secret may be revealed to the greater society. This is the case with the Reiki symbols, which are now readily available in print and online. I decided to include illustrations of the Reiki symbols in this book because I believe that the symbols need the power of an attunement behind it for the symbols to be used for healing purposes. I also considered people who purchase this book to be dedicated Reiki healers, alleviating my hesitation regarding publishing the Reiki symbols as illustrations. Although the secrecy of the symbols may not be as relevant as it once was, Reiki symbols maintain their sacred nature. Therefore, if you choose to display Reiki symbols in your healing space or home, please remember to treat these symbols with respect and honor their sacred essence.

Here are suggestions for using these sacred symbols during Reiki healing treatments:

- Draw the Reiki symbols on the palm of your hands using your index and middle finger as you start your Reiki treatment.

- Visualize the Reiki symbols in white light moving from the palms of your hands and into object or person receiving the Reiki energy.
- Draw the Reiki symbols with your tongue on the roof of your mouth and visualize the symbols traveling down to your heart center, through your arms, and out of your hands into the object or person receiving the Reiki energy.
- Close your eyes and draw the Reiki symbols with your eyeballs. Then, visualize the symbols traveling down to your heart center, through your arms, and out your hands into the object or person receiving the Reiki energy.

Experimenting with Using the Reiki Symbols

Pick a few methods of using the Reiki symbols from the previous listing that you wish to use in your self-healing session today.

Set the stage for your Reiki practice by finding a quiet place free of distractions and silence your cell phone.

Set your timer for five minutes and take a comfortable seated position.

Turn on Reiki using your unique method of connection and feel the infusion of Reiki energy into your being. Set your intention to send Reiki healing energy to yourself. Using the standard self-healing hand positions or your intuition, begin experimenting with the different methods of using the Reiki symbols during a healing session.

At the close of your Reiki healing session, pause for a few moments in quiet reflection.

Journaling Practice

Journal your direct experience of utilizing different Reiki symbol methods.

Which ways of drawing the symbols resonated with you? Which ones did you find most effective? Which ones were less effective?

Did you notice any energy shifts physically, emotionally, mentally, or energetically?

How might this information be helpful in future Reiki healing sessions?

Reiki Exploration Day 40

Daily Intention Review

Congratulations on completing this forty-day immersion experience! To help establish the mood for your day, take a moment to reconnect with your heartfelt intention and recommit to your healing path by reciting it aloud.

The Power of Reflection

Reflection is the process of deep thought or careful consideration. Unfortunately, in our fast-paced society, we often don't spend the time to pause and reflect before diving in to a new endeavor or challenge. Yet, reflection is an integral part of the learning process giving us space to ponder new concepts and deepen our understanding which can lead to wisdom.

On this day of our forty-day cycle, let's pause and reflect on your experiences over this immersion experience. Are there topics you'd like to revisit? Next, take a few moments to re-read your Reiki journal and reconnect with your personal experiences. Finally, consider your motivation for exploring Reiki healing. Does it still resonate with you, or have your incentives changed?

Reflect and Revisit the Past

Consider everything you have explored over the past thirty-nine days. Next, revisit your Reiki journal and select a day you'd like to review. Release all judgment and expectations before repeating that exercise.

Journaling Practice

Journal your direct experience of the exercise you selected. Complete that journaling practice. Next, compare your direct experience today with your experience the first time you completed the practice. Are there any differences? Similarities? What does this inform you about yourself and your growth as a Reiki practitioner?

Part 5

Reiki Mastery: Reiki Level Three

Chapter 15

What Is Reiki Level Three?

Reiki Level Three further increases both the power and effectiveness of your Reiki healing by introducing the Reiki Master symbol. It also includes instructions for circulating Ki, life force energy, and the dynamic Violet Breath. In addition, we explore advanced energy anatomy, including the five elements and additional chakras to complement your Reiki healing sessions.

Reiki Level Three is usually divided into two parts: Reiki Master attunement and the Reiki Master-Teacher class, the latter of which provides direction on how to pass the Reiki attunements to others.

At this level of Reiki, your spiritual connection becomes more robust, which may lead to additional changes in your lifestyle, relationships, and values. In addition, your personal energetic vibration will be raised during this process, enhancing your intuition and strengthening your psychic abilities.

What Is a Reiki Master?

I am hesitant to call myself a Reiki Master; I am a student of Reiki and of life, continually evolving and growing. Remaining humble and continuing to develop your Reiki skills are crucial to mastering the art of Reiki healing. My ideal Reiki Master is an experience Reiki healer who is proficient in all elements of Reiki healing, including using the Reiki symbols, developing a deep understanding of the energy body anatomy, cultivating intuition, and developing psychic senses. In addition, a Reiki Master should remain curious and continue their personal development and growth as they integrate Reiki into their daily lives.

What Is the Difference Between a Reiki Master and a Reiki Master-Teacher?

An individual can be a Reiki Master without becoming a Reiki Master-Teacher. Only pursue the Reiki Master-Teacher path if you feel compelled to instruct others in learning this healing modality. The qualities of an exceptional Reiki Master-Teacher include the following:

- Mastery of the three levels of Reiki
- Command of the Reiki symbols
- Experience in Reiki healing: both in person and distance healings
- Ability to create Reiki training materials
- Ability to organize and lead training sessions
- Ability to receive feedback from students without judgment
- Effective time management skills
- Ability to clearly express and explain Reiki concepts
- Desire to form and maintain meaningful relationships with their Reiki students

If you feel the call to teach Reiki to others but are not comfortable with any of the above statements, actively pursue these skills. The more well-rounded you are as a Reiki healer and as an individual, the better teacher you will become.

Why Advance to Reiki Level Three?

There are many reasons why you may want to extend your Reiki training to this final level, including the following:

- To deepen your spiritual connection
- To assist others with spiritual growth
- To actively raise your personal vibration to a higher frequency
- To continue to develop your intuition and psychic senses
- To teach Reiki to others

When Are You Ready to Advance to Reiki Level Three?

As with the transition from Reiki Level Two to Reiki Level Three, there are no definitive rules regarding the length of time you should wait before pursuing the Reiki Master level. Although it is your personal choice, you may want to complete the twenty-one-day self-healing practice at minimum, allowing your energetic body to become accustomed to the Reiki energy of Level Two before receiving your Reiki Master attunement. Additionally, I recommend taking the time to integrate all the concepts of Level Two before proceeding further. These key concepts should include the following:

- The basic chakra system
- The hand positions of self-healing
- The hand positions for healing others
- Knowledge of the three Reiki symbols and proficiency in using those symbols
- Proficiency in conducting distance healing sessions

This integration can be obtained by completing the forty-day immersion experience in part four. Above all, allow your intuition to guide you on the best time to move further along your Reiki path.

Reiki Level Three Attunement Process

During your Reiki Level Three attunement, similar to previous Reiki attunements, you will be attuned to a new Reiki symbol, the Master symbol, Dai Ko Myo (pronounced *dye-koh-myoh*). This powerful process dramatically elevates your personal vibration frequency and further increases the effectiveness of your Reiki healing sessions. After your attunement, you should practice Reiki self-healing for a minimum of twenty-one days and engage in daily meditation. Keeping a Reiki journal to track your progress and record your insights is highly recommended.

Similar to previous attunements, you may experience any of the following results:

- Shifts in relationships: as your personal energy changes, you might find new relationships forming and older, unhealthy relationships falling away
- Changes in eating and drinking habits: You may be drawn to eating more organic, healthier food options

- Changes in reading materials, music, and television preferences
- Changes in energy levels
- Changes in sleep patterns, including vivid dreams
- Desire to act more ethically
- A deeper connection to the Divine
- Strengthening of psychic senses
- A deeper connection to your spirit guides

Chapter 16

The Master Reiki Symbol and Additional Reiki Level Three Symbols

As a reminder, a symbol is both a form, the shape of a symbol, and a force, the power behind the symbol.[18] Symbols are not simply two-dimensional images. Instead, picture them as three-dimensional entities with dynamic energies.

Remember: the Reiki symbols should be memorized so they can be drawn accurately during Reiki healing sessions.

---

18. Butler, *The Magician*, 41.

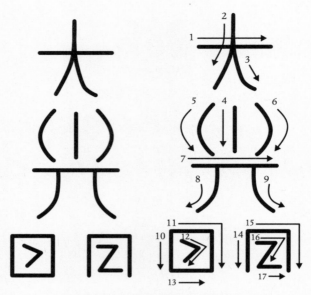

The Master Symbol: Dai Ko Myo

Dai Ko Myo is also known as the Master symbol, and its purpose is for spiritual healing. There are several variations of this symbol; feel free to use the version that resonates with you. In addition, this symbol is not unique to Reiki and can be viewed in Buddhist temples worldwide.

The name of this symbol translates to "shining light" or "enlightenment," providing us with insights regarding the power of this symbol.[19] This "great bright light" may reference the light we can shine on our higher selves and give us direction about our spiritual growth and development. Additionally, this light may provide illumination, shedding light on aspects of ourselves that we keep hidden in the darkness.

Since the energy of Dai Ko Myo is of a higher vibration and contains the essence of the three traditional Reiki symbols, it may replace the three symbols used in in-person Reiki healing sessions. This symbol's energy signature is of the Reiki source energy itself and is quite empowering.

The activation of the Dai Ko Myo symbol occurs during your attunement process. To use the Dai Ko Myo symbol in healing sessions, draw the character while silently intoning "Dai Ko Myo" three times. Experiment with different methods of drawing this symbol:

---

19. Powers, *Reiki*, 178.

- Draw the symbol with your pointer finger or both your pointer and index finger.
- Draw the symbol with your outstretched hand.
- Draw the symbol with your eyes.
- Draw the symbol on the roof of your mouth with your tongue.

I start all healing sessions by drawing the Dai Ko Myo symbol on the palms of my hands and visualize beaming the symbol into my healing participant.

Some suggested uses for the Dai Ko Myo symbol are listed here, but the full range of opportunities to use this symbol is limited only by your imagination.

- Empowering the Cho Ku Rei, Sei He Kei, and Hon Sha Ze Sho Nen symbols
- Purifying of food and drink
- Energetic balance
- Enhancing the mind-body-spirit connection
- Healing spiritual issues
- Healing the spiritual causes of illness
- Connecting with your higher self
- Assistance with identifying your soul purpose

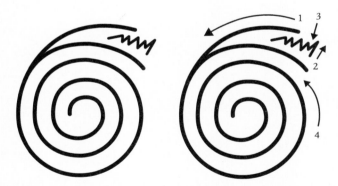

The Dumo and the Tibetan Master Symbol

Over time, I began experimenting with more contemporary symbols and gravitated toward a more modern version of the Master symbol that resonated with me deeply. As a result, Dumo is the version of the Master symbol I currently use in my Reiki healing sessions.

Raku, the Grounding Symbol

This symbol, pronounced *rah-koo*, can be used both during Reiki healing sessions and the attunement process. For Reiki healing sessions, this symbol can be used at the close of a treatment to ground the energy of the healing participant and end the energetic connection between the Reiki practitioner and the healing participant. Likewise, this symbol is used during the Reiki attunement process to cut the energetic connection between the Reiki student and Reiki Master-Teacher after transmitting the Reiki symbols.

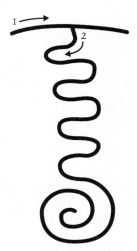

Nin Giz Zida, the Serpent of Fire Symbol

This symbol of Tibetan origin may be used in healing sessions and during the attunement process. Pronounced *nin-geez-zee-dah*, this symbol's purpose is to clear the central energy channel of the sushumna nadi, allowing access for kundalini energy to rise. Kundalini energy is a form of spiritual energy centered in your root chakra located at the base of your spine. When this energy is released, it travels up the sushumna nadi, enabling the individual to experience a spiritual awakening and deep transformation.

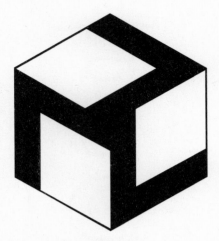

Antahkarana

The origin of this symbol, like many symbols in Reiki, is disputed. Pronounced *an-tah-kah-rah-nah*, this symbol is associated with the body's primary energy channel, the sushumna nadi. It is not used directly in Reiki healing sessions but as a catalyst to connect to the Divine. When used as the focus of meditation, this symbol can strengthen and clear the subtle body's energetic pathways, balance the chakras, and create a channel to communicate with healing guides and angels. When placed under a Reiki table, it can increase the Reiki energy of a healing session.

Chapter 17

Non-Traditional Healing Symbols

All Reiki and other healing symbols have been channeled through meditation or divine inspiration. Reiki symbols are inherently healing by nature and can't be misused or cause harm. However, this blanket statement isn't true about other symbols. That doesn't mean other symbols shouldn't be used during Reiki healings, but it does mean that you should take the time to use other healing symbols for self-healing for first-hand experience of the symbols' energy and how their power manifests during a healing session. Based on your experience, you can determine for yourself whether it is appropriate for you to share with others during Reiki healing sessions.

Many contemporary schools of Reiki, such as Karuna Reiki and Shamballa Reiki, use various modern symbols. Additionally, new symbols have been channeled by healers and mystics such as Christopher Penczak, as detailed in his 2004 *Magick of Reiki*. The symbols in this section are not a complete listing of all the healing symbols used by Reiki practitioners and healers of various Reiki traditions. Instead, it represents a sampling of the types of symbols you may consider exploring. As you meditate and perform healings, notice images that appear. Consider jotting these symbols down and reflect on their potential healing power. If you feel called to do so, experiment using them in self-healing sessions and track your experiences: physically, emotionally, mentally, energetically, and spiritually.

Om

Pronounced *aum*, om is an ancient and sacred symbol with roots in Hinduism, Buddhism, and Jainism. It's chanted in yogic circles, and its image can be seen on jewelry and clothing. Om is often called the sound of creation. By chanting "om," one can obtain a state of inner peace and connection to the universe. It corresponds to the state of oneness and therefore to supreme spiritual actualization.

This symbol can be drawn at the crown chakra in healing sessions to deepen a connection to the Divine and the universe. It can also be drawn over the brow chakra to bring peace of mind or the heart chakra to bring peace to emotional issues.

Ankh

The Ankh is an ancient Egyptian symbol of life, and Egyptian deities are often portrayed holding an ankh. This character is a powerful image representing all life: both human and divine—and the universe as a whole. It represents the key to hidden wisdom, knowledge, and ancient mysteries.

The ankh may be used in healing sessions to bring new life or energetic renewal to help provide wisdom and insights. Additionally, the Ankh can be used for participants with terminal illnesses to assist with their transition and connection to the Divine. Considering drawing this symbol over the entire body of yourself or your healing participant. Alternatively, you can draw this symbol over the brow chakra for sacred knowledge and divine awareness.

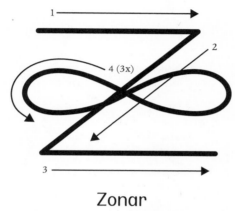

Zonar

Zonar is a symbol found in several modern Reiki traditions. Shaped in a letter Z with three infinity symbols, it is used to heal karmic-related issues and past-life traumas. The feelings of trauma are often held deeply within our being, even on the cellular level. This symbol can assist with breaking patterns of behavior that may have a karmic or past-life origin—for example, addiction, anger issues, abandonment issues, and toxic relationships—by gently releasing the emotions held deeply within.

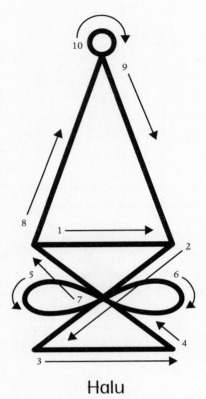

Halu

This Reiki symbol is a more intense version of the Zonar symbol, with the triangle representing increased mental energy. It can be drawn after the Zonar symbol for maximum effect. This symbol has a protective quality and heals on the physical, mental, and spiritual levels. Consider using this symbol to reinforce boundaries, prevent emotional manipulation, guard against psychic attacks, and eliminate harmful influences.

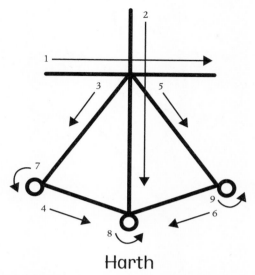

Harth

This Reiki symbol contains the energy of love, truth, harmony, and balance. This symbol heals the heart chakra, our energy center associated with love and compassion for others as well as ourselves. It assists with creating the inner changes that allow healthy relationships to develop and self-destructive behaviors transmuted into positive, life-affirming habits. Additionally, this symbol helps with forming loving connections with our spirit guides.

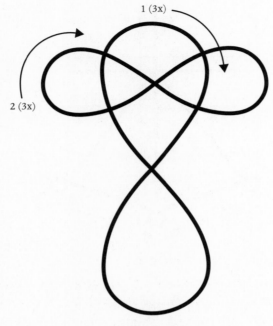

Len So My

The energy of Len So My resonates with the divine power of pure, unconditional love. This symbol aids in releasing and healing deep emotional pain associated with grief, loss, and abandonment. It can also assist with opening the heart to new relationships and increasing self-love and acceptance.

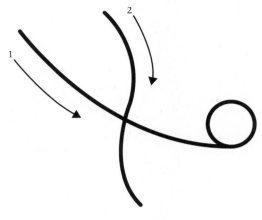

Al Luma

This symbol was channeled by Christopher Penczak and referenced in his book *Magick of Reiki*. This symbol can be used during healing sessions to assist your healing participant in relaxing, turning their focus inward, and receiving guidance from their spirit guides. I have successfully used this symbol during personal meditation sessions and in my Reiki healing treatments with successful results.

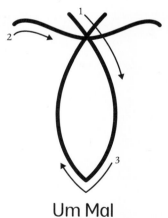

Um Mal

Um Mal is another symbol channeled by Christopher Penczak referenced in his book *Magick of Reiki*. This symbol may be used to heal any disconnect between our physical lifestyle and our spiritual beliefs. It assists with accessing repressed and neglected parts of ourselves. This symbol is also a potent tool for accessing hidden fears. Profound healing can occur once these unconscious fears are brought to the surface.

Infinity Compass

The Infinity Compass is a symbol gifted to me by my healing guides. It assists with healing the parts of yourself preventing you from following your life path and your connection to your higher self. This symbol can be used during your meditation practice or during healing sessions to assist your healing participant with walking their unique path with confidence, clarity, and alignment with their soul's purpose.

Chapter 18

Reiki and the Elements

In addition to the chakra map of the energy body, there are other maps you'll find to be just as helpful as you progress along your healing path. One of those maps is related to the elements: earth, water, fire, air, and ether/space. The ancient cultures of Greece, India, China, and the Americas recognized the elements as the basic building blocks of all material forms. Knowing the qualities of these elements and how to assist with balancing these energies within the body are powerful tools for a Reiki healer.

The ancient traditions of the East and the West have different element systems. We will explore the Western approach, which has roots in ancient Greece. In addition, I have developed a profound connection to the elements using an Eastern approach developed in ancient India known as the tattvas. The tattvas (also spelled tattwas) are symbols used to represent the elements and can be used as a focal point during meditation to develop insights into the essence of the element. For your reference, the tattvas are included in the elemental correspondence tables in the sections below.

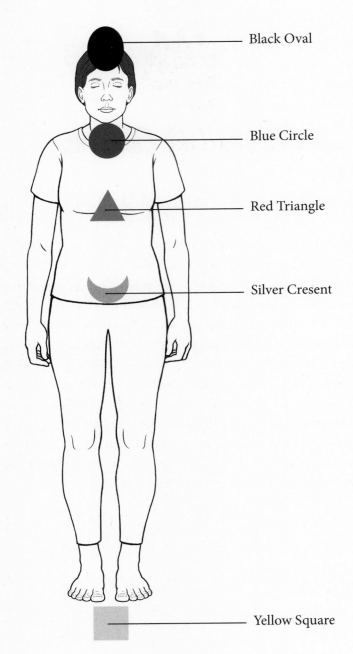

Black Oval

Blue Circle

Red Triangle

Silver Cresent

Yellow Square

Earth

Symbol: ▽ Upside down triangle with a horizontal line through the center
Tattva: Yellow square
Color: Green
Energy state: Solid
Astrological signs: Taurus, Virgo, and Capricorn
Direction: North
Archangel: Uriel (also spelled Auriel)
Finger: Ring finger

The earth element is the densest and most tangible of the five elements. It corresponds to the material world. The energy associated with the earth element is that of manifesting and creating on the physical plane. Individuals with a strong earth element are often grounded, practical, realistic, and cautious. These individuals persevere until their goals are attained and are motivated by tangible results. They appreciate routines and are aware of their limitations. When the earth element is dominant, life is approached slowly, deliberately, and cautiously.

However, imbalanced earth energy can cause issues both personal and professional. An excess of earth energy may be present if you feel stuck and unable to move forward. It might also express itself in overly conservative personality types who are afraid to take risks or are averse to change. On the other hand, too little of this element can lead to an un-grounded person who cannot handle responsibility or commitments. Without the earth element, we can't manifest our inner visions into reality.

On the elemental map of the human body, the earth element can be pictured as a yellow square containing your feet and legs or a yellow square directly beneath your feet.

Methods to Heal and Strengthen the Earth Element

- Walk barefoot on the grass, sand, or soil feeling the soles of your feet connecting to the earth.
- Explore nature by hiking, walking, cycling, or simply sitting outside.
- Gardening.
- Receive a massage.
- Meditate with the tattva associated with earth: a yellow square on a red background.

Water
Symbol: ▽ Upside down triangle
Tattva: Silver crescent
Color: Blue
Energy state: Liquid
Astrological signs: Cancer, Scorpio, Pisces
Direction: West
Archangel: Gabriel
Finger: Pinky finger

The water element is the second densest of the five elements and corresponds to the emotional plane. The energy associated with the water element is fluid and related to our feelings. Individuals with a balanced water element are often nurturing, intuitive, compassionate, and receptive. These individuals desire connection on the soul level and may be called to serve others. If the water element is dominant, individuals may be profoundly intuitive and may perceive information through their psychic senses more easily.

Unbalanced water energy can cause numerous issues. For example, an excess of water energy may be present if you feel overprotective, clingy, and needy in your personal relationships. It might also express itself as overly emotional individuals or those with issues regarding boundaries. On the other hand, too little water can lead to superficial relationships, a lack of emotional depth, or being cut off from feelings entirely. Without this element, we can't form meaningful connections with others or honor our own feelings.

On the elemental map of the human body, the water element can be pictured as a silver crescent moon located at your lower belly.

Methods to Heal and Strengthen the Water Element

- Spend time near a nature body of water such as a river, stream, lake, or the ocean.
- Take a bath with sea salt or essential oils.
- Meditate while listening to the sound of rain.
- Listen to music that moves you on an emotional level.
- Meditate with the tattva associated with water: a silver crescent on a black background.

Fire

Symbol: △ Upright triangle
Tattva: Red triangle
Color: Red
Energy state: Plasma
Astrological signs: Aries, Leo, Sagittarius
Direction: South
Archangel: Michael
Finger: Thumb

The fire element is the third densest of the five elements and corresponds to vital life force energy. The energy associated with the fire element is assertive and radiating. Individuals with a strong fire element are optimistic, energetic, passionate, creative, and self-confident. They enjoy challenges and competitive situations. Finally, these individuals take action in their lives and are often independent.

However, imbalanced fire energy can produce issues that may affect daily life. For example, an excess of fire energy may be present if you feel aggressive and domineering in your personal relationships. It might also express itself as acting impulsively without forethought. On the other hand, too little fire can lead to an overall lack of energy and an inability to enjoy life.

On the elemental map of the human body, imagine fire as a red triangle at your core.

Methods to Heal and Strengthen the Fire Element

- Spend time outdoors in the sunlight using the appropriate safety precautions such as sunscreen.

- Sit by a campfire.

- Meditate using a lit candle as the focus of your meditation.

- Engage with your competitive nature by playing a sport or game.

- Meditate with the tattva associated with fire: a red triangle on a green background.

Air

Symbol: △ Upright triangle with a horizontal line
Tattva: Blue circle
Color: Yellow
Energy state: Gas
Astrological signs: Gemini, Libra, Aquarius
Direction: East
Archangel: Raphael
Finger: Index finger

The air element is the fourth element and corresponds to the mental and intellectual plane. The energy associated with this element is that of breath and movement. Individuals with a strong air element are communicative, curious, intelligent, and versatile. They may enjoy traveling and exploring new places. Rational thought, objectivity, and strong social skills are hallmark marks of those who have a solid connection to the air element.

Imbalanced air energy can have negative consequences. For example, an excess of air energy may be present if you feel scattered or ungrounded. It might also express itself as gossip or overanalyzing a situation. Too little air can lead to difficulties in learning or processing information. Additionally, these individuals may experience poor concentration and communication skills.

On the elemental map of the human body, air element can be pictured as a blue circle at your throat center.

Methods to Heal and Strengthen the Air Element

- Write in a journal.
- Fly a kite on a windy day.
- Read a book.
- Meditate with the tattva associated with air: a blue circle on an orange background.

Ether (Space)
Symbol: ✸ Circle with four intersecting lines at the center
Tattva: Black oval
Color: Black or white
Energy state: Vibration
Astrological signs: Transcends the zodiac
Direction: The center of the universe
Archangel: Metatron
Finger: Index finger

Ether is the fifth element and corresponds to space. The energy associated with the element is that of connection and potential. Ether is the substance from which the four elements are derived. This element is balanced when the other four elements are in harmony. However, I have found that skygazing is a way to connect with ether's unlimited potential.

Chapter 19

Advanced Chakra Anatomy

The seven-chakra system explored in part one is the most common chakra system used today, found in yoga classes and New Age circles everywhere. However, expanding our view to include two more major chakras brings us a deeper connection to the earth and the heavens. These two chakras exist outside the human body.

Chakra 0: Earth Star Chakra

Location: Six to twelve inches below the feet

Color: Brown, black, or gray

Purpose: To connect with the energy and wisdom of Mother Earth and our ancestors. This energy vortex also provides the grounding for the chakra system. Additionally, it is the gateway to assessing information regarding karmic patterns and past lives.

When balanced, we are open to receiving information directly from the earth, including our collective history as humans, our ancestral heritage, our place as part of the whole earth, and the deep wisdom of the planet herself. We care about the well-being of the earth and feel an innate, deep connection to the natural world. A balanced Earth Star chakra roots us into our daily lives and allows us to access Earth's energies for optimal health. This chakra is significant to Reiki healers since this connection will enable us to release negative energies to Mother Earth so they can be transmuted into positive energy.

When this energy center is not functioning properly, we may feel disconnected from our collective past and our place on this planet. We may abuse, waste, or pollute the earth's natural resources. Genetic health issues and issues associated with negative ancestral patterns may be present. Without the anchor of a balanced Earth Star chakra, we may live unbalanced lives and lack a strong connection to humanity.

Chakra 8: Soul Star Chakra

Location: Approximately six inches above your head
Color: Pink or white
Purpose: To connect with the wisdom and insights from the Divine and your higher self, the timeless part of you, without the filter of the ego associated with your current incarnation on this planet.

This chakra is accessed when the seven chakras below it are unblocked and the energy pathways flow freely. This chakra assists with understanding our soul's purpose for this lifetime. Through this chakra, we can access our higher self, the aspect of ourselves that is not limited by personal ego and personality. It is also through this chakra that we can access the Akashic Record, also known as the Book of Life. This chakra is either opened or closed. To open the Soul Star chakra, consciously unblock, strengthen, and heal the other major chakras.

Minor Chakras

Although not as well-known as the major energy centers in the subtle body anatomy, the minor chakras play vital roles in your overall health. Some mystics say there are hundreds of major and minor chakras within our energetic body. For our purposes, I've included minor chakras that I've found invaluable as a Reiki healer.

Hand Chakras

The hand chakras are located at the center of the palms of each hand. These are the energy centers related to healing as Reiki energy is transmitted through these energy centers. As energy pathways, the nadis connect the heart chakra to the hand chakras and create a powerful connection between the loving, compassionate energy of the heart flowing into the hands. Conversely, the energy we absorb through our hand chakras is transmitted to our heart center.

When our hand chakras are optimally functioning, we have a sense of openness and connection to the world around us. Our creativity is freely expressed, often with tangible results. Balanced hand chakras assist us with perceiving subtle energies around us, providing valuable insights that can be used in Reiki healing sessions.

The energy centers of the hands can be awakened by massage and activities that require manual dexterity, such as playing the piano or guitar. Additionally, creative pursuits such as pottery, sculpting, and finger painting can activate the hand chakras. Finally, consider taking tai chi, qi gong, or yoga classes to energize your energy centers, including your hand chakras.

Foot Chakras

The foot chakras are located in the middle of the soles of the feet. These energy centers are directly connected to the energy of the earth. Earth energy flows through the foot chakras and up to the root chakra. Our sense of stability and grounding is enhanced when our foot chakras are open to receiving this energy flow.

There are many ways to activate the foot chakras. Walking barefoot on the grass, sand, or dirt directly connected to the earth's energy awakens these energy centers. Foot massage or reflexology can also stimulate these energy centers. Exercises for your feet, such as pointing and flexing your feet, curling and extending your toes, and picking up an object such as a sock or dishcloth with your feet, are all excellent ways to open and balance your foot chakras while maintaining the health of your feet.

High Heart Chakra

This chakra is located in the thymus gland, between the heart and throat chakras. It connects these two energy centers enabling you to communicate honestly about your feelings and matters of the heart. It bridges the gap between our emotions and our intellect. The High Heart chakra assists with compassion and connection to others, setting the stage for positive social relationships. It also helps achieve understanding and forgiveness for yourself. Additionally, this energy center is connected to your immune system.

The High Heart chakra can be balanced by meditating on your heart center, spending time in nature, practicing random acts of kindness, and telling yourself daily, "I love you."

Chapter 20

The Microcosmic Orbit and the Violet Breath

The Violet Breath is a powerful technique used for healing and for passing attunements to others. To best understand how to perform the Violet Breath, we'll review each part of the process in detail. The terms used to describe the energy points and flow of energy pay homage to the origins of these practices, which are rooted in Taoist, Buddhist, and Traditional Chinese Medicine traditions. Don't let the new vocabulary overwhelm you; the concepts are similar to the chakra system that we explored in Reiki Level One.

Hara Line/Sushumna Nadi: This energy channel is the main energetic pathway in the human energy system. It can be visualized as a silver cord or column in the exact location of your spine. You can imagine this cord extending up to heaven through the crown of your head and extending down into the earth from your tailbone. Through the Hara line or sushumna nadi, we can draw cosmic energy down through the crown of our heads and pull earthly energy up through our root chakra.

Meridians/Nadis: The meridians or nadis are the energetic pathways that run throughout the human body. The stimulation of these energetic channels is used during acupuncture and acupressure practices. It is through these energetic highways that Reiki energy travels.

Dantian or Hara Center: The energy center is located at the lower belly and is home to the reservoir of ki, your personal life force energy.

Conception Vessel (Ren Mai): This meridian line runs down the front of the body, starting just below the eyes. This energy pathway travels around the mouth to the chest and abdomen before ending at the perineum. The energy associated with the Conception Vessel has a yin, passive, feminine quality.

The purpose of the Conception and Governor Vessels is to transport ki or life force energy to the major organs and to maintain the energetic balance within the body.

Governor Vessel (Du Mai): This meridian line runs up from the perineum to the tailbone traveling up the back body and ending at the back of the head. This energy pathway moves down the front of the face to the canine teeth of the upper jaw. The energy associated with the Governor Vessel has a yang, active, masculine quality.

The purpose of the Conception and Governor Vessels is to transport ki or life force energy to the major organs and to maintain the energetic balance within the body.

Hui Yin Point: The Hui Yin point is an energetic point located at your perineum. This vibrant energy center is where the Governor Vessel and Conception Vessel connect. During the Violet Breath process, the muscles surrounding the Hui Yin point are contracted, as if you were stopping the flow of urination. This contraction or lifting up of the pelvic floor muscles, known as mula bandha in yoga circles, prevents energy from leaking out of your energy field by way of the root chakra for the duration of the muscle contraction. This energy is instead directed upward from the root chakra toward the crown chakra.

Microcosmic Orbit: This practice has many variations, but all consist of visualization and circulating energy around our auric field. The Microcosmic Orbit creates a complete energy circle through the body by connecting the Conception and Governor Vessels, balancing our yin and yang energies. This technique enhances our connection to our own life force energy and assists with increasing our ability to receive and channel ki, which is a necessary component of passing Reiki attunements to others. This practice can be done every day as part of your meditation practice.

To practice the Microcosmic Orbit, contract the Hui Yin point as if you were restricting the flow of urination and place the tip of your tongue at the roof of your mouth behind the front teeth. These actions prevent energy from leaking through the root chakra and the crown chakra, allowing the ki to build within the subtle body. Next, imagine a ball of light at your Dantian, located at your lower belly. With each inhale, visualize the ball of light intensifying, and with each exhale, picture the ball of light becoming brighter. When you are ready to proceed, imagine the ball moving downward from the Dantian to the root chakra at your tailbone, then up the back body to the crown of your head. Pause the ball of light at the crown of your head before picturing it descending the front of your body until it returns to the Dantian. Pause before repeating the orbital cycle. The ball of light represents your life force energy, and this practice circulates your personal energy throughout your auric field.

An extension of the Microcosmic Orbit is the Macrocosmic Orbit, which extends the visualization to include your legs, feet, and arms. For this version, picture the ball of light at your Dantian traveling down to the root chakra where the ball of light splits into two balls of energy. Next, these two balls of energy descend the back of your thighs to the soles of your feet to each big toe. From that point, the balls of light travel up the inner thighs and back to the root chakra. Now, the ball of light ascends the spine until it reaches the shoulders, where it divides into two balls of light that travel down the inside of both arms to the palms of the hands to the middle fingers. Next, the balls of light travel up the front of the hands and both arms until the two balls of light merge into one at the shoulder blades. The ball of light then travels up the back of the neck to the crown of the head before descending the front body back to the Dantian. Always take a moment to ground your energy after performing the Micro- and Macrocosmic Orbit.

Kundalini Energy: Kundalini is a dynamic, powerful energy that coils around the root chakra at the base of the spine. The origins of the word *kundalini* is from the Sanskrit words *kund*, to burn, and *kunda*, to coil.[20] For most individuals, this energy remains untapped but can be awakened during certain spiritual practices, including yoga and meditation. The imagery associated with kundalini is a coiled serpent that, when awakened, rises from the root chakra and travels up the spine through all the chakras. This energy's awakening may feel like an electrical current, wave, or heat flash. Kundalini energy is closely related to spiritual growth and development.

Putting It All Together: The Violet Breath

The Violet Breath combines breath work, visualization, and the stimulation of meridian points for powerful results, including a more robust energy flow, a vibrant auric field, and the potential to release kundalini energy.

---

20. Willow Kumar, *Kundalini Awakening for Beginners: Activate Your Kundalini Energy and Increase Your Psychic Abilities with Yoga Breathing Exercises and Chakra Meditation Poses to Strengthen Your Body, Mind, and Soul* (Self-published, 2022), 7.

The color violet is associated with spiritual development and the frequency of higher love.[21] It is the color connected with the crown chakra and the wisdom of our higher self, the eternal aspect of our being not limited by our personal ego.

There are many different variations of the Violet Breath technique. Below is a simple one for you to try.

1. Contract the Hui Yin point as if you were restricting the flow of urination, and place the tip of your tongue on the roof of your mouth behind the teeth.

2. On your inhale, visualize drawing up red energy from the Earth through your root chakra and drawing down blue celestial energy from the heavens into your crown chakra. On your exhale, picture these two colors swirling within your auric field, creating a vibrant violet energy. Repeat this process several times until you feel your entire body fill with violet light.

3. Visualize this violet energy condensing into a violet ball of energy located at your Dantian (lower abdominal area). This violet ball of light descends the front of your body to the root chakra before traveling up your spine to the crown of your head in a circular motion. Repeat this visualization several times.

4. Visualize this healing ball of violet light moving towards your heart center and picture the Dai Ko Myo symbol in white light inside the purple mist.

5. If using the Violet Breath for healing sessions, you can energetically send the Dai Ko Myo symbol from your heart center through your hands for healing. If meditating with the violet breath, you can simply sit with the Dai Ko Myo symbol in your heart center. Using the Violet Breath during the attunement process, the Dai Ko Myo symbol is blown through the Reiki student's crown chakra.

There are many ways to use the power of the Violet Breath, including when passing Reiki attunements to others. The Violet Breath can be used during meditation sessions for spiritual growth and development or in Reiki self-healing treatments as a powerful way of clearing your own auric field and enhancing the effectiveness of your Reiki sessions. It is helpful to use the Violet Breath during Reiki sessions when you feel extra energy is needed or a concentration of Reiki energy needs to be sent to a particular area.

---

21. Richard Gerber, *A Practical Guide To Vibrational Medicine*, 244.

Chapter 21

Next Step: Intention Setting

Now, it's time to pause and reflect on the concepts of Reiki Level Three. In our goal-driven society, we often don't take the time to slow down and reflect on what we have learned before moving on to our next objective. When we pause, we can better assimilate the concepts and develop true mastery of the material. So, let's consider the fundamental concepts of Reiki Level Three.

- List the five main themes of Reiki Level Three that connect with you the most.
- List five topics that do not resonate with you at this time.
- List five topics that you wish to research further.
- Finally, reflect on where you envision your Reiki path leading. List your hopes, dreams, and wishes for your upcoming forty-day immersion experience.

Now it's time to craft your heartfelt intention for the upcoming forty days. Like your previous intentions, it should be based on your unique goals. In addition, you may consider developing a more profound understanding of the topics that appeal to you and an appreciation for those areas that do not interest you at this time. As a reminder, your heartfelt intention assists us with aligning our daily actions with our long-term goals and desires.

Sample Heartfelt Intention

I, [your name], agree to follow the daily practices in these pages, including meditation, journaling, and self-healing, for a minimum of forty days. I will be open to developing a deeper understanding of the Reiki symbols of Reiki Level Three and how to use these powerful symbols. Although I do not currently connect to modern Reiki symbols, I will have an open mind about using these symbols for self-healing to explore their potential. I will say *yes* to activities, choices, and thoughts that align with my goals of developing mastery of Reiki as a healing modality for my own self-healing and so that I can be of service to others.

Today, with a grateful heart for my unique journey, I am ready to commit myself to my further study of Reiki healing, my own self-exploration, and the integration of Reiki energy into my daily life.

Signed: _____

Date: _____

Craft your heartfelt intention in your Reiki journal.

Part 6

Reiki Forty-Day Immersion Experience: Reiki Mastery

Reiki Exploration Day 1

Daily Intention Review

With a grateful heart for your dedication to your growth as a Reiki healer, read out loud your heartfelt intention.

Dai Ko Myo: The Master Symbol and Enlightenment (Focus on Form)

Enlightenment is the realization of spiritual knowledge and has been the ultimate goal of spiritual seekers and religions throughout time and across cultures. There are numerous names for enlightenment: illumination, nirvana, self-realization, the promised land, or entering the kingdom within.[22] It is said that attaining enlightenment is the highest pursuit one can have during this lifetime.

The Master symbol, Dai Ko Myo, may be translated as "Great Enlightenment" or "Bright Shining Light." The primary purpose of this symbol is for spiritual healing, and it represents a method of direct, divine connection to the Source. When we are connected to the Source, enlightenment is possible. This connection to the Divine can assist with self-actualization, personal growth, understanding of our purpose, and spiritual development.

There are two forms of this symbol that you may wish to use in your practice. The first is the traditional symbol which has roots in Japan. The non-traditional symbol has origins in Tibet and is used as a substitute for the original version. Experiment to see which symbol provides the best results for you.

Dai Ko Myo Meditation Practice

To form a deep understanding of the power of the Dai Ko Myo symbol, let's first consider the traditional symbol's shape. Set the intention to create a deep connection to the power of the Dai Ko Myo symbol. Then, draw the Dai Ko Myo symbol seven times as accurately as possible. Scan the images you created and pick the one you are most drawn to working with for your meditation. Next, consider the image you have drawn. Does this image speak to you in some way? Does it stir up any emotions, memories, or random thoughts?

---

22. Eknath Easwaran, *Meditations: A Simple Eight-Point Program for Translating Spiritual Ideas into Daily Life* (Tomales, CA), 28.

Begin your meditation practice by setting a five-minute timer and finding a comfortable seated position. Then, take a few centering breaths, and with a soft gaze on the Dai Ko Myo image, invite your mind to focus on the symbol. If your mind wanders during this practice, simply re-focus your attention on the Dai Ko Myo symbol. After your meditation, sit for a moment or two to absorb the benefits of the practice.

If you'd like to experiment with the non-traditional Master symbol, repeat this exercise and compare your results.

Journaling Practice

Journal your direct experience of your meditation. Did drawing the Dai Ko Myo symbol multiple times awaken any new insights? How did you feel during this part of the practice? Did it stir up emotions or random thoughts? What insights, if any, did you receive during your meditation? How might you use this more profound awareness of the Master symbol during your Reiki healing sessions?

Reiki Exploration Day 2

Daily Intention Review

Take several deep breaths and allow your mind to settle. From this place of serenity, read your heartfelt intention out loud.

Dai Ko Myo: The Master Symbol (Focus on Force)

As a reminder, the Reiki symbols' force, or dynamic energy, is initially activated during the Reiki attunement process. It is then turned on when you draw the character and recite its name, "Dai Ko Myo," (pronounced *dye-koh-myoh*) three times silently or out loud.

The force behind the Dai Ko Myo is etheric, purifying, spiritual, and deeply healing. This subtle energy is directed based on your intervention and focus. Suggested uses for the Dai Ko Myo symbol are listed here, but the opportunities to use this symbol are only limited by your imagination.

✿ Spiritual Healing

- Replacement for the three Reiki Level Two symbols
- Healing the spiritual component of a physical, emotional, or mental illness

- Increases the power and effectiveness of the other Reiki symbols
- Clearing of karmic-related issues and karmic debt
- Assists with enlightenment
- Assists with meditation
- Assists with psychic and intuitive development
- Assists with sealing in Reiki energy at the close of a Reiki session
- Cleanses crystals
- Increases the benefits of medications, herbs, flower essences, etc.
- Purifies the energy of food and drink
- Passing Reiki attunements to others

Dai Ko Myo Chanting Practice

Continuing our journey to form a deep connection to the power of the Dai Ko Myo symbol, we will use the power of intonation or vibration. By chanting the symbol's name, we can tap into the essence of the symbol and begin to experience the potential of its power.

Find a comfortable seated position and set the intention to connect to the energy of the Dai Ko Myo symbol. Spend a few moments centering yourself by taking a few deep breaths. Set a five-minute timer and begin slowly, mindfully repeating "Dai Ko Myo" aloud. At the end of your chanting practice, sit for a few moments to observe any after-effects you may experience.

Journaling Practice

Describe your direct experience of your chanting practice. What effects did this practice have on you physically, emotionally, mentally, and energetically? What, if any, shifts in energy occurred in your physical location? Did you receive any insights regarding the potential of this symbol's power? How might you use these insights in your Reiki healing sessions?

Reiki Exploration Day 3

Daily Intention Review

Take a few cleansing breaths and connect with your soul's purpose. When you are ready, read your heartfelt intention out loud.

The Higher Self and the Dai Ko Myo Symbol

Consider the concept of your higher self. What does this term mean to you? Your higher self isn't separate from you; it's the part of your being that is eternal in nature and closely connected to the Divine. The higher self is perfectly complete and has access to divine knowledge and profound understanding.

When we connect to our higher self, we understand our true nature and relationship to the cosmos. We know our divine purpose and make decisions and take action from this place of inner wisdom.

The Dai Ko Myo symbol can help us connect to our higher self. When using Dai Ko Myo in a healing session, you do not need to use the three symbols from Reiki Level Two. If using Dai Ko Myo, draw it over your healing participant's body and tap the symbol into your healing participant three times with your index and middle fingers.

Dai Ko Myo Self-Healing Practice

Find a comfortable seated position and settle in for a few moments. Set a timer for five minutes, the duration of your targeted self-healing session today. Take a complete inventory of yourself at this moment in time. Notice how you feel physically, emotionally, mentally, energetically, and spiritually.

Turn on Reiki using your unique method of connection and feel the infusion of Reiki energy into your being. Set your personal healing intention to connect with your higher self and receive deep spiritual healing. Release your expectations about Dai Ko Myo and allow your experience to unfold.

Using the traditional Dai Ko Myo symbol or the Tibetan variation, begin your Reiki healing session.

After your healing session, take a few moments to scan your body and observe any subtle shifts of energy that may have occurred.

Journaling Practice

Journal your direct experience of your self-healing session. What was your experience using only the Dai Ko Myo symbol during your self-healing practice? What shifts in energy did you experience physically, emotionally, mentally, and energetically? Did you experience a connection to your higher self or sense a deeper spiritual connection forming? If so, describe that experience. How might this information be helpful in future Reiki healing sessions?

Reiki Exploration Day 4

Daily Intention Review

As a reminder of why you've embarked on this journey of healing, read out loud your heartfelt intention.

Raku: The Grounding Symbol (Focus on Form)

Consider the zigzag shape of the Raku symbol, which resembles a flash of lightning. The image of a lightning bolt may bring to mind memories of Harry Potter and his adventures, but there is an ancient, rich symbolism associated with lightning. According to *An Illustrated Encyclopedia of Traditional Symbols*, lightning has been associated with the following:

- Spiritual illumination
- Enlightenment
- Revelation
- Descent of power
- Destruction of ignorance

Similar to the sun's power, the lightning bolt is described as both destructive and fertilizing.[23] Simply put, it is the descent of fire from the heavens. Lightning is a sign of power and strength, the manifestation of an energy that restores equilibrium.[24]

---

23. Cooper, *An Illustrated Encyclopedia of Traditional Symbols*, 97.
24. Chevalier and Gheerbrant, *Dictionary of Symbols*, 607.

Raku Meditation Practice

To begin our journey to form a profound understanding of the power of the Raku symbol, we will consider its shape. Set the intention to develop a deep connection to the essence of this symbol. Then, draw the Raku symbol seven times as accurately as you can. Scan what you've created and pick the one you are most drawn to working with for your meditation. Next, consider the image you have drawn. Does it speak to you in any way or stir up any emotions, memories, or random thoughts?

To begin your meditation practice, set a timer for five minutes and find a comfortable seated position. Take a few centering breaths, and with a soft gaze on the Raku image, invite your mind to focus on the symbol. If your mind wanders during this practice, simply refocus your attention on the symbol. At the conclusion of your meditation, sit for a moment or two to absorb the benefits of the practice.

Journaling Practice

Journal your direct experience of your meditation. Did drawing the Raku symbol multiple times awaken any new insights? How did you feel during this part of the practice? Did you experience any shifts in your emotional state or notice random thoughts? What insights, if any, did you receive during your meditation? How might you use this more profound awareness of the Raku symbol in future Reiki healing sessions?

Reiki Exploration Day 5

Daily Intention Review

Consider your goals and desires for continuing your study of Reiki healing. When you are ready, read your heartfelt intention out loud.

Raku: The Grounding Symbol (Focus on Force)

As a reminder, the Reiki symbols' force, or dynamic energy, is initially activated during the Reiki attunement process. It is then "turned on" when you draw the symbol and recite its name three times silently or out loud.

The force behind the Raku is grounding and separating.

Suggested uses for the Raku symbol appear in the following list, though it's typically used at the close of a Reiki session and after the attunement process. I have also used it to assist with severing energetic cords, the invisible etheric cords of connection between people. Feel free to experiment with ways to use this symbol's power.

- To sever the energetic connection between healer and healing participant at the end of a Reiki session
- To assist with grounding of Reiki energy
- To cut energy cords

Raku Chanting Practice

Continuing our journey to form a deep connection to the power of the Raku symbol, we will use the power of intonation or vibration. By chanting the name of the symbol, Raku (pronounced *rah-koo*), we can tap into the essence of the symbol and begin to experience the potential of the symbol's power.

Begin your chanting practice by silencing your cell phone and finding a comfortable seated position. Set the intention to connect to the energy of the Raku symbol. Spend a minute or two centering yourself by taking a few deep breaths. Set a timer for five minutes and slowly, mindfully repeat the word "Raku" aloud, allowing the vibrations of the word to wash over you. At the end of your chanting practice, sit for a few moments observing any after-effects you may experience.

Journaling Practice

Describe your direct experience of your chanting practice. What effects did this practice have on you physically, emotionally, mentally, and energetically? Did you experience any intuitive hits regarding potential uses for the force behind the Raku symbol? How might you use these insights in your Reiki healing sessions?

Reiki Exploration Day 6

Daily Intention Review

Appreciate your dedication and commitment to your development as a Reiki healer. Recommit yourself to your healing path by stating your heartfelt intention aloud.

Severing Connections and the Raku Symbol

During Reiki healing sessions and when performing Reiki attunements on others, there can be a merging of auric fields between healer and receiver. A vast amount of valuable psychic information can be gained when this entwining of energies occurs, which can assist with the healing process. However, at the session's completion or the end of the attunement, these attachments must be severed to maintain the energetic well-being of the healer. The Raku symbol is the tool available to us to cut these energetic connections.

I have found another practical use for the Raku symbol—cutting energetic cords. Energetic cords are the invisible attachments that link us to others in our lives. You can think of these cords as energetic connections or as emotional ties. I visualize them as colorful streams of energy.

Sometimes these connections are no longer beneficial, and some ties might even be toxic in nature. For example, consider the painful relationships you might have in your life, such as a relationship with a former spouse or partner, a difficult coworker, or a destructive friendship. The Raku symbol, along with your intention, can be used to sever the connections with these unhealthy relationships and allow for personal healing to occur.

Raku Cord-Cutting Practice

Find a comfortable seated position and settle in for a few moments. Set a timer for five minutes, the duration of your targeted self-healing session today. Then, bring to mind a relationship past or present that causes you emotional pain or drains your energy.

Turn on Reiki using your unique method of connection and feel the infusion of Reiki energy into your being. Set your personal healing intention to sever the energetic connection with this toxic relationship and restore energetic balance.

Now picture in your mind's eye the person from whom you are ready to sever your energetic connection. Next, scan your physical body, front and back, to intuitively find where the energetic cord tying you to the person exists. Finally, picture this cord connecting you with the other person.

Using the Raku symbol, visualize cutting the energetic cord. Then imagine the place in your body where the energetic cord is attached and fill it with white light as the remaining attachment dissolves completely from your body. Now, use the Dai Ko Myo symbol to send healing energy to the place where the attachment was located. After your healing session, take a few moments to notice any shifts in energy that may have occurred.

Journaling Practice

Journal your direct experience of your cord-cutting session. What was your experience using the Raku symbol to cut the energetic cord? What was your experience using the Dai Ko Myo to heal the place of attachment? What sensations did you experience physically, emotionally, mentally, and energetically? How might this information be beneficial in future Reiki healing sessions?

Reiki Exploration Day 7

Daily Intention Review

Reflect on the progress you are making on your journey of healing and self-discovery. When you are ready, recite out loud your heartfelt intention.

Nin Giz Zida: The Serpent of Fire Symbol (Focus on Form)

This symbol is related to kundalini energy, the sleeping serpent coiled at the root chakra located at your tailbone. This power lies dormant, waiting to be awakened, sparking radical spiritual growth and development.

The serpent, or snake, has a rich tradition in the history of medicine and the healing arts. The symbol of two serpents intertwining a staff is the symbol of the caduceus, often referred to as the staff of Hermes. This symbol has a rich history and was carried by messengers during ancient times as a symbol of peace and protection. Its many correspondences include its association with modern medicine, the wand symbolizing power, the wings representing transcendence, and the two serpents of healing and poison, sickness and wellness.[25] The caduceus is similar to the staff held by Asclepius, the Greek god of medicine. Asclepius's staff is a long rod with one snake wrapping around the length of the staff. The serpent may invoke fear in many, but it symbolizes healing, immortality, transformation, and the life-death-rebirth cycle. Consider the shape of the symbol. What does it represent to you?

The shape first reminded me of a snake, but after reflection, I developed a different connection to this powerful symbol: The top line suggests the great abyss that separates the known—or our limited understanding of our world—from the unknown, the highest levels of the Divine. The descending motion of the serpent speaks to me about divine energy and inspiration moving from the heavens into the mundane world. The three

25. Cooper, *An Illustrated Encyclopedia of Traditional Symbols*, 28.

coils of the spiral represent the kundalini energy and the potential for metamorphosis. In summary, I interpret this symbol as calling down divine energies to assist with awakening our kundalini energy so we can actively participate in our personal transformational process and assist others with their own metamorphosis.

Nin Giz Zida: The Serpent of Fire Meditation Practice

To assist with forming a deep connection to the Nin Giz Zida symbol, consider the shape of the symbol. Next, set the intention to develop a personal understanding of the power of the Serpent of Fire symbol. When you feel ready, draw the Nin Giz Zida symbol seven times as accurately as you can.

Look over the images you created and pick the one you are most drawn to working with for your meditation. Next, consider the image you have drawn. Does this image speak to you in some way? Does it stir up any emotions, memories, or random thoughts?

Begin your meditation practice by setting a five-minute timer and finding a comfortable seated position. Take a few centering breaths and with a soft gaze on the Serpent of Fire image, invite your mind to focus on the symbol. If your mind wanders during this practice, re-focus your attention on the Nin Giz Zida symbol.

After your meditation, sit for a moment or two to absorb the benefits of the practice.

Journaling Practice

Journal your direct experience of your meditation. Did drawing the Nin Giz Zida symbol multiple times awaken any new insights? How did you feel during this part of the practice? Did it awaken any emotions or random thoughts? What insights, if any, did you receive during your meditation? How might you use this more profound awareness of the Fire Serpent symbol in future Reiki healing sessions?

Reiki Exploration Day 8

Daily Intention Review

Reflect on your deepening connection to Reiki energy. When you feel ready, read your heartfelt intention out loud.

Nin Giz Zida: The Serpent of Fire Symbol (Focus on Force)

As a reminder, the Reiki symbols' force, or dynamic energy, is initially activated during the Reiki attunement process. It is then "turned on" when you draw and recite the name of the Fire Serpent symbol, "Nin Giz Zida," three times silently or out loud.

The force behind Nin Giz Zida, the Fire Serpent symbol, is electric, energizing, and active. This subtle energy is directed based on your intervention and focus. Here are some uses for the Serpent of Fire symbol:

- During the Reiki attunement process
- To align the chakras
- To increase the subtle energy within the body
- To increase vitality or energy
- To increase metabolism and your inner fire
- To assist with the awakening of kundalini energy

Nin Giz Zida Chanting Practice

Continuing our journey to cultivate a deep understanding of the power of the Fire Serpent symbol, we will use the power of intonation or vibration. By chanting Nin Giz Zida (pronounced *nin-geez-zee-dah*), we can tap into the essence of the symbol and begin to experience the potential of the symbol's power.

Begin your chanting practice by finding a comfortable seated position and silencing your cell phone. Set the intention to connect to the energy of the Fire Serpent symbol. Spend a few moments centering yourself by taking a few deep breaths. Set a five-minute timer and begin slowly, mindfully repeating "Nin Giz Zida" aloud. At the end of your chanting practice, sit for a few moments observing any after-effects you may experience.

Journaling Practice

Describe your direct experience of your chanting practice. What effects did this practice have on you physically, emotionally, mentally, and energetically? Did you notice any shifts in energy within your chakras? Did you feel any physical sensations, such as increased heat or vitality? Did you develop a deeper awareness of the power behind the Fire Serpent symbol? How might you use these insights during your Reiki healing sessions?

Reiki Exploration Day 9

Daily Intention Review

Take a moment to reflect on your heartfelt intention and how your healing practice has led to personal growth and expansion. Then, when you are ready, read your heartfelt intention aloud with an appreciation for your evolution as a healer.

Nin Giz Zida: the Serpent of Fire Symbol (Focus on Healing)

Snakes or serpents continue to grow throughout their lifetimes. To accommodate this growth process, the outside layer of scales and skin is shed during a process lasting several days. The rich symbolism of regeneration and rebirth is significant for healing.

Consider the unhealthy lifestyle choices and modes of behavior that can lead to illness. If these habits and practices were "shed," we could experience a sense of rebirth and revitalization as we embrace renewed health and well-being. Moreover, we can actively engage in removing energetic blockages and negative or limiting thought patterns to allow for new personal growth. As a result, we could undergo a dramatic transformation in our energetic and physical bodies.

Fortunately, using Reiki healing techniques, we have the tools available to assist us in pursuing healing on all levels of our being. As we continue to practice Reiki daily, the potential for regeneration, rebirth, and greater health is within our reach.

Nin Giz Zida: Serpent of Fire Healing Session

Find a comfortable seated position, settle in for a few moments, and silence your cell phone. Consider your chakras from your root chakra to your crown chakra. Do a self-assessment on each of these energy centers using your intuition or a pendulum. Write down whether each energy center is open, blocked, underperforming, or overactive. Also, write down in your Reiki journal your personal healing goal for each energy vortex.

Set a timer for ten minutes, the length of today's targeted self-healing session. Turn on Reiki using your unique method of connection and feel the infusion of Reiki energy into your being. Set your healing intention to balance and heal your chakras. Release your expectations about the Fire Serpent symbol and allow your experience to unfold.

Draw the Fire Serpent symbol over your entire being, starting at the crown of your head and ending with the spiral at your root chakra, and begin your Reiki self-healing session.

After your healing session, take a few moments to scan your energy centers and observe any subtle shifts of energy that may have occurred.

Journaling Practice

Journal your direct experience of your self-healing session. What was your experience using the Fire Serpent symbol during your self-healing practice? What was the state of each chakra before the healing session? How did each of your chakras respond to your Reiki treatment? Did you receive any insight regarding the potential for healing using the Fire Serpent symbol? How might this information be beneficial in future Reiki healing sessions?

Reiki Exploration Day 10

Daily Intention Review

You are ten days into your second healing immersion. Congratulations! Take a moment to connect with your heartfelt intention. Read it aloud. Does it still resonate with you? Does it still reflect your goals for your Reiki journey? If it feels appropriate, feel free to modify or reword your intention.

Antahkarana

This symbol is associated with amplification and focus. Although not used directly in Reiki healing sessions, the symbol can be placed under the Reiki healing table or displayed in your healing space to create a dynamic environment for healing to take place. Meditating upon the Antahkarana symbol creates a connection between the brain and the crown chakra, facilitating a relationship to divine energies and accessing powerful insights. It also automatically starts the Microcosmic Orbit, healing and energizing your auric field and the chakras.

Consider the shape of the symbol. What does it represent to you? When I reflect on the shape, I see the structure of a cube and sense dynamic movement in the form of a triskele. The symbol of a triskele is an ancient one found in many cultures. According to *An Illustrated Encyclopedia of Traditional Symbols*, the triskele may represent the movements of the sun as it rises, reaches its zenith, and sets. It may also relate to the lunar phases representing the renewal of life.[26] Both meanings reference divine movement and cosmic energies.

---

26. Cooper, *An Illustrated Encyclopedia of Traditional Symbols*, 181.

Antahkarana Meditation Practice

To assist with forming a deep connection to the Antahkarana symbol, start by considering the shape of the symbol. Next, set the intention to create a personal understanding of the power of the Antahkarana symbol. When you feel ready, draw the Antahkarana symbol seven times as accurately as you can.

Look over the images you created and pick the one you are most drawn to working with for your meditation. Next, consider the image you have drawn. Does this image speak to you in some way? Does it stir up any emotions, memories, or random thoughts?

To begin your meditation practice, set a timer for five minutes and find a comfortable seated position. Then take a few centering breaths, and with a soft gaze on the Antahkarana image, invite your mind to focus on the symbol. If your mind wanders during this practice, re-focus your attention on the Antahkarana symbol. After your meditation, sit for a moment or two to absorb the benefits of the practice.

Journaling Practice

Journal your direct experience of your meditation. Did drawing the Antahkarana symbol multiple times awaken any new insights? How did you feel during this part of the practice? Did it awaken any emotions or random thoughts? What insights, if any, did you receive during your meditation? How might you use this more profound awareness of Antahkarana in your Reiki healing sessions?

Reiki Exploration Day 11

Daily Intention Review

Take a few moments to reflect on your goals and desires as a Reiki healer. When ready, read your heartfelt intention out loud.

Contemporary Reiki Symbols: Embracing the New

Without judgment, reflect on your unique approach to life. For example, would you consider yourself a traditionalist who prefers the established path, or are you more of a pioneer who embraces change at every turn? Of course, there are benefits and drawbacks to both approaches to life.

Traditionalists may be overly focused on past practices and shun modern techniques simply due to their newness. However, it can be equally problematic to ignore proven methods and traditions, disregarding them as antiquated and having no benefits in today's modern world.

I prefer a balanced approach to life. I believe in understanding the historical context in which practices and ideas originated, but I also feel strongly that knowledge isn't static. As we evolve as individuals and as a collective, new healing modalities emerge and older healing traditions may be reinterpreted for modern society.

Whatever your personal preference is, taking the time and energy to understand and integrate both the traditional and contemporary approaches to healing and the symbols used in healing modalities enables and empowers you to become a well-balanced healer.

Non-Traditional Symbol Meditation and Self-Healing Practice

Select a symbol from the non-traditional healing symbols. Draw the image and sit with it for a few moments while noticing your gut reaction to the symbol: How does it speak to you?

Now set a timer for five minutes and turn off your cell phone. Sit in a comfortable position and settle in for a few moments. Turn on Reiki and feel the infusion of Reiki energy into your being. Finally, begin your self-healing session by incorporating the new symbol into your treatment. At the conclusion of your self-healing session, sit for a moment or two to absorb the benefits of the practice.

Journaling Practice

Journal your direct experience of your self-healing session using a modern Reiki symbol. What was your reason for selecting this symbol? Did it call to you in some way? Did it awaken any emotions or random thoughts as you drew the symbol? What was your direct experience of your self-healing session using this new Reiki symbol? Did you notice any energetic changes or physical sensations? How might you use the insights you received in future Reiki healing sessions?

Reiki Exploration Day 12

Daily Intention Review

Take a few deep breaths and connect to the energies of both the heavens and the earth. Then, from this place of awareness, state your heartfelt intention aloud.

Sushumna Nadi: The Central Channel

A nadi is the name for an energetic pathway or channel within the subtle body. The primary energetic pathway is the sushumna nadi (sometimes called the Hara line). This channel begins at the root chakra at your tailbone and travels up your spine to the crown of your head. The seven main chakras are located along this energetic pathway.

The role of the sushumna nadi is distributing the flow of life force energy throughout the subtle body. It is also the line of connection between the earth and the heavens allowing us to draw wisdom and energy from both. When kundalini energy rises from the root chakra up the spine, it travels along the sushumna nadi, often referred to as the path to enlightenment.

Clearing the Central Channel Practice

Find a comfortable seated position and settle in for a few moments. Silence your cell phone.

Set a timer for five minutes and bring your awareness to your spine. Sit up straight with your head held in a neutral position.

Close your eyes and invite your awareness to descend to your root chakra at your tailbone. Imagine a brilliant ball of healing white light there. On the inhale, picture this healing ball of white light rising up your spine through the seven main chakras to the crown of your head. On the exhale, visualize that healing ball of light descending down to your tailbone. Repeat this process for the duration of your meditation practice.

After your meditation, take a few moments to notice any shifts in energy that may have occurred.

Journaling Practice

Journal your direct experience of your meditation practice. For example, were you able to connect to the sushumna nadi? What sensations did you experience physically, emotionally, mentally, and energetically? Did you receive any insights during this practice? How might this information be useful in Reiki healing sessions?

Reiki Exploration Day 13

Daily Intention Review

Take a moment to connect with Mother Earth's nurturing energies. From this place of warmth and support, recite your heartfelt intention out loud.

Earth Star Chakra

The Earth Star chakra, located approximately six to twelve inches below your feet, is considered a sub-personal energy center, since it exists below the physical body. Its color is a rich, earthy brown, with specks of deep red or black, reflecting its grounding properties. In addition to establishing and maintaining a connection to our home planet, this energy vortex assists with releasing negative or excess energy back into the earth, where these energies can be transmuted and recycled. You can also tap into this chakra to draw up the earth's healing energy whenever you feel depleted or need an energy boost.

Let's explore your connection to your own Earth Star chakra. Consider these statements:

- "I feel a deep connection to Mother Earth."
- "I am fascinated by my ancestry and family tree."
- "I quickly release negative or excess energy."
- "I value the planet and am attracted to environmental causes."
- "I love animals and feel connected to all the creatures on this planet."
- "I often act from a state of mental and emotional stability."
- "I consider myself deeply grounded."

If you noticed a statement does not feel true for you now, consider paying extra attention to your Earth Star chakra. In addition to Reiki self-healing sessions and other energetic healing treatments, there are many methods of balancing this energy center. You can explore the suggestions here for ways to support your Earth Star chakra.

❀ Affirmations

- "I am nurtured and supported by Mother Earth."
- "I easily release negative energies back to Mother Earth where they can be transmuted into something positive."
- "I am connected to my heritage and past generations."

Consider exploring the various metaphysical tools available to assist you with balancing and strengthening your Earth Star chakra. Here are some recommendations.

🪷 *Essential Oils*

- Cypress
- Patchouli
- Myrrh
- Hematite
- Red jasper
- Black kyanite

Earth Star Chakra Self-Healing Session

Find a comfortable seated position and settle in for a few moments. Set a timer for five minutes, the duration of your targeted self-healing session today.

Take a complete inventory of yourself at this moment in time. Notice how you feel physically, emotionally, mentally, energetically, and spiritually. Then, bring your awareness to your Earth Star chakra, located approximately six to twelve inches below your feet.

Turn on Reiki using your unique method of connection and feel the infusion of Reiki energy into your being. Set your intention to perform Reiki healing on your Earth Star chakra.

With your intuition to guide you, use the self-healing hand positions and the Reiki symbols that resonate with you, being sure to spend time healing your Earth Star chakra. After your healing session, take a few moments to scan your body and observe any subtle shifts of energy that may have occurred.

Journaling Practice

Consider your Earth Star chakra. Describe your connection to this energy center. How does your Earth Star chakra currently function? What color do you intuitively feel reflects the energy of your Earth Star chakra? Did you have any random thoughts, emotions, or sensations during your healing session? Did an energy shift occur? Did you receive insights regarding your Earth Star chakra? How might this information be helpful in future Reiki healing sessions?

Reiki Exploration Day 14

Daily Intention Review

Take a few deep breaths and consider your relationship to the divine feminine and the feminine qualities within yourself. From this place of honoring the feminine aspects of your own nature, state aloud your heartfelt intention.

Ida Nadi and Conception Vessel: The Divine Feminine

The ida nadi is the energy channel related to our feminine energies. This energy channel begins below the root chakra and ends at the left nostril. The ida nadi intersects with its counterpart, the pingala nadi, between the chakras centers by crisscrossing around the central channel (the sushumna nadi) in a figure-eight pattern. The color associated with the ida nadi is yellow, and its planetary correspondence is the moon.

The ida nadi is responsible for our flow of feminine energies related to receptivity, intuition, creativity, and understanding. It is the yin of the yin/yang symbol. It is the lunar energies that balance the solar aspects. These feminine energies are associated with the left side of the body and the right hemisphere of the brain.

The principle of the divine feminine can also be found in the Conception Vessel, the meridian or energy pathway responsible for the distribution of ki or life force energy within the body as it relates to the feminine; yin energies are passive, receptive, and lunar in nature. Staring just below the eyes, this meridian line travels down the front of the body, circles around the mouth to the chest and abdomen, and ends at the Hui Yin point at the perineum.

In our society, we have not placed a high value on the feminine aspects of ourselves. As a result, many individuals have lost their connection to the divine feminine, the manifestation of the feminine energies of the cosmos. We can reestablish this divine connection by tapping into and cultivating our own divine feminine energies.

Activating Your Divine Feminine Energies

Find a comfortable seated position and settle in for a few moments. Silence your cell phone. Set a timer for five minutes and bring your awareness to the left side of your body, your feminine side. Sit up tall with your head held in a neutral position.

Gently close your eyes and spread the fingers on your right hand. Using your thumb, gently close off your right nostril and breath slowly using only your left nostril. Try keeping your inhales and exhales the same length, promoting a calm, focused mind. This breathing technique activates your feminine lunar energies and stimulates the ida nadi. After your meditation, take a few moments to notice any subtle shifts in energy that may have occurred.

Journaling Practice

Journal your direct experience of your meditation practice. What is your relationship with your feminine qualities? Were you able to connect to the ida nadi? What sensations did you experience physically, emotionally, mentally, and energetically? Did you receive any insights during this practice? How might this information be useful in Reiki healing sessions?

Reiki Exploration Day 15

Daily Intention Review

Take a few deep breaths and consider your relationship to the divine masculine and masculine qualities within yourself. From this place of honoring the masculine aspects of your own nature, state aloud your heartfelt intention.

Pingala Nadi and Governor Vessel: The Divine Masculine

The pingala nadi is the energy channel related to our masculine energies. The color associated with this nadi is red, and its planetary correspondence is the sun. This energy channel begins below the root chakra and ends at the right nostril. The pingala nadi intersects with its counterpart, the ida nadi, between the chakras centers by crisscrossing around the central channel, the sushumna nadi, in a figure-eight pattern.

The pingala nadi is responsible for our flow of masculine energies related to action, force, vitality, logic, and knowledge. It is the yang of the yin/yang symbol. It is the solar energies that balance the lunar qualities. These masculine energies are associated with the right side of the body and the left hemisphere of the brain.

The concept of the divine masculine can also be found in the Governor Vessel, the meridian or energy pathway responsible for the distribution of ki within the body as it relates to the masculine, yang energies that are active, stimulating, and solar in nature. This meridian line travels up the Hui Yin point from the perineum to the tailbone and up the back body to the top of the head. It then descends down the front of the face to the canine teeth in the upper jaw.

Our culture has placed a high value on masculine qualities, especially as they are linked to productivity, domination, and the cultivation of power. These are not bad or evil qualities, but if they are left unchecked, the consequences can be devastating. The lack of feminine energies has led to imbalances across society in politics, the workplace, and relationships. By achieving balance internally between our divine masculine and divine feminine qualities, we can assist with healing these energies in the larger world.

Activating Your Divine Masculine Energies

Find a comfortable seated position and settle in for a few moments. Silence your cell phone. Set a timer for five minutes and bring your awareness to the right side of your body, your masculine side. Sit up tall with your head held in a neutral position.

Gently close your eyes and spread the fingers on your left hand. Using your thumb, gently close off your left nostril and breath slowly using only your right nostril. Try keeping your inhales and exhales the same length to promote a calm, focused mind. This breathing technique activates your masculine solar energies and stimulates the pingala nadi.

After your meditation, take a few moments to notice any changes in energy that may have occurred.

Journaling Practice

Journal your direct experience of your meditation practice. What is your relationship to your masculine qualities? Were you able to connect to the pingala nadi? What sensations did you experience physically, emotionally, mentally, and energetically? Did you receive any insights during this practice? How might this information be useful in Reiki healing sessions?

Reiki Exploration Day 16

Daily Intention Review

Connect with your purpose for studying Reiki healing. From this place of dedication to your healing path, recite your heartfelt intention out loud.

Soul Star Chakra

The Soul Star chakra is a transpersonal energy center located approximately six to twelve inches above your head within your auric field. It is referred to as the seat of the soul. Through this energy center, we can access the Divine, the Akashic Records, our past lives, and our purpose for this incarnation on planet Earth.

Let's explore your connection to your own Soul Star chakra. Consider the statements below:

- "I am open to receiving inspiration from the Divine."
- "I am connected to my soul's purpose."
- "I feel a connection to the consciousness of the universe."
- "I am connected to my higher self and open to receiving its guidance."
- "I am living an authentic life."

If you notice a statement does not feel true for you now, consider paying extra attention to your Soul Star chakra. In addition to Reiki self-healing sessions and other energetic healing treatments, there are many methods of balancing this energy center. You can explore the suggestions below for ways to support this energy center.

Affirmations

- "I honor my soul's journey."
- "I am open to receive guidance from my higher self."
- "I am living an authentic life in alignment with my soul's purpose."

Consider exploring the various metaphysical tools available to assist you with balancing and strengthening your Soul Star chakra. Here are some recommendations.

Essential Oils

- Neroli
- Frankincense
- Jasmine

Crystals

- Selenite
- Clear quartz
- Lithium quartz

Soul Star Chakra Self-Healing Session

Find a comfortable seated position and settle in for a few moments. Set a timer for five minutes, the duration of your targeted self-healing session today. Take a complete inventory of yourself at this moment in time. Notice how you feel physically, emotionally, mentally, energetically, and spiritually. Then, connect to your Soul Star chakra, located approximately six to twelve inches above your head.

Turn on Reiki using your unique method of connection and feel the infusion of Reiki energy into your being. Set your intention to perform Reiki healing on your Soul Star chakra. Intuitively use the self-healing hand positions and the Reiki symbols that resonate with you, but spend time healing your Soul Star chakra. After your healing session, take a few moments to scan your body and observe any subtle shifts of energy that may have occurred.

Journaling Practice

Journal your direct experience of your self-healing session. Consider your Soul Star chakra. Describe your connection to this energy center. How does your Soul Star chakra currently function? Using your intuition, what color would best describe your Soul Star energy center? Did you experience any random thoughts, emotions, or sensations during your healing session? Did any shifts in energy occur during your self-healing session? Did you receive insights regarding your Soul Star chakra? How might this information be helpful in future Reiki healing sessions?

Reiki Exploration Day 17

Daily Intention Review

Bring your awareness to your Dantian, your Hara center, located at your lower belly. Recite aloud your heartfelt intention from this place of connection to your own life force energy.

The Dantian and the Hara Center

Located in the lower abdominal region, the energy center referred to as the Dantian or Hara center is an important energy center used in Reiki, especially when passing Reiki attunements to others. Although the Dantian or Hara center are from two complementary Eastern traditions, for our purposes as Reiki healers, the essence of this energy center as the reservoir of our own life force energy remains consistent whether you refer to it as the Dantian or the Hara center.

The Hara center or Dantian is the center of the ki or chi body and is the gateway to our internal ocean of energy and personal vitality. *Chi* or *ki* are often translated into English as "energy," "breath," "air," "vital essence," or the "activating energy of the universe."[27] This energy permeates all beings and is distributed throughout the body through the meridians or nadis. Reiki energy also uses these energetic pathways.

By accessing our own Dantian or Hara center, we can better understand and regulate our own energetic body and be more powerful channels for Reiki energy as we heal and pass attunements on to others.

Connecting with Your Dantian or Hara Center

Find a comfortable seated position, silence your cell phone, and settle in for a few moments. Set a timer for five minutes and bring your awareness to your lower abdominal region. Close your eyes and place both hands on your lower belly, right below your navel. Bring to mind your own Dantian or Hara center, the reservoir of your vital life force. Let your awareness drop to this region of your body and focus your attention there as you slowly inhale and exhale. If your mind wanders during your meditation, gently refocus your awareness on your Dantian. After your meditation, take a few moments to notice any shifts in energy that may have occurred.

Journaling Practice

Journal your direct experience of your meditation practice. Were you able to connect with your Dantian? If so, describe your experience of your reservoir of vital, life force energy. What sensations did you experience physically, emotionally, mentally, and energetically? Did you receive any insights during this practice? How might this information be useful in Reiki healing sessions?

Reiki Exploration Day 18

Daily Intention Review

Take a few deep, clearing, breaths, anchoring yourself in this present moment. From this place of inner stillness, read out loud your heartfelt intention.

---

27. Powers, *Insight Yoga*, 15.

Kundalini

Kundalini energy has been popularized over the past few decades. It refers to the spiritual energy that typically remains dormant within all of us. It is typically pictured as a serpent coiled up three times around a lingam at the root chakra. The coiled serpent represents the divine feminine energies, and the lingam represents the divine masculine energies. Kundalini energy can be awakened by yogic or spiritual practices, including Reiki. The energy rises from the root chakra through all the energy centers along the sushumna nadi until it reaches the crown chakra.

It would be best if you don't force the kundalini energy to rise. It will rise spontaneously when the right energetic conditions are met, and the chakras are functioning in a balanced way. It will also rise when you are performing Reiki attunements.

Symptoms of kundalini awakening:

- Involuntary muscle movements such as shaking or twitching
- Unexplained temperature changes within the body, such as heat or cold
- Unexplained sensations of tingling or electrical currents running through the body
- New sensitivity to stimuli such as light and noise
- Introverted behaviors such as socially isolating for a time
- Changes to eating and sleeping patterns

If kundalini is forced to rise before it's ready, you may experience periods of hallucinations and other illnesses. Trust that any effects of Kundalini rising are temporary in nature and will resolve as your energetic body assimilates to this new energetic frequency.

Integrating kundalini energy into your energy body may produce the following results:

- A deeper connection to the Divine
- Increased mental and emotional bandwidths
- A newfound sense of inspiration, determination, and drive
- Awakening or strengthening of psychic senses
- Clarity
- Enlightenment

Kundalini Meditation Practice

Find a comfortable seated position and settle in for a few moments. Silence your cell phone. Set your intention for exploring your kundalini energy using visualization and start a timer for five minutes. Visualize the lingam, a phallic shape located at your root chakra. The lingam represents your divine masculine energies. Picture it as clearly as you can. How does it feel? What color is it? Now, visualize a serpent coiled around the lingam three times. Again, picture the serpent as clearly as you can. How does she feel? What color is it?

Using this symbol of kundalini energy as the focal point for the five-minute meditation. Notice if your sense of the serpent changes over time. Be aware if she starts to move up your sushumna nadi; if she does, notice if the energy meet resistance in any of your chakra centers.

After completing your meditation, sit in quiet contemplation for a few moments.

Journaling Practice

Journal your direct experience of your meditation practice. Were you able to connect with your untapped kundalini energy? Describe the appearance of the lingam and serpent. Consider drawing a picture to record your experience.

What sensations did you experience physically, emotionally, mentally, and energetically? Did your kundalini energy move or rise during your meditation? If so, did it run into any energetic blocks or obstructions? Did you receive any insights during this practice? How might this information be useful in Reiki healing sessions and the attunement process?

Reiki Exploration Day 19

Daily Intention Review

Take a deep, centering breath, hold it for a moment, and then exhale completely. Now, with clarity of mind, state aloud your heartfelt intention and connect with the progress you are making on your own journey of healing.

Hand Chakras

There are two powerful energy vortexes located in the palm of each hand. Although considered minor chakras, they are significant for all energy healers, especially Reiki healers, since Reiki energy is primarily transmitted through the hand chakras. The hand chakras and heart chakra are connected by an energetic channel called the Pericardium meridian. This powerful energetic connection transmits loving energy from the heart center to the hands. (This could be the reason why holding hands is such a loving gesture of connection.) The hand chakras are also related to creativity and our ability to make our creative visions tangible.

Let's explore your connection to your own hand chakras. Consider these statements:

- "I feel the connection between my loving heart and the compassionate touch of my hands."
- "I appreciate my hands' abilities to express my creative nature."
- "When I turn on my connection to Reiki energy, I easily sense the energy in the palms of my hands."
- "My hands are a method of exploring the world through my sense of touch."

If you notice a statement that does not feel true for you now, consider paying extra attention to your hand chakras. In addition to Reiki self-healing sessions and other energetic healing treatments, there are many methods of balancing this energy center. You can explore the suggestions that follow for ways to support your hand chakras.

Affirmations

- "My hands are an extension of my loving and compassionate heart."
- "I easily express my creative nature with the assistance of my hands."
- "Reiki healing energy flows freely and openly through my hand chakras."

Consider exploring the various metaphysical tools available to assist you with balancing and strengthening your hand chakras. Here are some recommendations similar to the ones for the heart chakra.

Essential Oils

- Jasmine
- Rose
- Pine
- Bergamot

✿ *Crystals*

- Rose quartz
- Kunzite
- Malachite

Hand Chakra Self-Healing Session

Find a comfortable seated position and settle in for a few moments. Set a timer for five minutes, the duration of your targeted self-healing session today. Take a complete inventory of yourself at this moment in time. Notice how you feel physically, emotionally, mentally, energetically, and spiritually. Then, connect to your hand chakras at each palm's center.

Turn on Reiki using your unique method of connection and feel the infusion of Reiki energy into your being. Set your intention to perform Reiki healing on your hand chakras. Using your intuition, use the self-healing hand positions and the Reiki symbols that resonate with you, but spend time healing each hand chakra.

After your healing session, take a few moments to scan your body and observe any subtle shifts of energy that may have occurred.

Journaling Practice

Journal your direct experience of your self-healing session. Consider your hand chakras, and describe your connection to these energy centers. How do your hand chakras currently function? Using your intuition, what colors are these energy centers? Did you have any random thoughts, emotions, or sensations during your healing session? Did any shifts in energy occur? Did you receive any insights regarding your hand chakras? How might this information be helpful in future Reiki healing sessions?

Reiki Exploration Day 20

Daily Intention Review

Congratulations on reaching the twentieth day of your Reiki immersion experience! Reflect for a few moments on your growth as a Reiki healer. When ready, recite aloud your heartfelt intention.

Building Up Your Personal Energy and Preventing Energy Leaks

Our energetic body is in a constant state of flux. Consider your energy levels throughout the day. Some activities, like taking a walk or engaging in a lively conversation with friends, may increase your energy. Other activities, such as holding on to anger or encountering a problem at work, may deplete energy reserves. Maintaining energetic balance throughout the day is one of Reiki's benefits. Our energy also naturally leaks out at the root and crown chakras. This feature of our energetic body releases energy back into the environment as we receive new energy into our subtle body.

However, there are instances when we want to increase our internal energy or ki consciously, such as when building up our inner power to pass attunements on to others and for intensive Reiki healing sessions. We accomplish this action by closing off the gateways at the root and throat chakras, allowing our personal energy to build up at our core.

To close the root chakra gateway, we contract the Hui Yin point located at the perineum. In yoga, this practice is called mula bandha and is the same as restricting the flow of urination. When you become familiar with this type of muscle engagement, you can experience this contraction as a lifting of the pelvic floor.

The throat chakra is another gateway that must be closed to keep your energy from rising up through the throat chakra and out through the crown of your head. This restriction can be accomplished by pressing the tip of your tongue against the roof of your mouth behind your front teeth. During this practice, breathing through the nose is recommended.

Building Up Your Ki Practice

Find a comfortable seated position and settle in for a few moments. Silence your cell phone. Take notice of your current energy level. How would you describe it? Set your intention for increasing and experiencing your ki. When you are ready, start a timer for five minutes.

Take a few cleansing breaths through your nose and bring your awareness to your perineum. Next, begin to contract your perineum. Now, bring your attention to your mouth. Gently but firmly, press the tip of your tongue to the roof of your mouth, and breathe softly and deeply while holding this position. After completing your meditation, sit in quiet contemplation for a few moments.

Journaling Practice

Journal your direct experience of this energetic practice. Describe your energy levels before and after this meditation. Could you connect to the Hui Yin point and maintain the contraction during the meditation? (If not, this is an area of growth that will become easier with practice over time.) Were you able to maintain the connection of the tip of your tongue to the roof of your mouth? (If not, this might be an area where you can use more focus.) Did you receive any insights during this practice? How might this information be useful in Reiki healing sessions and the attunement process?

Side note: Repeat this exercise while walking for five minutes. It's essential to hold the Hui Yin contraction and maintain the connection of the tip of the tongue to the roof of the mouth while walking during the attunement process.

Reiki Exploration Day 21

Daily Intention Review

Take a moment to consider your personal energy level at this moment in time. Then from this place of awareness, state your heartfelt intention out loud.

Microcosmic Orbit

The Microcosmic Orbit practice is the continuous, circular movement of energy through the front and back of the body. By exploring this orbital pattern, we can tap into the nature of our own internal universe.

To practice the Microcosmic Orbit, contract the Hui Yin point as if you were restricting the flow of urination and place the tip of your tongue at the roof of your mouth behind your front teeth. These actions prevent energy from leaking through the root chakra and the crown chakra, effectively allowing ki to build within the subtle body. Next, imagine a ball of light at your Dantian (lower belly). With each inhale, imagine the ball of light intensifying, and with each exhale, visualize the ball of light becoming brighter. When you are ready to proceed, visualize the ball moving downward from the Dantian to the root chakra at your tailbone, then up the back of your body to your crown. Pause the ball of light at the top of your head before descending the ball of light down the front of your face and chest until it returns to the Dantian. Pause before repeating the orbital cycle. The ball of light represents your ki, and this practice effectively circulates your personal energy throughout your auric field.

The benefits of practicing the Microcosmic Orbit include:

- Improving overall health and well-being
- Mental and emotional balance
- Balancing the internal divine feminine and divine masculine energies

Microcosmic Orbit Meditation Practice

Find a comfortable seated position, silence your cell phone, and settle in for a few moments. Take notice of your current energy level. Start a five-minute timer.

Take a few cleansing breaths and bring your awareness to your perineum. Begin to contract your perineum. Now, bring your attention to your mouth behind your front teeth. Gently but firmly, press the tip of your tongue to the roof of your mouth, and breathe softly and deeply through your nose, holding this position. Imagine a ball of light at Dantian, your lower belly. Imagine this ball of light growing larger with each inhale and brighter with each exhale. When ready, imagine this ball of light descending to your root chakra. On an inhale, imagine the ball of light rising up your back body to the crown of your head. On your exhale, visualize the ball of light descending down your front body to your root chakra. Repeat this visualization for the remainder of the five minutes. At the end of the five minutes, release the Hui Yin point contraction and allow your tongue to relax inside your mouth. Finally, picture the ball of light returning to your Dantian. After completing your meditation, sit in quiet contemplation for a few moments.

Journaling Practice

Journal your direct experience of this energetic practice. Describe your energy levels before and after this meditation. Were you able to feel your energy circulate around your body? Did you receive any insights during this practice? How might this information be useful in Reiki healing sessions and the attunement process?

Reiki Exploration Day 22

Daily Intention Review

Connect with the energy of the earth. When you are ready, recite your heartfelt intention out loud from this place of support and stability.

Foot Chakras

Located at the sole of each foot are two energy centers. These are considered minor chakras, but they are essential to Reiki healers. Foot chakras link our root chakra to the Earth Star chakra beneath our feet. As Reiki healers, maintaining our energetic balance during Reiki sessions is of the utmost importance. Our foot chakras can assist us with maintaining optimal energy levels. It is through these vortexes we can release unwanted energies and receive beneficial energies from the earth.

Let's explore your connection to your foot chakras. Consider the statements below:

- "I easily draw up nurturing and healing energies from the earth."
- "I effortlessly release any energies that do not serve me."
- "I am deeply connected to Mother Earth."
- "I typically feel grounded, stable, and supported."

If you notice a statement that does not feel true for you now, consider paying extra attention to your foot chakras. In addition to Reiki self-healing sessions and other energetic healing treatments, there are many methods of balancing this energy center. Explore the suggestions that follow for ways to support your foot chakras.

✿ *Affirmations*

- "I am supported by Mother Earth and easily receive her nurturing energies."
- "I am grounded and supported."
- "I easily release excess and unwanted energies back to Mother Earth."

Consider exploring various metaphysical tools with balancing and strengthening your foot chakras. Here are some recommendations similar to the ones for the root and Earth Star chakras.

✿ *Essential Oils*

- Cypress
- Vetiver
- Patchouli

❀ *Crystals*

- Black kyanite
- Lodestone
- Pyrite

Feet Chakra Self-Healing Session

Find a comfortable seated position and settle in for a few moments. Set a timer for five minutes, the duration of your targeted self-healing session today. Take a complete inventory of yourself at this moment in time. Notice how you feel physically, emotionally, mentally, energetically, and spiritually. Then, connect to your foot chakras at each sole.

Turn on Reiki using your unique method of connection and feel the infusion of Reiki energy into your being. Set your intention to perform Reiki healing on your foot chakras. Using your intuition, use the self-healing hand positions and the Reiki symbols that resonate with you, but spend time healing each foot chakra.

After your healing session, take a few moments to scan your body and observe any subtle shifts of energy that may have occurred.

Journaling Practice

Journal your direct experience of your self-healing session. Consider your foot chakras. Describe your connection to these energy centers. How do your foot chakras currently function? Using your intuition, what colors are these energy centers? Did you have any random thoughts, emotions, or sensations during your healing session? Did a shift in your energy occur? Did you receive insights regarding your foot chakras? How might this information be helpful in future Reiki healing sessions?

Reiki Exploration Day 23

Daily Intention Review

With a thankful heart for all the progress you have made along your healing path, recommit to your healing goals by stating your heartfelt intention out loud.

Color Healing and the Violet Breath

The Violet Breath is part of the attunement process but can also serve as a stand-alone meditation practice that taps into the healing energies of the heavens and the earth.

Consider the colors associated with the Violet Breath: Red is a primary color, that along with blue and yellow, are the source of all other colors on the color wheel. It is associated with the active fire element, the sun, passion, vitality, and blood, a symbol of our humanity.[28] It also corresponds to the root chakra, our sense of stability and safety. Red is a warming color, and visualizing it brings in the earth element and its associated characteristics of security and grounding.

Blue, another primary color, is associated with the passive water element, truth, piety, peace, the Great Void of the heavens or the sea, representing divine or cosmic energies.[29] It is also connected to the throat chakra, our communication center. The color blue is a cooling and calming color. Visualizing this color can assist with developing a sense of openness, imagination, inspiration, and increased sensitivity levels.

The color violet, a harmonious mixture of red and blue, symbolizes temperance, knowledge, devotion, clarity of mind, and the balance between Heaven and Earth.[30] The chakras associated with violet is the crown chakra, our personal connection to the Divine. Picturing this color promotes spiritual growth and development while calming the body and the mind. It can also assist with creativity.

By using colors during meditation, you can modify your internal energies to resonate with the frequency of the energies of the associated colors. For example, the Violet Breath is a way to use the energies of these three colors to produce a state of being connected to both the earth and the Divine.

Violet Breath Meditation Practice

For this practice, we will not be using the contraction of the Hui Yin point or the connection of the tongue to the roof of the mouth as we would in an attunement. Instead, we will focus on first drawing up earth energies into our auric field and then drawing down heavenly energies. These two types of energies will become mixed into a vibrant violet color.

Find a comfortable seated position, silence your cell phone, and settle in for a few moments. Then, take notice of your current energy level. When you are ready to begin, start a timer for ten minutes.

Take a few cleansing breaths. Next, visualize the rich red energies of the earth. This energy resonates with the vibrations of stability and grounding. On your inhale, imagine

---

28. Cooper, *An Illustrated Encyclopedia of Traditional Symbols*, 40.
29. Ibid.
30. Chevalier and Gheerbrant, *The Penguin Dictionary of Symbols*,1068–1069.

drawing up the earth's red color into your being, and on each exhale, imagine this red energy filling up your entire body and permeating your auric field. After a few cycles of breath, pause and feel the vibrancy of the earth's energy. Next, bring your awareness to the heavens and picture blue, calming energy beginning to descend. Imagine drawing down this celestial blue color into your being on each inhale. On each exhale, imagine this blue energy filling your entire body and spreading into your auric field. After a few cycles of breath, pause and feel your response to the frequency of this cosmic energy. Now, visualize drawing up the red energy of the earth and drawing down the celestial blue energy of the heavens simultaneously during your inhale. On the exhale, picture the colors mixing and blending to produce a vibrant violet hue. When you feel that your auric field is filled with violet energy, simply sit with the visualization of the violet color until your meditation session is complete.

Sit in quiet contemplation for a few moments before proceeding to the journaling exercise.

Journaling Practice

Journal your direct experience of the Violet Breath meditation practice. Describe your energy levels before and after this meditation. What was your experience connecting with the red energy of the earth? How did you feel physically, emotionally, mentally, and energetically? What was your experience connecting with the blue energy of the cosmos? How did you feel physically, emotionally, mentally, and energetically? What was your experience combining these energies into the violet color? How did you feel physically, emotionally, mentally, and energetically? Did you receive any insights during this practice? How might this information be useful in Reiki healing sessions and the attunement process?

Reiki Exploration Day 24

Daily Intention Review

Settle in for a moment, noticing how you are showing up today. Then, honoring who you are at this moment, state your heartfelt intention out loud.

The Elements Overview

The ancient Greeks believed that all creation is composed of four elements. This theory dates back to around 450 BCE and was introduced by the Greek philosopher Empedocles. The four original elements were earth, water, fire, and air. Each has its unique attributes and qualities. Later, the theory was adjusted to include a fifth element, ether or space, by Aristotle, a student of Plato.

Although modern science no longer ascribes to this theory of what composes matter, the elements are a valuable tool to assess an individual's unique composition. Similar to the chakra system, the elements can provide a helpful map used to determine the energetic qualities of an individual.

Qualities of Earth: Grounded, practical, focused, responsible

Qualities of Water: Emotional, fluid, sensitive, nurturing, intuitive

Qualities of Fire: Passionate, dramatic, driven, enthusiastic, impulsive

Qualities of Air: Communicative, intellectual, rational, curious

Qualities of Ether: Spacious, etheric, expansive, unlimited potential

The Elements: Self-Assessment

Consider your unique elemental makeup using the following self-assessment. If you are drawn to more than one answer, feel free to select more than one response.

Which activity brings you the most joy?

A. Walking barefoot on soft, green grass

B. Spending time at the ocean or a lake

C. Competing in a challenging sport or game

D. Curling up with a good book

E. Going to a concert

I feel most connected to this part of myself:

A. My physical body

B. My emotions

C. My personal power

D. My mind

E. My inner essence

A characteristic that I'd like to change about myself is:

A. I have a stubborn streak

B. I can be overly emotional

C. I can be arrogant and vindictive

D. I have great ideas but difficulty manifesting my inner vision

E. I spend most time engaging in spiritual activities at the expense of more practical pursuits

An important goal in my life is:

A. Achieving financial stability and security

B. Finding emotional connections

C. Following my passions

D. Continuing to learn and develop new skills

E. Understanding myself and my place in the universe

Currently, I am most interested in pursuing:

A. Knowledge about my ancestors

B. Pleasurable pursuits

C. Cultivating my own willpower and authority

D. Developing my communication skills

E. Developing my meditation skills

The statement that best describes me is:

A. "I am dependable and practical and enjoy accomplishing my daily to-do list."

B. "Deep emotional currents color my life, and I experience vivid dreams often."

C. "I approach life enthusiastically and face life challenges head-on."

D. "I approach life rationally and expect others to do the same."

E. "I am one with all that is."

Mostly As: Strong Earth Element Connection

Mostly Bs: Strong Water Element Connection

Mostly Cs: Strong Fire Element Connection

Mostly Ds: Strong Air Element Connection

Mostly Es: Strong Ether Element Connection

Journaling Practice

Journal your direct experience of your Self-Assessment Quiz. Consider your responses. Is one element prominent in your unique makeup? Is there a lack of an element? How might these insights be helpful to you in your personal healing and development? How might this information be useful in Reiki healing sessions?

Reiki Exploration Day 25

Daily Intention Review

With a grateful heart for all the progress you've already made, recommit to your healing goals by stating your heartfelt intention out loud.

Knee Chakras

The minor energy centers at the knees are worth exploring due to the number of knee-related health issues. The knees are one of the most complex joints in the human body. From an energetic perspective, our knees are related to our personal ego and sense of pride. When these energies become imbalanced, we can become rigid in our beliefs, attitudes, and behaviors. Inflexibility is a hallmark characteristic of blocked knee chakras, which are located at the back of each knee.

Let's explore your connection to your knee chakras. Consider these statements:

- "I flow with the rhythms of my life."
- "I am open to new ideas and concepts."
- "My ego is a part of my identity but does not define me."
- "I walk through life with confidence and ease."

If you notice a statement that is not true for you now, consider paying extra attention to your knee chakras. In addition to Reiki self-healing sessions and other energetic healing treatments, there are many methods of balancing these energy centers. You can explore the suggestions below for ways to support your knee chakras.

✤ *Affirmations*

- "My knees support me through life's twists and turns."
- "I walk my path with ease and grace."
- "I flow in harmony with the rhythms of my life."

Consider exploring the various metaphysical tools to assist with balancing and strengthening your knee chakras.

✤ *Essential Oils*

- Roman chamomile
- Grapefruit
- Bergamot

✤ *Crystals*

- Tree agate
- Watermelon tourmaline
- Garnet

Knee Chakra Self-Healing Session

Find a comfortable seated position and settle in for a few moments. Set a timer for five minutes, the duration of your targeted self-healing session today. Take a complete inventory of yourself at this moment in time. Notice how you feel physically, emotionally, mentally, energetically, and spiritually. Then, connect to your knee chakras at the back of each knee.

Turn on Reiki using your unique method of connection and feel the infusion of Reiki energy into your being. Set your intention to perform Reiki healing on your knee chakras. Using your intuition, use the self-healing hand positions and the Reiki symbols that resonate with you, but spend time healing each knee chakra.

After your healing session, take a few moments to scan your body and observe any subtle shifts of energy that may have occurred.

Journaling Practice

Consider your knee chakras. Describe your connection to these energy centers. How do your knee chakras currently function? Using your intuition, what colors are these energy centers? Did you have any random thoughts, emotions, or sensations during your healing session? Did any shifts in energy occur? Did you receive insights regarding your knee chakras? How might this information be helpful in future Reiki healing sessions?

Reiki Exploration Day 26

Daily Intention Review

Take a few moments and connect to the earth element. From this place of groundedness, state aloud your heartfelt intention.

Earth Element

The first and most tangible element is the earth element. The earth element is associated with stability, grounding, stillness, and manifestation. The earth element is also connected to your relationship with finances and your home environment.

Let's explore your connection to the earth element. Consider these statements:

- "I enjoy gardening."
- "I consider myself a caretaker of this planet."
- "I am connected to my physical body."
- "I feel safe and secure."
- "I am in a state of financial health."
- "I enjoy spending time at home."
- "My friends would describe me as dependable and practical."

If you noticed a statement does not feel true for you at this time, consider spending extra attention cultivating the earth element within you. In addition to Reiki self-healing sessions and other energetic healing treatments, there are many methods of connecting to the earth element. You can explore the suggestions below for ways to support you in this endeavor.

❀ *Affirmations*

- "I easily attract abundance."
- "I am deeply rooted in the nurturing energies of Mother Earth."

Explore the various metaphysical tools available to assist you with connecting with the earth element. Below are some recommendations.

❧ *Essential Oils*

- Cedar wood
- Vetiver
- Juniper

❧ *Crystals*

- Jasper
- Petrified wood
- Smoky quartz

Earth Element Meditation Practice

For this practice, you will need colored pencils, colored markers, crayons, or paint. Additionally, you'll need a blank index card or a piece of cardstock. You'll be creating a tattva, a representation of the earth element used for meditation. Originating in spiritual traditions of India, they have gained popularity in the West over the last hundred years.

Create a yellow square on a purple background with your art materials. It doesn't have to be perfect but try to be as precise as possible.

Sit in a comfortable position. Silence your cell phone and set a timer for five minutes. Take a few deep breaths and bring your awareness to the present moment. Set your intention to connect with the earth element on a deep and personal level. Allow your gaze to soften, and begin to focus on the earth tattva card you created. If your mind wanders during your practice, invite it back to the focus of your meditation.

When you have finished your meditation, sit for a minute or two afterward in observation, noticing any shifts in energy that have occurred.

Journaling Practice

Reflect on your practices today. What is your current relationship with the earth element? Is there an opportunity to strengthen your connection to this element? How might that manifest in your life? Journal about your direct experience with the earth tattva meditation practice. Did you notice any shifts in energy?

How might you use your knowledge about the earth element as part of your Reiki healing sessions?

Reiki Exploration Day 27

Daily Intention Review

Take a moment to connect with your emotional landscape. From a place of feeling, recite your heartfelt intention aloud.

Water Element

Next is the water element. It is less dense than earth but has more substance when compared to the remaining three elements. It is associated with emotions, fluidity, dreams, and the ability to nurture others and yourself.

Let's explore our connection to the water element. Consider these statements:

- "I enjoy spending time near bodies of water."
- "I am deeply connected to my emotions and express them easily."
- "I enjoy taking luxurious baths."
- "I seek out the pleasures of life."
- "I consider myself a sensual being."
- "I enjoy cultivating deep relationships with family and friends."
- "I am emphatic and intuitive."

If you noticed a statement that is not true for you now, consider spending extra attention cultivating the water element within you. In addition to Reiki self-healing sessions and other energetic healing treatments, there are many methods of connecting to the water element. You can explore the suggestions below for ways to support you in this endeavor.

⚘ Affirmations

- "I am open to feeling and expressing my emotions."
- "I am a deeply intuitive being, and I trust my intuition."

Explore the various metaphysical tools available to assist you with connecting with the water element. Here are some recommendations.

🪷 *Essential Oils*

- Chamomile
- Bergamot
- Sandalwood

🪷 *Crystals*

- Agates
- Rose quartz
- Aquamarine

Water Element Meditation Practice

For this practice, you will need colored pencils, colored markers, crayons, or paint. Additionally, you'll need a blank index card or a piece of cardstock. Again, you'll be creating a tattva for use in meditation, this time a representation of the water element. With your art media, create a silver (or white if you don't have silver) crescent on a black background. It doesn't have to be perfect, but try to be as precise as possible.

Sit in a comfortable position. Silence your cell phone and set a timer for five minutes. Take a few deep breaths and bring your awareness to the present moment. Set your intention to connect with the water element in a deep and personal way. Allow your gaze to soften and focus on the water tattva card you created. If your mind wanders during your practice, invite it back to the focus of your meditation. When you have finished your meditation, sit for a minute or two afterward in observation, noticing any shifts in energy that have occurred.

Journaling Practice

Reflect on your practices today. What is your current relationship with the water element? Is there an opportunity to strengthen your connection to this element? How might that manifest in your life? Journal about your direct experience with the water tattva meditation practice. Did you notice any shifts in energy? How might you use your knowledge about the water element as part of your Reiki healing sessions?

Reiki Exploration Day 28

Daily Intention Review

Take a few deep, cleansing breaths to center yourself. When you are ready, recommit to your Reiki path by stating your heartfelt intention out loud.

Shoulder Chakras

Our shoulders are where we carry our responsibilities. The minor energy centers located at each shoulder assist us with these burdens. When these energies become imbalanced, we can become overwhelmed by our commitments. Additionally, some obligations we carry belong to others, not ourselves. Our shoulder chakras can assist us in joyfully participating in all aspects of our life, fulfilling our responsibilities with zest, and allowing others to assume ownership of their burdens.

Let's explore your connection to your shoulder chakras. Consider these statements:

- "I am shouldering my responsibilities with ease and grace."
- "I embrace even the more challenging aspects of life in a lighthearted way."
- "I release all burdens that are not mine to carry."

If you notice a statement that does not feel true for you now, consider paying extra attention to your shoulder chakras. In addition to Reiki self-healing sessions and other energetic healing treatments, there are many methods of balancing and strengthening these energy centers. You can explore the suggestions below for ways to support your shoulder chakras.

⚘ *Affirmations*

- "I approach my responsibilities with strength, purpose, and joy."
- "I release all burdens that are not mine to carry."

Consider exploring the various metaphysical tools available to assist you with balancing and strengthening your shoulder chakras.

⚘ *Essential Oils*

- Rosemary
- Ginger
- Eucalyptus

✿ Crystals

- Blue aragonite
- Angelite
- Onyx

Shoulder Chakra Self-Healing Session

Find a comfortable seated position and settle in for a few moments. Silence your cell phone and set a timer for five minutes, the duration of your targeted self-healing session today. Take a complete inventory of yourself at this moment in time. Notice how you feel physically, emotionally, mentally, energetically, and spiritually. Then, connect to your shoulder chakras.

Turn on Reiki using your unique method of connection and feel the infusion of Reiki energy into your being. Set your intention to perform Reiki healing on your shoulder chakras. Using your intuition, use the self-healing hand positions and the Reiki symbols that resonate with you, but spend time healing each shoulder chakra.

After your healing session, take a few moments to scan your body and observe any subtle shifts of energy that may have occurred.

Journaling Practice

Journal your direct experience of your self-healing session. Consider your shoulder chakras. Describe your connection to these energy centers. How do your currently shoulder your responsibilities? Do you take on the burdens of others? How do your shoulder chakras currently function? Using your intuition, what colors are these energy centers?

Did you have any random thoughts, emotions, or sensations during your healing session? Did a shift in energy occur? Did you receive any insights regarding your shoulder chakras? How might this information be helpful in future Reiki healing sessions?

Reiki Exploration Day 29

Daily Intention Review

Take a moment to connect with your own inner fire. From this place of inspiration and passion, read your heartfelt intention out loud.

Fire Element

The fire element falls in the middle of the five elements. It is less dense than water and more tangible than air. It is associated with drive, determination, passion, and inspiration.

Let's explore your connection to the fire element. Consider these statements:

- "I approach life with enthusiasm."
- "I have a competitive nature."
- "I am self-confident."
- "I enjoy being in leadership roles."
- "I am comfortable standing in my personal power."
- "I am excited to dive into new situations."
- "My friends would describe me as inspirational and courageous."

If you noticed a statement that does not feel true for you now, consider spending extra attention cultivating the fire within you. In addition to Reiki self-healing sessions and other energetic healing treatments, there are many methods of connecting to this element. Following are some suggestions for ways to support you in this endeavor.

Affirmations

- "I follow my passions with enthusiasm."
- "I confidently stand in my personal power."

There are various metaphysical tools available to assist you with connecting to the fire element. Here are some recommendations.

Essential Oils

- Cinnamon
- Basil
- Black pepper

Crystals

- Citrine
- Pyrite
- Peridot

Fire Element Meditation Practice

For this practice, you will need colored pencils, colored markers, crayons, or paint. Additionally, you'll need a blank index card or a piece of cardstock. You'll be creating a tattva for meditation representing the fire element. Using your art materials, create a red triangle on a green background. It doesn't have to be perfect, but try to be as precise as possible.

Sit in a comfortable position. Silence your cell phone and set a timer for five minutes. Take a few deep breaths and bring your awareness to the present moment. Set your intention to connect with the fire element in a deep and personal way. Allow your gaze to soften and begin to focus on the fire tattva card you created. If your mind wanders during your practice, invite it back to the focus of your meditation.

When you have finished your meditation, sit for a minute or two afterward in observation, noticing any shifts in energy that have occurred.

Journaling Practice

Reflect on your practices today. What is your current relationship with the fire element? Is there an opportunity to strengthen your connection to this element? How might that manifest in your life? Journal about your direct experience with the fire tattva meditation practice. Did you notice any shifts in energy? How might you use your knowledge about the fire element in future Reiki healing sessions?

Reiki Exploration Day 30

Daily Intention Review

Take a few deep breaths and call to mind why you embarked on this path of inner exploration and healing. From this place of connection to your goals, recite your heartfelt intention aloud.

Hip Chakras

Hip issues are commonplace in today's society. As a result, it's beneficial to consider the energy centers located at each hip point. The hip joints are ball-and-socket joints that provide mobility and stability. Health issues related to the hips, specifically hip mobility issues, are often associated with the inability to move forward in life or the reluctance to make important life decisions. The minor chakras located at each hip point assist with helping us make important choices so we can move forward along our life's path.

Let's explore your connection to your hip chakras. Consider these statements:

- "I am comfortable making important decisions in my life."
- "I make goals and work toward them with confidence and purpose."
- "When I feel stuck, I determine the root cause, so I continue moving along my life's path."
- "I embrace the endless opportunities of this lifetime."

If you notice a statement that does not feel true for you at this time, consider paying extra attention to your hip chakras. In addition to Reiki self-healing sessions and other energetic healing treatments, there are many methods of balancing these energy centers. You can explore the suggestions below for ways to support your hip chakras.

❀ Affirmations

- "I confidently make decisions that align with my best and highest good."
- "I make personal goals and actively work to achieve them step by step, day by day."
- "I easily make choices that are best for me."

Consider exploring the various metaphysical tools available to assist you with balancing and strengthening your hip chakras.

❀ Essential Oils

- Wild orange
- Grapefruit
- Tangerine

❀ Crystals

- Amber
- Aragonite
- Tantalite

Hip Chakras Self-Healing Session

Find a comfortable seated position and settle in for a few moments. Set a timer for five minutes, the duration of your targeted self-healing session today. Take a complete inventory of yourself at this moment in time. Notice how you feel physically, emotionally, mentally, energetically, and spiritually. Then connect to your hip chakras located at each hip point.

Turn on Reiki using your unique method of connection and feel the infusion of Reiki energy into your being. Set your intention to perform Reiki healing on your hip chakras. Using your intuition, use the self-healing hand positions and the Reiki symbols that resonate with you, being sure to spend time healing each hip chakra.

After your healing session, take a few moments to scan your body and observe any subtle shifts of energy that may have occurred.

Journaling Practice

Journal your direct experience of your self-healing session. Consider your hip chakras. Describe your connection to these energy centers. How do your hip chakras currently function? Using your intuition, what colors are these energy centers? Did you have any random thoughts, emotions, or sensations during your healing session? Did a shift in energy occur? Did you receive insights regarding your hip chakras? How might this information be helpful in future Reiki healing sessions?

Reiki Exploration Day 31

Daily Intention Review

Bring your awareness to your mind and appreciate your ability for deep thought and introspection. From this place of connection to your mental body, state your heartfelt intention aloud.

Air Element

The air element is less tangible than the earth, water, and fire elements. In nature, air can't be seen with your physical eyes but can be felt and experienced. The air element is related to the mind, intellect, movement, and breath.

Let's explore your connection to the air element. Consider these statements:

- "I enjoy learning new things."
- "Reading is one of my favorite pastimes."
- "Communication is one of my strengths."
- "My friends would describe me as talkative and intelligent."

If you noticed a statement that does not feel true for you at this time, consider spending extra attention cultivating the air element within you. In addition to Reiki self-healing sessions and other energetic healing treatments, there are many ways of strengthening and balancing your internal air element. Explore the following suggestions for methods of support in this endeavor.

❀ *Affirmations:*

- "I am an effective communicator."
- "I easily learn and retain information."

There are various metaphysical tools available to assist you with connecting with the air element. Here are some recommendations.

❀ *Essential Oils*

- Clary sage
- Lemongrass
- Frankincense

❀ *Crystals*

- Amethyst
- Fluorite
- Blue sapphire

Air Element Meditation Practice

For this practice, you will need colored pencils, colored markers, crayons, or paint. Additionally, you'll need a blank index card or a piece of cardstock.

You'll be creating a tattva, this time representing the air element. Create a blue circle on an orange background using your art media. It doesn't have to be perfect, but try to be as precise as possible.

Now sit in a comfortable position. Silence your cell phone and set a timer for five minutes. Take a few deep breaths and bring your awareness to the present moment. Set the intention to connect with the air element in a deep and personal way. Allow your gaze to soften and focus on the air tattva card you created. If your mind wanders during your practice, invite it back to the focus of your meditation. When you have finished your meditation, sit for a minute or two afterward in observation, noticing any shifts in energy that have occurred.

Journaling Practice

Reflect on your practices today. What is your current relationship with the air element? Is there an opportunity to strengthen your connection to this element? How might that manifest in your life? Journal about your direct experience with the air meditation practice. Did you notice any shifts in energy? How might you use your knowledge about the air element as part of your Reiki healing sessions?

Reiki Exploration Day 32

Daily Intention Review

Connect with your heart by feeling your capacity for love and compassion. From this place of warmth and tenderness, recite your heartfelt intention out loud.

High Heart Chakra

The High Heart energy center is not considered a major chakra, but knowledge about this energy center is invaluable to Reiki healers. It is located in the thymus gland at your sternum between your heart and throat chakras.

Let's explore your connection to your own High Heart chakra. Consider these statements:

- "I easily give and receive love."
- "I can express my feelings to others without judgment."
- "I easily forgive myself for my past mistakes."
- "I value myself and take care of my needs."
- "I love myself unconditionally."
- "I am truthful to myself about how I am feeling."

If you noticed a statement does not feel true for you now, consider paying extra attention to your own High Heart chakra. In addition to Reiki self-healing sessions and other energetic healing treatments, there are many methods of balancing this energy center. Explore the suggestions below for ways to support your High Heart chakra.

✿ *Affirmations*

- "I honor my emotions and truthfully express my feelings to others."
- "I am worthy of my own love and compassion."
- "I forgive myself completely."

Consider exploring various metaphysical tools available to assist you with balancing and strengthening your High Heart chakra. Here are some recommendations.

✿ *Essential Oils*

- Jasmine
- Rose
- Neroli

✿ *Crystals*

- Rose quartz
- Green calcite
- Blue tourmaline

High Heart Chakra Self-Healing Session

Find a comfortable seated position and settle in for a few moments. Silence your cell phone and set a timer for five minutes, the duration of your targeted self-healing session today. Take a complete inventory of yourself at this moment in time. Notice how you feel physically, emotionally, mentally, energetically, and spiritually. Connect to your High Heart chakra, located at your sternum.

Turn on Reiki using your unique method of connection and feel the infusion of Reiki energy into your being. Set your intention to perform Reiki healing on your High Heart chakra. Using your intuition, use the self-healing hand positions and the Reiki symbols that resonate with you, but spend time healing your High Heart chakra. After your healing session, take a few moments to scan your body and observe any subtle shifts of energy that may have occurred.

Journaling Practice

Journal your direct experience of your self-healing session. Consider your High Heart chakra. Describe your connection to this energy center. How does your High Heart chakra currently function? Did you have any random thoughts, emotions, or sensations during your healing session? Did a shift in energy occur during your self-healing session? Did you receive any insights regarding your High Heart chakra? How might this information be helpful in future Reiki healing sessions?

Reiki Exploration Day 33

Daily Intention Review

Consider your relationship with the cosmos. Then, from this place of divine connection, state your heartfelt intention aloud.

Ether (Space) Element

The ether element is the subtlest of all the elements. It is associated with the void of space, infinite potential, and connection with the Divine and the cosmos.

Let's explore your connection to the ether element. Consider these statements:

- "I enjoy meditation."
- "I consider myself to be a part of a larger, universal whole."
- "I am connected to my higher self."
- "The Divine inspires me."
- "I actively cultivate my unlimited potential."
- "My friends would describe me as living in harmony with the universe."

If you noticed a statement that is not true for you at this time, consider spending extra attention cultivating the ether element within you. In addition to Reiki self-healing sessions and other energetic healing treatments, there are many methods of connecting to the ether element. Explore the suggestions here for ways to support you in this endeavor.

⚘ Affirmations

- "I am connected to all that is."
- "I easily commune with my higher self."

There are various metaphysical tools available to assist you with connecting with the ether element. Here are some recommendations.

❀ *Essential Oils*
- Lavender
- Star anise
- Peppermint

❀ *Crystals*
- Clear quartz

Ether Element Meditation Practice

For this practice, you will need colored pencils, colored markers, crayons, or paint. Additionally, you'll need a blank index card or a piece of cardstock. You'll be creating a tattva, a representation of the ether element used for meditation. With your art media, create a purple oval on a yellow background. It doesn't have to be perfect but try to be as precise as possible.

Sit in a comfortable position. Silence your cell phone and set a timer for five minutes. Take a few deep breaths and bring your awareness to the present moment. Set your intention to connect with the ether element in a deep and personal way. Allow your gaze to soften and begin to focus on the ether tattva card you created. If your mind wanders during your practice, invite it back to the focus of your meditation.

When you have finished your meditation, sit for a minute or two afterward in observation, noticing any shifts in energy that have occurred.

Journaling Practice

Reflect on your practices today. What is your current relationship with the ether element? Is there an opportunity to strengthen your connection to this element? How might that manifest in your life? Journal about your direct experience with the ether meditation practice. Did you notice any shifts in energy? How might you use your knowledge about the ether element as part of future Reiki healing sessions?

Reiki Exploration Day 34

Daily Intention Review

As a reminder of your healing path, read your heartfelt intention aloud.

The Power of the Sacred *Yes*

As human beings, we have agency, the power to make our own choices about our lives both big and small. Consider all the aspects of life you say *yes* to experiencing. For example, you have said *yes* to following the healing path of Reiki. As a result, you have given yourself permission to actively engage in your own healing process and help others with their healing journeys.

Reiki is a practice that requires consent. It's tempting to think we know what's best for others, but each person must stand in their personal power and make choices for themselves. Whether or not others want to pursue their own healing is their choice. Before beginning every Reiki healing session whether in person or remote, always confirm that this individual is willing to accept Reiki healing energy.

As a Reiki healer, you are only responsible for receiving consent and performing the Reiki healing session to the best of your ability. You are not responsible for the outcome of the session. Sometimes healing occurs in a way we don't expect or anticipate. Other times, the individual may have verbally said *yes* to receiving Reiki energy but was unwilling to say *yes* to the changes needed in their lifestyle to ensure long-term healing benefits. Therefore, it's essential to be able to separate yourself from your healing participant's outcome.

Additionally, as a Reiki healer, you must maintain energetic health and balance. Be sure to say *yes* to activities that nurture your body, mind, and soul to ensure that you can continue to provide support to others.

Sacred *Yes* Affirmation Practice

Find a comfortable seated position and settle in for a few moments. Set a timer for five minutes. The affirmation for today's practice is: "I enthusiastically say *yes* to activities that support my goals and my needs while honoring the free agency of others to do the same." Repeat that affirmation silently to yourself. If your mind wanders, gently invite it back to your affirmation. After your affirmation session, spend a few moments in quiet reflection.

Journaling Practice

Journal your direct experience of your affirmation practice. During your affirmation practice, did you notice any shifts in energy that occurred? Did you have any random thoughts, feelings, or sensations? What activities do you currently say *yes* to regularly? How do those activities support you? What practices should you say *yes* to that you have been putting off? Are there instances where you step in, believing that you know what's best for another? How might you show greater respect for others' rights to say *yes* or *no*? How might this information be helpful in future Reiki healing sessions?

Reiki Exploration Day 35

Daily Intention Review

Take a few deep breaths and draw your attention inward. Pause to consider your progress along your healing path and the insights you have gained thus far on your personal journey. When you are ready, state your heartfelt intention out loud.

The Power of the Sacred *No*

Saying *no* to activities is just as important as your right to say *yes*. For those of us who are people-pleasers, the idea of saying *no* can stir up feelings of guilt and cause stress. Therefore, maintaining boundaries and the ability to say *no* are critical components of being a Reiki healer. Consider the following questions:

- How many Reiki sessions can you perform daily and maintain your work-life balance and vibrant health?
- What time do you carve out as personal time?
- Do you maintain professional relationships with your healing participants?
- Do you allow healing participants to contact you between sessions for advice and guidance?
- Do you feel it necessary to continue treating a healing participant who is habitually late or routinely misses/cancels appointments?
- Are you compelled to continue a healing session if a healing participant is rude or acts inappropriately toward you?

These are scenarios that you should consider as you continue along your path as a Reiki healer. You are the only one responsible for maintaining your boundaries. You have the authority to discontinue providing Reiki healing services to anyone who does not respect your time or makes you uncomfortable. You also have the agency to set your own schedule to ensure that you can fully participate in your own life while being of service to others. Although saying *no* may be challenging at times, we are embracing our authority and standing in our personal power to make choices that are best for us.

Sacred *No* Affirmation Practice

Find a comfortable seated position and settle in for a few moments. Silence your cell phone and set a timer for five minutes. Here's the affirmation for today's practice: "Without apologies, I embrace the sacred *no* to protect my personal boundaries and to maintain my energetic health." Repeat that affirmation silently to yourself. If your mind wanders, gently invite it back to your affirmation. After your affirmation session, spend a few moments in quiet reflection.

Journaling Practice

Journal your direct experience of your affirmation practice. For example, did you notice any shifts in energy that occurred during your affirmation practice? Did you have any random thoughts, feelings, or sensations? What activities do you currently say *no* to regularly? Do you consider yourself a people-pleaser, and if so, does it adversely affect areas of your life? Is saying *no* difficult for you? If so, why? What activities do you say *yes* to that you should decline? How might this information be helpful in future Reiki healing sessions?

Reiki Exploration Day 36

Daily Intention Review

Connect with your heart by feeling your capacity for love and compassion. From this place of warmth and tenderness, recite your heartfelt intention out loud.

Reiki Openings and Closings

In my experience, the parts of Reiki healing sessions people most frequently remember are the beginnings and the endings. While it may seem a little counterintuitive since the actual healing occurs in the middle, it does underscore the importance of how each session is opened and closed.

Items you may want to include in your opening:

- Acknowledging your healing participant for taking an active role in their healing process.
- Express gratitude for the gift of Reiki.
- Inviting in spirit guides, angels, and ancestors.
- Stating your intention for the healing session.

Here's a sample Reiki opening:

Thank you, Dr. Usui, for sharing the gift of Reiki healing with us. With an open heart, I invite my spirit guides, ancestors, the ascended masters, archangels Michael, Raphael, and Uriel, as well as any other angels or divine beings of 100 percent pure light who wish to join me in this healing work. I respectfully ask that this healing session is in alignment with the best and highest good of [healing recipient's name here].

Items you may want to include for your closing:

- Gratitude for the gift of Reiki.
- Thank the spirit guides, angels, and ancestors for their presence.
- A closing prayer such as the metta prayer of lovingkindness.

Here's a sample Reiki closing:

With a grateful heart, I give thanks for the gift of Reiki and to all guides, angels, ancestors, and beings of 100 percent pure light who guided me during this session. May all beings be peaceful. May all beings be happy. May all beings be safe. May all beings awaken to the light of their true nature. May all beings be free.

Reiki Openings and Closings Practice

For this practice you will need a piece of paper and a pen. Find a comfortable seated position and settle in for a few moments. Consider the opening of your Reiki healing session. What would be a few statements that you feel would set the tone for your Reiki healing session? Write down your version of a Reiki opening. Next, consider what words would encapsulate the message that you would like to send as you end a Reiki session. Write down your personalized Reiki closing.

Set a timer for five minutes and begin your self-healing session using the Reiki opening that you just created. At the close of your Reiki self-healing session be sure to use your Reiki closing remarks. After your healing session, spend a few moments in quiet reflection.

Journaling Practice

Journal your self-healing session. What was your experience using your Reiki opening declaration? Did it set a certain tone or focus for your Reiki healing? Are there parts of your Reiki opening that you'd like to modify? What was your experience of your self-healing session? Did you experience any random thoughts, feelings, or sensations? Describe your experience using your Reiki closing remarks. Are there elements of your Reiki closing that you'd like to adjust? Did you receive any insights into the value of utilizing opening and closing remarks during Reiki healing treatments? How might this information be helpful in future Reiki healing sessions?

Reiki Exploration Day 37

Daily Intention Review

Begin today by remembering why you embarked on this adventure of self-healing and discovery. When you are ready, state your heartfelt healing intention aloud.

The Role of a Teacher

Whether or not you become a Reiki Master-Teacher is a personal decision that deserves careful consideration. First, think of a teacher whom you admire. What qualities does this individual possess that made a positive impression on you? I've been fortunate to have some excellent teachers in my lifetime. Here are some characteristics I consider valuable qualities in a Reiki teacher:

- Knowledgability: A teacher should have mastered all the concepts of Reiki before teaching this healing modality to others.
- Approachability: Students should feel comfortable approaching their teacher with questions.
- Patience: Everyone learns at a different pace, and a teacher should be able to adjust for those students who learn more slowly as well as keep the interest of those individuals who learn more quickly.
- Cultivating curiosity: A teacher should spark students' inquisitive nature.

- Accommodation of different learning styles: Some individuals learn best through auditory means, some learn visually, and others learn best through hands-on experience. A teacher should be able to accommodate different learning styles.
- Preparedness: A teacher should have a prepared agenda and a plan to address all relevant topics.
- Organization: A teacher should know how many students will be attending class and have available the appropriate amount of materials, such as handouts.
- Creativity: This is a powerful tool for teachers. When a teacher uses their imagination to find inspiring ways to present the topics of Reiki, it encourages students to use their own creativity in their Reiki healing sessions by way of example.

As you consider whether you will become a Reiki Master-Teacher, cultivate the qualities within yourself that will best assist you if (or when) you take that step along your healing path.

Thank You Letter Practice

You will need a pen and a piece of paper for this exercise. Find a comfortable seated position and settle in for a few moments. Now, call to mind a teacher whom you admire. What qualities made this person an excellent teacher? What did this individual bring out in you? How did your interaction with this teacher change your life for the better? Then, craft a thank-you letter for this teacher, recounting your experiences and noting the positive difference this individual made in your life. If this person is still alive, consider mailing them this letter in appreciation.

Journaling Practice

Journal your direct experience writing your thank-you letter to an influential teacher. What qualities do you think make for an exceptional teacher? What do you feel you could offer as a Reiki teacher? Describe what you think would be your strengths as a Reiki teacher. What areas might need a little more attention before you become a Reiki teacher? Is this a course of action you are ready to explore now? Why or why not?

Describe the Reiki trainings you attended. What were elements of the training sessions that you thought worked well? What areas would you change and why? How might this information determine whether you will teach Reiki healing to others?

Reiki Exploration Day 38

Daily Intention Review

As a reminder of why you began this journey of Reiki healing, take a moment to reconnect with your heartfelt intention and recommit to your healing path by reciting it aloud.

The Benefits of a Refresher

A refresher is any activity that revises or updates one's skills or knowledge. My favorite example of the need for a refresher relates to TV shows. After the end of a season of your favorite TV show, the wait for the new season's premiere may seem to drag on and on. After the long wait, the premiere usually starts with a recap of the previous season, bringing you up to speed so you can actively follow along with the current storyline. Unfortunately, I had the annoying experience of a TV series that didn't follow this format, so I spent the first half hour trying to figure out what was happening; I was utterly lost.

As a Reiki Master, you should be fluent in all elements of Reiki healing. The topics of Reiki Level One may seem elementary, but it's beneficial to give yourself a refresher on these subjects. In this sense, a refresher is a short but powerful re-examination of fundamental concepts necessary to successfully maintain or deepen one's level of understanding. In addition, your perspective may have changed over time, and this practice may provide you with an opportunity to discover new knowledge and a more profound connection to the material.

Reiki Level One Refresher Practice

Consider all the topics covered in part one of this text. Next, revisit your Reiki journal from part two, the immersion experience associated with Reiki Level One, the Foundations of Reiki. After you review your journal, select a day you'd like to revisit. Release all judgment and expectations before repeating that exercise.

Journaling Practice

Journal your direct experience of your Reiki Level One refresher. Has your knowledge regarding these topics changed? Have you developed a deeper understanding of the concepts of Reiki Level One? What areas might you want to continue to explore?

Now, consider the exercise you completed. How did your direct experience today compare to your direct experience the first time you finished the practice? What differences are there? What similarities? What does this tell you about yourself and your growth as a Reiki practitioner? How might you use the concept of a refresher in your daily life and during future Reiki healings?

Reiki Exploration Day 39

Daily Intention Review

To help establish the mood for your day, take a moment to reconnect with your heartfelt intention and recommit to your healing path by reciting it aloud.

The Process of Reviewing

Whereas a refresher works best for topics that are most familiar to you, the process of reviewing materials periodically assists with mastery of Reiki. One definition of the word "review" is "an evaluation of something to initiate change." In this case, what we are attempting to change is our own understanding of Reiki.

It's common that once we finish a class or a course, we feel a sense of completion and accomplishment. The ending of the class signals the end of our journey, and we might not feel the need to continually review the materials presented during the training. However, during the review process, we retain and remember what we have learned. By establishing a practice of periodically reviewing our Reiki notes, books, and course materials, we develop a strategy to help us transition information from our short-term memory to our long-term memory. It can also promote critical thinking skills and provide insights into additional ways to include Reiki in your daily life.

Reiki Level Two Review Practice

Consider all the topics you have covered during part three of this text associated with the concepts of Reiki Level Two. Next, revisit your Reiki journal from part four, the immersion experience associated with Reiki Level Two: Beyond the Basics. Now, select a topic you'd like to review in more detail. Next, re-read that section of the text and the associated daily practice on that topic. Once you have read the appropriate material, release all judgment and expectations before repeating the daily exercise related to your selection.

Journaling Practice

Journal your direct experience of your Reiki Level Two review. Has your knowledge regarding these topics changed? Have you developed a deeper understanding of the concepts of Reiki Level Two? What areas might you want to continue to review?

Now, consider the exercise you completed. How did your direct experience today compare to your direct experience the first time you finished the practice? What differences are there? What similarities? What does this inform you about yourself and your growth as a Reiki practitioner? Can you identify opportunities to establish periodic review sessions? How might this practice assist you in your development as a Reiki healer?

Reiki Exploration Day 40

Daily Intention Review

Congratulations on completing your last forty-day immersion experience! To help establish the mood for your day, take a moment to reconnect with your heartfelt intention and state it aloud.

Reflection and Your Inner Light

Reflection needs a light source. For example, the experience of looking into a mirror is different if the room is well-lit or dark. The lack of light in a dark room prevents us from seeing the image in the mirror. Personal reflection works similarly. It requires that we shine our inner light on aspects of ourselves, even the parts that we prefer to remain in the shadows. This practice of looking inward is directly related to our personal growth and development. In the reflection process, we can assess where we are and determine where we want to go. Reflection allows us to know ourselves on a deep, intimate level.

After this final forty-day cycle, let's pause and reflect on your experiences over this immersion experience. Consider your personal growth, development of your Reiki skills, and the new knowledge you've gained during this immersion experience. Finally, reflect on the progress you've made along your path.

Reflection Practice

Consider all the topics you have covered over the past thirty-nine days of part six of this text, the Reiki Level Three immersion experience. Next, scan your Reiki journal and select a day you want to revisit. Finally, release all judgment and expectations before repeating that exercise.

Journaling Practice

Journal your direct experience of the exercise you selected. Complete that journaling practice. Next, compare your direct experience today with your direct experience the first time you completed the practice. What differences are there? What similarities? What does this tell you about yourself and your growth as a Reiki practitioner?

What role does reflection play in your life? Is there an opportunity to schedule time for personal reflection, for example at the end of the day? How might you use the concept of reflection in future Reiki healing sessions?

Conclusion

Congratulations on completing your final forty-day immersion experience! The insights and experiences you have gained will continue to support your growth as a Reiki healer. Although this book is at a close, your personal Reiki journey will continue.

To support your development as a Reiki healer, read on to see some of my favorite resources.

Reiki

Magick of Reiki: Focused Energy for Healing, Ritual, & Spiritual Development by Christopher Penczak is an excellent resource for Reiki healers interested in trying different healing symbols during Reiki healing sessions as well as any healers who wish to add an element of magic to their healing sessions.

The Art of Psychic Reiki: Developing Your Intuitive and Empathic Abilities for Energy Healing by Lisa Campion is a good text for healers who want to dive deeper into their psychic skills development for the purpose of healing.

Chakras and the Energy Body

Wheels of Life: A User's Guide to the Chakra System by Anodea Judith is a comprehensive guide to the seven main chakras. This book has been a favorite of mine, and I believe it is an indispensable resource for healers who wish to develop an in-depth knowledge of the classic chakra system.

The Subtle Body: An Encyclopedia of Your Energetic Anatomy by Cyndi Dale extensively details all components of the energetic body and is a must-read for all energy healers.

Essential Oils

The Essential Guide to Aromatherapy and Vibrational Healing by Margaret Ann Lembo is a practical and informative text providing insights into essential oils' healing and energetic properties.

Angels

Angels and Archangels: A Magician's Guide by Damien Echols is an essential guide to the angelic realms and provides guidance on how these powerful allies can assist us in our daily lives.

Crystals

The Book of Stones: Who They Are and What They Teach by Robert Simmons and Naisha Ahsian is a definitive text providing invaluable information on many crystals' background and metaphysical properties.

Intention Setting

The Power of Intention: Learning to Co-Create Your World Your Way by Wayne W. Dyer is a helpful guide in harnessing the power of intention to assist you with achieving your goals.

Websites

The International Association of Reiki Professionals' website is an online resource that provides support for your Reiki business, including liability insurance and relevant articles about Reiki. https://iarp.org.

The International Reiki Association is an organization that provides guidance on growing and promoting your Reiki practice, in addition to essential tips to thrive as a Reiki healer. https://www.reikiassociation.com.

Reiki Rays is an informative website on all things Reiki-related, including many free resources. https://reikirays.com.

Appendix

Sample Waiver of Liability Release Form

In consideration for being allowed to participate in Reiki healing sessions at (insert business name here), I acknowledge and agree to the following:

- Reiki healing is intended to reduce stress, promote relaxation, and enhance overall health and well-being.
- Reiki practitioners do not diagnose medical conditions, perform medical treatments, or interfere with any treatments I may receive or currently be receiving from a licensed medical professional.
- Reiki healing is not a substitute for medical or psychological diagnosis or treatment but can act as a complementary treatment to my current medical care.
- I understand that relaxation enhances healing treatments.
- I understand that long-term energetic imbalances may sometimes require multiple Reiki healing sessions to address.
- I understand that Reiki healers are conducting Reiki healing sessions upon my request and are not responsible for the outcome of any healing session.
- I further agree to release and hold harmless the (insert business name here) from all claims and liabilities associated with any damages to myself or my property resulting from my participation in Reiki healing sessions.

Name: _____

Signature: _____

Date: _____

Bibliography

Andrews, Ted. *How to Meet and Work with Your Spirit Guides (Llewellyn's Practical Guide to Personal Power)*. St. Paul, MN: Llewellyn Publications, 2002.

Armady, Naha. *Everyday Crystal Rituals: Healing Practices for Love, Wealth, Career, and Home*. Emeryville, CA: Althea Press, 2018.

Arroyo, Stephen. *Astrology, Psychology and the Four Elements: An Energy Approach to Astrology & Its Use in the Counseling Arts*. Sebastopol, CA: CRCS Publications, 1975.

Block, Douglas and Demetra George. *Astrology For Yourself: How to Understand and Interpret Your Own Birth Chart*. Berwick, ME: Ibis Press, 2006.

Butler, W. E. *The Magician: His Training and Work*. North Hollywood, CA: Melvin Powers Wilshire Book Company, 1969.

Campion, Lisa. *The Art of Psychic Reiki: Developing Your Intuitive and Empathic Abilities for Energy Healing*. Oakland, CA: Reveal Press, 2018.

Chevalier, Jean, Alain Gheerbrant, et al. *The Penguin Dictionary of Symbols*. London: Penguin, 1996.

Chopra, Deepak. *Quantum Healing: Exploring the Frontiers of Mind/Body Medicine*. New York: Bantam Books, 2015.

Choquette, Sonia. *The Psychic Pathway: A Workbook for Reawakening the Voice of Your Soul*. New York: Crown Publishing Group, 1995.

Clifford, Frank C. *Getting to the Heart of Your Chart: Playing Astrological Detective*. London: Flare Publications, 2017.

Cooper, J. C. *An Illustrated Encyclopedia of Traditional Symbols*. New York: Thames and Hudson, 1979.

Covington, Candice. *Essential Oils in Spiritual Practice: Working with the Chakras, Divine Archetypes, and the Five Great Elements.* Rochester, VT: Healing Arts Press, 2017.

Dale, Cyndi. *Llewellyn's Complete Book of Chakras: Your Definitive Source of Energy Center Knowledge for Health, Happiness, and Spiritual Evolution.* Woodbury, MN: Llewellyn Publications, 2016.

———. *Subtle Energy Techniques.* Woodbury, MN: Llewellyn Publications, 2017.

———. *The Subtle Body: An Encyclopedia of Your Energetic Anatomy.* Boulder, CO: Sounds True, 2009.

Dyer, Wayne W. *The Power of Intention: Learning to Co-Create Your World Your Way.* Carlsbad, CA: Hay House, 2004.

Easwaran, Eknath. *Meditation: A Simple Eight-Point Program for Translating Spiritual Ideas into Daily Life.* Tomales, CA: Nilgiri Press, 1991.

Echols, Damien. *Angels and Archangels: A Magician's Guide.* Boulder, CO: Sounds True, 2020.

Emmons, Robert A., and Michael E. McCullough. "Counting Blessings Versus Burdens: an Experimental Investigation of Gratitude and Subjective Well-Being in Daily Life." *Journal of Personality and Social Psychology* vol. 84, 2 (2003): 377–89. doi:10.1037//0022-3514.84.2.377.

Frazier, Karen. *Complete Reiki: The All-in-One Reiki Manual for Deep Healing and Spiritual Growth.* Emeryville, CA: Rockridge Press, 2020.

———. *The Ultimate Guide to Psychic Abilities: A Practical Guide to Developing Your Intuition.* Beverly, MA: Quarto Publishing Group, 2021.

Fueston, Robert. *The History and System of Usui Shiki Reiki Ryoho.* Twin Lakes, WI: Lotus Press, 2017.

Gerber, Richard. *A Practical Guide to Vibrational Medicine: Energy Healing and Spiritual Transformation.* New York: HarperCollins Publishing, 2000.

Godwin, David. *Godwin's Cabalistic Encyclopedia.* Woodbury, MN: Llewellyn Publications, 2017.

Govinda, Kalashatra. *A Handbook of Chakra Healing: Spiritual Practice for Health, Harmony, and Peace.* Old Saybrook, CT: Konecky and Konecky, 2004.

Hauck, Dennis William. *The Emerald Tablet: Alchemy for Personal Transformation.* New York: Penguin Group, 1999.

Hay, Louise. *Heal Your Body: The Mental Causes for Physical Illness and the Metaphysical Way to Overcome Them.* Carlsbad, CA: Hay House, 1988.

Hirschi, Gertrud. *Mudras: Yoga in Your Hands.* San Francisco: Red Wheel/Weiser, 2000.

International Center for Reiki Training, staff. *An Evidence Based History of Reiki.* Southfield, MI: International Center for Reiki Training, 2015.

Illes, Judika. Encyclopedia of Spirits. New York: HarperOne, 2009

Judith, Anodea. *Chakra Balancing.* Boulder, CO: Sounds True, 2003.

———. *Eastern Body, Western Mind: Psychology and the Chakra System as a Path to Self.* New York: Crown Publishing Group, 2004.

———. *Wheels of Life: A User's Guide to the Chakra System.* Woodbury, MN: Llewellyn Publications, 2015.

Kavanagh, Ambi. *Chakras and Self-Care: Activate the Healing Power of Chakras with Everyday Rituals.* New York: Penguin Random House, 2020.

Klotsche, Charles. *Color Medicine: The Secrets of Color Vibrational Healing.* Flagstaff, AZ: Life Technology Publishing, 1992.

Kumar, Willow. *Kundalini Awakening for Beginners: Activate Your Kundalini Energy and Increase Your Psychic Abilities with Yoga Breathing Exercises and Chakra Meditation Poses to Strengthen Your Body, Mind, and Soul.* Self-published, 2022.

Lembo, Margaret Ann. *The Essential Guide to Aromatherapy and Vibrational Healing.* Woodbury, MN: Llewellyn Publications, 2018.

Pfender, April. *The Complete Guide to Chakras: Activating the 12-Chakra Energy System for Balance and Healing.* Emeryville, CA: Rockridge Press, 2020.

Penczak, Christopher. *Magick of Reiki: Focused Energy for Healing, Ritual, & Spiritual Development.* Woodbury, MN: Llewellyn Publications, 2004.

Powers, Lisa. *Reiki Level I, II and Master Manual.* Self-published, 2018.

Powers, Sarah. *Insight Yoga: An Innovative Synthesis of Traditional Yoga, Meditation, and Eastern Approaches to Healing and Well-Being.* Boulder, CO: Shamabala Publications, 2008.

Prabhu, K. V. *Power of Symbols: Reiki & Other Spiritual Symbols: Reiki & Other Spiritual Symbols: Reiki & Other Spiritual Symbols.* Chennai, India: Notion Press, 2019.

Quest, Penelope. *The Reiki Manual: A Training Guide for Reiki Students, Practitioners, and Masters.* New York: Penguin Group, 2011.

Scheffer, Mechthild. *The Encyclopedia of Bach Flower Therapy.* Rochester, VT: Healing Arts Press, 2001.

Shay, Shoshana. *Reiki History: Real Reiki from Japan to the Western World*. St. Petersburg, FL: Radiance Associates, 2019.

Stein, Diane. *Essential Reiki: A Complete Guide to an Ancient Healing Art*. New York: Crossing Press, 1995.

Stevenson, Angus, editor. *Oxford Dictionary of English*. Oxford, UK: Oxford University Press, 2010.

Stewart, R. J. *Earth Light: The Ancient Path to Transformation*. Rockport, MA: Element Books, 1992.

Stiene, Frans. *The Inner Heart of Reiki: Rediscovering Your True Self*. Winchester, UK: Ayni Books, 2015.

Tipton, Melissa. *Llewellyn's Complete Book of Reiki: Your Comprehensive Guide to a Holistic Hands-On Healing Technique for Balance and Wellness*. Woodbury, MN: Llewellyn Publications, 2020.

Vaudoise, Mallorie. *Honoring Your Ancestors: A Guide to Ancestral Veneration*. Woodbury, MN: Llewellyn Publications, 2019.

Virtue, Doreen. *Angel Medicine*. Carlsbad, CA: Hay House, 2005.

To Write to the Author

If you wish to contact the author or would like more information about this book, please write to the author in care of Llewellyn Worldwide Ltd. and we will forward your request. Both the author and publisher appreciate hearing from you and learning of your enjoyment of this book and how it has helped you. Llewellyn Worldwide Ltd. cannot guarantee that every letter written to the author can be answered, but all will be forwarded. Please write to:

Dawn McLaughlin
℅ Llewellyn Worldwide
2143 Wooddale Drive
Woodbury, MN 55125-2989
Please enclose a self-addressed stamped envelope for reply,
or $1.00 to cover costs. If outside the U.S.A., enclose
an international postal reply coupon.

Many of Llewellyn's authors have websites with additional information and resources. For more information, please visit our website at http://www.llewellyn.com.

Notes

Notes

Notes

Notes

Notes